The Poetics of Gender

GENDER AND CULTURE
Carolyn G. Heilbrun and Nancy K. Miller,
editors

GENDER AND CULTURE
A series of Columbia University Press
Edited by
Carolyn G. Heilbrun
and
Nancy K. Miller

The Poetics of Gender

NANCY K. MILLER, Editor

Columbia University Press

New York

Jane Gallop's "Annie Leclerc Writing a Letter, with Vermeer" first appeared in *October* (Summer 1985), 33:103–18. Reprinted by permission of MIT Press.

Sandra M. Gilbert and Susan Gubar's "Tradition and the Female Talent" first appeared in *Literary History: Theory and Practice. Proceedings of the Northeastern University Center for Literary Studies*, vol. 2, 1984. Reprinted with permission of the Department of English, Northeastern University.

Library of Congress Cataloging-in-Publication Data
Main entry under title:

The Poetics of gender.

  (Gender and culture)
  Includes bibliographies.
    1. Women and literature—Congresses.   2. Sexism in language—Congresses.   I. Miller, Nancy K.
  II. Series.
  PN481.P64   1986   809'.89287   85-29904
  ISBN 0-231-06310-5
  ISBN 0-231-06311-3 (pbk.)

Columbia University Press
New York   Oxford
Copyright © 1986 Columbia University Press
All rights reserved

Printed in the United States of America
p 10 9 8 7 6
c 10 9 8 7 6 5 4 3 2

Contents

Foreword

In rereading the essays in this volume, as in attending the Poetics of Gender Colloquium itself, I felt like the protagonist (always male, of course) in a Frank Capra movie, the kind of film that formed one's consciousness when I was young. In those hideously sentimental films the hero had an impossible dream, idealistic, fair, honorable (all in male terms, of course), and in the end of the film, that dream had become a reality. Capra assured my generation that virtue is rewarded, good triumphs, honesty pays off, never mind whose good, what virtue, what honesty. All this we knew to be hogwash. And yet my new, graduate-school self in 1950, permitted in the last reel to attend the Poetics of Gender colloquium in 1985, would have been, like the James Stewart–Gary Cooper type in those phony films, convinced of angelic powers.

Old now, I must still believe in triumphs: of feminist guts, criticism, theory, friendship, and community. A miracle on 116th street? Certainly. Let us take the matter of pronouns. Monique Wittig writes: "It is without justification of any kind, without questioning, that personal pronouns somehow engineer gender all through language, taking it along with them quite naturally, so to speak, in any kind of talk, parley, or philosphical treatise. And although they are instrumental in activating the notion of gender, they pass unnoticed."

My early days as a graduate student at Columbia were spent in the shadow, indeed at the foot, of the greatest pronounder of them all: Lionel Trilling. Yet he did not, as Wittig says, "support the notion of gender while pretending to fulfill another function." Trilling's

pronoun was "We," and he proclaimed its function: to encompass the
entire male intellectual community, at the least, his "own brighter
students at Columbia" (all male, of course, in those days). In hearing
Wittig deconstruct that pronoun, I have completed an intellectual
journey. Mr. Smith went to Washington, and I stayed at Columbia.

But I basked not only in the transformation of my "we,"
but also in the presence of an elegant, reputable, Riffaterrian colloquium dedicated to gender: this has never happened at Columbia
before. While the University is, at this moment, still struggling to
decide upon a program of Women's Studies, we have spoken of how
we write, and discover, and rename. Michael Riffaterre, who, to his
honor, questioned the poetics of Trilling's "we," said this was the "most
successful of all the colloquia." And next year's, he announced, will be
on anger. I think he saw a natural order, and he was right.

Yet, almost as though the beneficence of the Capra era
clung to me through this colloquium, I was happily aware that there
was little anger. No one was condemned, or attacked from a podium
of self-righteousness, or made to feel like a trespasser on the lawns
of the patriarchy. There was a sense of community, of working together
that, while it could not last—who, in her right mind, would live even
in a feminized Capra world?—nurtured and stimulated us. I said at
the time of welcoming everyone to this colloquium on poetics and
theory that I felt rather like the ringmaster at a circus who had never
herself hung from a trapeze or tamed a lion. I had heard many accounts,
and have since heard more, of conferences where women scholars felt
misapprehended, not always answered with the deliberation they expected. But I stayed to find that no ringmasters were needed, and
there were no lions to be tamed.

Virginia Woolf was mentioned more often than any other
single figure at the conference, and that made me, personally, feel
both welcome and brave. There has been a certain amount of dialogue,
not to say confrontation, between theorists of literature, often of the
French or Freudian persuasion, who tend to speak in polysyllabic
metasemiotics, and those who prefer to set forth their more old-
fashioned formulations in writing characteristic of the English novel
and essay at its most graceful. I have long urged: let there be commerce
between these two modes of critical discourse, as Pound said to

Whitman in a not so different connection. At this conference, none felt excluded, all felt stimulated, provoked, enabled. Ours was the right to walk upon the patriarchal lawn, and Mary Ann Caws, to take but one instance, ignoring her twenty-six books of theory and abstruse originality, moved us all with her Brit lit accounts of men who had tried to rewrite women's lives after their deaths. The Gilbert and Gubar essay in this volume speaks of the powerful reaction male writers in the modern period have had to female assumption of the pen and the voice. But in each case, our awareness was not of what men had done to us, but of what we here offered each other.

Which is not to say, with Wittig, that we must still work on those pronouns—we must, as she has tried to do, transform them. "We" must do that.

CAROLYN G. HEILBRUN

Preface

Does gender have a poetics? The language of the question and the framing of its answers are bound up with the events of a particular context: a series of colloquia on poetics initiated by Michael Riffaterre and held annually at Columbia's Maison Française. At the eighth meeting of the series, November 15–17, 1984, the subject was gender. In the previous seven years the colloquia had been devoted to the poetics of: poetry, the text, intertextuality, the reader, the author, the body, and ideology. In many interesting and often paradoxical ways the colloquium on the poetics of gender may, I think, be said to have reviewed and revised all of the above, since these major points of focus in contemporary literary studies have also been and continue to be crucial areas of reflection and debate within the history of feminist criticism. But the question of the poetics of gender is also a different question. Feminist criticism has shown that the social construction of sexual difference plays a constitutive role in the production, reception, and history of literature. In this second decade of feminist criticism, it has become equally (if problematically) clear that the very conventions and categories of critical discourse within which we all operate, the acts of interpretation we perform and which come to embody us, are inextricably involved with the conventions and categories of identity itself.

What difference does difference make? Feminist criticism generally and necessarily asks what it might mean to read and write through the prism of gender, but over the course of these three days feminist critics both complicated the question and interrogated its answers through a broad range of topics and approaches: the social conditions of literary production; the politics of reception and the discourses of canon formation; female authorship and literary history; sexual difference and the languages of theory.

These general fields of inquiry of course regroup questions more specifically related to the current practice of feminist criticism in the United States, and the work of the conference was marked by a review of available textual strategies and their implications for that project. To take a few examples: Elaine Showalter characterizes her approach in this paper as "downhome, downright Yankee historical," as an example of what Alice Jardine calls an "American contextual feminism," and Susan Suleiman, "thematic reading." Suleiman in her discussion distinguishes between an " 'ultrathematic,' " referential approach, and a more textual thematics. Rehearsing the "current split" in "transatlantic feminist" criticism over the question of sexual difference, Naomi Schor proposes the practice of "reading double," reading for the operations of history in sexual difference itself. At an angle to the deconstructive poetics of the already read, I elaborate a model of "overreading" the underread texts of women's writing. And so on.

Looking back through these essays, it has seemed to me that this extreme self-consciousness about the critical politics of reading (Jardine's "ethics of reading," Elizabeth Berg's "frivolous reading"), an acute attention to what Suleiman calls the "ideological aims and implications. . . of *any* way of reading," and Nancy Vickers, "the points of convergence between multiple rhetorics," constituted the central preoccupation of the colloquium. From this perspective, the poetics of gender that underwrites the arguments of most of the papers is the common interrogation of the powers of the universal as they inhere in all diacritical and interpretive acts, including the workings of grammar itself. Thus, Catharine Stimpson analyzes the subversive force of Stein's "self-contradictory" poetics—taking on "patriarchal poetry"—and shows Stein's insistence, through the operation Stimpson calls "transposition," on the arbitrariness of gender arrangements in language. Against the massive fiction of the indifference of language, Monique Wittig argues for the legibility in fiction of *elles* as the "bearer of a universal point of view," and names the "mark of gender": "a mark

unique of its kind, the unique lexical symbol that refers to an oppressed group."

But if any poetics of gender must acknowledge its difference from the universal, from the universal's claim of impartiality, a
feminist poetics must go further still in the terms of its own project,
beyond the acknowledgment of the difference gender makes, and
recognize, in Berg's formulation, that it must itself "be a continual
reminder that there is nothing impartial." In this sense, underlining
the difference gender can mark within its own field of meaning, Jane
Gallop offers a critique of *écriture féminine* as a concept of writing that
runs the risk of effacing "the difference between women in view of
some feminine essence," of forgetting "the other woman." And Domna
Stanton interrogates the maternal metaphor privileged in French theories of the feminine to propose instead the "more concrete, contextual inscriptions of differences within/among women" made possible
by metonymy's tropological zones.

The essays on women's writing in fact dwell on the material
differences at work in its production and reception. This is part of what
Ann Jones means by "pre-poetics," the study of "the conditions necessary for writing at all," that many of the papers map with great
attention to the intersections of artistic, political, and economic practices. Thus Sandra Gilbert and Susan Gubar identify the moment in
England and America "when the middle-class woman began . . . to
enter the profession of letters" and read in the works of male modernist
writers rage at women's "usurpation of the marketplace"; Showalter
grounds her discussion of female culture and women's writing in the
specificity of a uniquely American tradition of quiltmaking in the
nineteenth century; and Schor insists upon the structuring force of
the "historical reality" of 1848 in Sand's pastoral. In the same way,
Vickers, arguing back through Woolf, shows through the example of
Cellini that within the dominant tradition a "masterpiece" must be
understood not as an "isolated product" but as a "process in context."
This is also to talk about the gender of poetics.

●

In his closing remarks, Michael Riffaterre, expressing, as
he said, a "personal sentiment," observed: "never before did we have

such large audiences, never before did we have such passionate audiences." It was a passionate event; this is not a commonplace occur-
rence in academic calendars, and I would like to thank him here for
taking up (or taking on) the poetics of feminist criticism, for sponsoring
the conference that in turn produced this volume. And because that
frame of reference—Columbia, the Maison Française, the history of
the other colloquia—lent, I think, so particular a coloration to the
work, rather than impose another strategy of reading through the table
of contents, I in the end decided to present the papers in the volume
according to the order (however arbitrary) in which they were presented
at the conference itself. I regret all the more, theréfore, that a certain
number of the papers important to the discussion at the conference
were unavailable to me for publication in this volume: Sandra Gilbert
and Susan Gubar's " 'Forward into the Past': The Complex Female
Affiliation Complex"; U. C. Knoepflmacher's "Becoming Cinderellas:
Male Appropriations of Female Fairytales"; Lawrence Lipking's "The
Rape of the Sybil: Wordsworth, Rilke, and Abandoned Women"; Robert
Scholes's "The Left Hand of Difference: Le Guin and Derrida."[1]

      In the context of the remarks above, Riffaterre announced
that the next colloquium would be on the Poetics of Anger, and that
he saw this choice of topic to some extent as a continuation of the
Poetics of Gender. This strikes me, in one way, as a logical line of
thought (or as Carolyn Heilbrun puts it in her foreword, "a natural
order") in the spirit of Virginia Woolf's reflections on sexual identity
and anger in A *Room of One's Own*—but not perhaps the whole story.

      A conference on gender in the future would, I think, want
to imagine "the other woman" of other literatures, colonial, for example, that present less familiar geographies and configurations of
difference. One might also imagine a future conference on the Poetics
of Respect, since that was almost tangibly the dominant mode of
interaction among the participants: feminist intertextualities.[2] As Mary
Ann Caws concludes about the tale of Christa T., it "was really about
being allowed to invent us, all of us, all over again, finding our several
voices through our metaphors, and with enough time to stay." In the
end, this self-authorizing permission to reinvent identities and refigure
their temporalities is perhaps the gender-bearing mark of another
poetics—or at least its question.

NANCY K. MILLER

NOTES

1. The papers (respectively) will appear (or are already in print) in: *Historical Studies in Literary Criticism*, ed. Jerome J. McGann (Madison: University of Wisconsin Press, 1985); as part of a new book tentatively entitled *Ventures into Childland* to be published by the University of Chicago Press; as part of a chapter in his forthcoming study, *Abandoned Women and Poetic Tradition*, University of Chicago Press (Women in Culture and Society Series, ed. Catharine R. Stimpson); in *Textual Power: Literary Theory and the Teaching of English*. (New Haven: Yale University Press, 1985), chapter 7.

2. I owe the notion of a Poetics of Respect to Jane Forress-Betty. I want to thank her here as well for her astute editorial advice, and generous assistance at the various stages of this project.

Although much of this discussion—questions, answers, commentary (and the occasional joke)—was either too punctual or contextual to reappear in the published versions, the staff of the Maison Française tape-recorded the proceedings and they are currently available for consultation.

Gertrude Stein
and the Transposition of Gender

CATHARINE R. STIMPSON

I

Among her other abilities, Gertrude Stein was a woman poet. She began to experiment with the theory and practice of poetry around 1910. She was 36 years old. By then, she had written and repressed one autobiographical novel; published three novellas with a vanity press; and embarked upon another autobiographical novel, an epic of family and nation, written for herself and strangers, *The Making of Americans*. She had also begun writing her portraits: combinations of the snapshot, the x-ray, the lyric poem, and conceptual art. Like a dolphin in a school of one, Stein was breathing in the sea of modern poetry—in French and English.

Ideas about gender were powerful crosscurrents in that sea. Simply speaking, gender is a way of classifying living things and languages, of sorting them into two groups: feminine and masculine. However, no system of classification is ever simple. Cultural laws of gender demand that feminine and masculine must play off against each other in the great drama of binary opposition. They must struggle against each other, or complement each other, or collapse into each other in the momentary, illusory relief of the androgynous embrace. In patriarchal cultures, the struggle must end in the victory of the masculine; complementarity must arrange itself hierarchically; androgyny must be a mythic fiction.

By 1910, the modern reformation of such patriarchal laws was a well-established, though not well-loved, cultural fact. It demanded that masculinity no longer have the strong, heavy beat of the arsis. Either femininity and masculinity were to have the equal beat of the spondee, or, even more radically, femininity and masculinity were to disappear altogether. Men and women were to create a new prosody of behavior. Such a code would necessarily articulate sexual differentiation. No one would stop being born either female or male. However, such a code would dismiss gender differentiation. Once at liberty, at one with liberty, no one would become feminine or masculine. By 1910, of course, the modern counterreformation in support of patriarchal laws had also begun. Among its most powerful popes and priests were otherwise avant-garde male modernists. As Sandra M. Gilbert has written: "For the male modernist. . . gender is most often an ultimate reality, while for the female modernists an ultimate reality exists only if one journeys beyond gender" (196).

Stein's negotiations with these crosscurrents are swimmingly self-contradictory. Even as her poetry moves against some patriarchal habits, it reconstitutes others. She is simultaneously disobedient and obedient, a reformer and a counterreformer. Her poetry is a series of propositions about the possibilities of transposing gender, about the possibilities of breaking up its orders, codes, and poses. However, her poetry also demonstrates the difficulties of such fundamental, capacious alterations. For Stein often transposes gender in another, less leaping sense. She merely moves gender's orders, codes, and poses from one point to another. She rearranges them.

As a result, if I may shift my metaphor from sea to mountain, water to earth, fluid to solid, the massive/massif Stein, with the deft slyness of the unconscious, reproduces a range of crevassed discourse about gender in the twentieth century. Her poetics, because self-contradictory, are an encyclopedia about the poetics of gender.

Significantly, one entry is missing from Stein's encyclopedia: misogyny. She can be sardonic about women. Look, for example, at the short poem in *Bee Time Vine*, "An Elegant Escape," a quick sketch about presences and absences, similarities and differences, including those between romantic heroines and New Women:

> In the midst of wind there is a milk bottle.
> Not now.
> And in the midst of the water there is a flower.
> So there is.
> There is a difference between Anna Karenina and Anne
> Veronica. (201)

However, Stein, far more apt to find pleasure in women, has little or nothing to do with the virulence and violence of women-bashing. Look, for example, at another fragment, "Attacks," a succinct tribute to women's being, and being in space:

> She is.
> She is the best way.
> She is the best way from here to there.
> (Bee Time Vine, 221)

Of course, some male poets refuse to write about women as nagging, castrating, or engulfing perils. However, such a refusal by a male poet is an act of generosity toward the other; by a female poet, toward the self.

II

The self-contradictions in Stein emerge as we map the veins of psychosexuality, ideology, and literary practice in her career. Attempting to create modern writing for modern history, a modern period for the modern period, Stein was in conflict with all literature as she knew it. More particularly, she was in conflict with patriarchal poetry in two ways. First, the mere fact of her femaleness challenged an arrogant equation of the creation of high poetry with a male poet. Next, much of the matter *and* manner of her poetry subverted patriarchal, heterosexual rules. Indeed, her poetry is perhaps more subversive than her other literary experiments—if only because her poetry is a primary place for her plays with language as language, for her attempts to treat language as an innocent system consisting of sentences that might be broken into clauses, clauses that might be broken into words, words that might be broken into phonemes and morphemes.

In the laboratory of the text, Stein was searching for the elementary particles of language, no matter how many of them there might be. The process is so wonderfully messy, the product so multi-textured, that together they challenge two patterns of thought on which gender depends: binarism, splitting the world into mutually reinforcing sets of dualistic categories, including that of feminine/masculine; and teleologicalism, believing that the world, and its narratives, spin toward certain ends, including the triumph of the willful masculine over the feminine.

Stein's tricky pages also illustrate a persuasive theory about women's writing. Mary Jacobus has argued that the woman writer, especially a member of the avant-garde, takes writing as the site of "challenge and Otherness" (10–21). If women are to speak, they will articulate difference. However, if they are to speak, they must enter what has been a male domain. Such a passage is risky, for the woman may destroy the femaleness (and its imperatives of silence) that has been the source of her difference. But, if she runs the risk, a woman will have her rewards. For her activity can be more than the "representation of female oppression" and of ancient silence. Her writing can mean the very discovery of difference. The "traversal of boundaries" necessarily "exposes boundaries" as well. In this exposure is the "multiplicity, joyousness and heterogeneity" of textuality itself.

Nevertheless, and despite her sexual preferences, Stein never ceased to believe in bourgeois heterosexuality: its decencies, norms, and families. This had at least two consequences. First, Stein equated the mind, especially that of the genius, with masculinity. She was a frequent Tory about who should labor in laboratories. Next, she equated sexuality with heterosexuality. Necessarily, such an ideology tore at her ambitions and sexual desires. She was at odds with her own compulsions for work and for love.[1]

In order to survive, Stein had to repair such rifts and renderings between ideology and self. She devised a series of coping strategies that were successful enough to permit her, in the last part of the first decade of the twentieth century, to believe in female creativity (Walker, 119–20.) Those coping strategies included the choice of a mate, Alice B. Toklas, who utterly supported her. Next, Stein internalized an alternative myth of the artist—the artist as a genderless worker, as voice/eye/ear in time present who lives to work, without hope of an immediate audience. Finally, Stein chose to live in a Bohemian milieu that included, because it was Bohemian, other female artists. Between 1908 and 1912, she wrote "Orta or the One Dancing," a portrait of one of those artists: Isadora Duncan. Here, the female, a principle of "fluid creativity," incorporates the qualities of thinking and feeling; listening and talking; anticipating, actualizing, and accepting. In brief, the female fuses polarities.

Honoring the female, Stein had to deconstruct the male. She did so through cutting loose from her brother Leo, a severing of ties she dramatizes in abstract form in "Two" (1910–12). Her Leo (he) is a vociferously hyperrational intellectual. Incapable of hearing (a metonymy for receptivity and understanding), he is deaf, and therefore, dumb. Stein's representation of her family drama is one of the first of her satires about patriarchs and the patriarchy, satires that were to become more joyously mocking as she grew older and more confident.[2]

Despite all this, Stein could not, did not, fully abandon the male. For her lesbian relationship with Toklas, which helped her expand her ideology of creativity to embrace the female as creator, also perpetuated the conventions of bourgeois marriage. Indeed, the couple swerved perilously close to perpetuating the social conventions of the Victorian bourgeois marriage. To be sure, Stein's poetry— whether eroticized or not—contains a number of polymorphous metaphors for her relationship with Toklas. Stein, lucky thing, is frequently "Baby," Toklas her parent. "In This Way, Kissing," croons:

> Next to me in me sweetly sweetly
> Sweetly Sweetly sweetly sweetly.
> In me baby baby baby
> Smiling for me tenderly tenderly.
> Tenderly sweetly baby baby.
> Tenderly tenderly tenderly tenderly.
> (*Bee Time Vine*, 199–200)[3]

Stein also invokes and renders diminutive Toklas' Jewishness. Toklas becomes a "little Jew." However, with the comforting, reassuring ease that can privilege obsession, Stein returns to binary metaphors to articulate her relationship. Stein is an admiral, a caesar, and, most frequently, a husband. Toklas is the happy wife. In burst after burst of rhyme, "Mrs." loves "kisses."

As husband, Stein is a proper gentleman. She is discreet in the descriptions of sexuality in the erotic poetry, using a tact that modern taboos about homosexuality helped to impose. However, she casually, but consistently, appropriates Toklas's voice. Although Toklas could insert herself into Stein's manuscripts, Stein's use of Toklas was by far the more common practice. Take, for example, the poem "All Sunday" (1915). The piece is a dialogue between author and wife, or "Mrs." However, the poem has no quotation marks. At least two inter-pretations exist for such diacritical lacunae. The first, more charitable, claims that the poem concerns a day in the life of a married couple so coupled that their identities, and voices, blur together. A punctua-tion mark would puncture this blissful, even symbiotic unity. Support-ing such a kindly reading is the fact that some columns of speech fragments are swatches of first-person plural discourse, of "we-ness":

> We said we agreed.
> Then what.
> We went everywhere.
> We were hot.
> We sat down.
> It was very pleasant.
> We said we were happy.
> (*Alphabets and Birthdays*, 124)

The second, less charitable, reading claims that the poem is a covert dramatic monologue. The author has simply sponged up the wife's voice. Of course, the wife talks. She confesses:

I am going to tell all my feelings. I love and obey. I am very sensible. I am sensitive to distraction. I like little handkerchiefs. I like to have mosquito netting over my bed. I can estimate the reluctance with which I am hurried . . . I like to do my nails. How do I do them. How do you do. (105)

However, the author inscribes the confession. By 1932, when Stein wrote *The Autobiography of Alice B. Toklas*, she was well-versed in turning her wife's "remarks" into literature.

Such poems reflect, not only Stein's adoption of a male role, but her commitment to still another, and complementary, myth of the writer: the writer as genius, as exemplary consciousness; as romantic, even ravenous, ego. She believed in the writer as the embracer of multitudes. Indeed, she praised Whitman for doing in the nineteenth century, and for the nineteenth century, what she was doing in, and for, the twentieth century. She refers both to "leaves of grass," and to "leaves of stone," a joke about the English translation of her last name. As the writer commanded the world, so self could merge with language. In "Poetry and Grammar," she tells of her love for grammar and of her schoolgirl delight in learning how to parse sentences. "I really do not know that anything has ever been more exciting than diagramming sentences" (*Lectures in America*, 210). For this unlikely frisson leads to "one completely possessing something and incidentally one's self" (211).

However, Stein's theories of language are no more unitary than her self-presentations and presentations of gender. The contradictions within those theories subtly, and unpredictably, reinforce the contradictions within those self-presentations and presentations. For she was also profoundly interested in language as language, in writing as writing, an interest compelling enough to help her avoid the more egregious solipsisms of a theory of *writer as language, of writer as writing*. In effect, in addition to saying "It's me there," she said, "It's it there." In the 1930s, Stein and Toklas, on their American lecture tour, were driving in the country in Western Massachusetts. Toklas pointed out a batch of clouds. Stein replied, "Fresh eggs." Toklas insisted that Stein look at the cloud. Stein replied again, "Fresh eggs." Then Toklas asked, "Are you making symbolical language?" "No," Stein answered, "I'm reading the signs. I love to read the signs" (in Rogers, 112).

The tension between a theory of the writer as writing and writing as writing is another head of the Hydra of the debate about the representational power, the referential status, of language. On the one hand, the Stein who believed heroically in the writer as writing also believed in the writer as representor, in language as representational and referential. Of course, customary descriptions might hang over and encrust contemporary realities. However, the modern writer was to break open the stale cakes of linguistic custom. A yeasty, rising literature could then give us compositions from and about the world, those patterns that our activities and perceptions create.

In the 1930s, Stein's lectures about poetry firmly commit the poem to being about the world. She insists that poetry is vocabulary, the lexicon of naming. In colleges, clubs, and lecture halls, she told her American audiences that her "struggle" was to "mean names without naming them" (LIA, 236). She wanted to generate—from the matrix of language—a word for the Forest of Arden without saying beech, fir, or tree. Famously, she declared: "Poetry is concerned with using with abusing, with losing with wanting, with denying with avoiding with adoring with replacing the noun" (231). Not surprisingly, her rhetoric is that of love. For she saw naming as an act of love—done for love, with love, in love. What, in brief, we do for love. Not surprisingly, for she is the woman writer only partly freed from patriarchal ideologies of work and love, her rhetoric is that of the conventional male role in a love affair: desire; command; fear of rejection; gratification; and abandonment. Once again, like the falcon circling and returning to its trainer, she could not resist the lure of the alluring bait of gender.

On the other hand, to say that a poem is "about" the world is slippery. "About," as adverb or preposition, is ominously vague. The sentence "I am about there" is far looser than "I am there." The Stein who heroically explored writing as writing, who so liked to read the signs, explored writing as a self-controlling and self-reflexive system. "Poetry and Grammar" also declares: "Language as a real thing is not imitation either of sounds or colors or emotions it is an intellectual recreation and there is no possible doubt about it and it is going to go on being that as long as humanity is anything" (LIA, 237–38). The pun on "recreation" ("re-creation" and "recreation") implies that language is both a mental construct and fun. Because so many of Stein's poems, be they fragments or extended meditations, seem to be immediately indecipherable, they tend to distance the reader from language-on-the-page; to assign that language-on-the-page to another, even inhuman, world. As Walker writes, *Tender Buttons* is "a brilliantly subversive demonstration of the unbreachable gulf that separates the chaotic plenitude of the sensory world from the arbitrary order of language" (xi).[4]

Simultaneously, two theoretical texts of the 1930s, *The Geographical History of America* and "What Are Masterpieces," speculate about the autonomy of the great text. In a ranking flurry of binary oppositions, Stein groups one quality over another: consciousness of the present over memory and foresight; the present over past and future; the gratuitous over the necessary; the thing itself over relations among things; objects over actions; the masterpiece over journalism and the media. She then associates the first terms with the realm of "entity" and human mind; the second terms with the messy, time-struck, bustling realm of "identity" and human nature. The masterpiece might be about identity, but it belongs to entity. The masterpiece might take human nature as its subject, but it is the product of human mind.

Even as she polarizes kinds of literature and kinds of experience, Stein entangles them in thickets of contradictions—about both literature and gender—that arise from webbing the traditional with the new. First, to illustrate what she means, she repudiates some of her own earlier protofeminist ideas. For example, in Lucy Church Amiably, published in 1930, she had stated firmly that women and children were changing faster than men. They were more modern. "If men have not changed women and children have. Men have not changed women and children have" (177). However, in her American lectures, she tells her audience to dismiss all that. "The thing that is important," she stresses, "is the way that portraits of men and women and children are written, by written I mean made. And by made I mean felt" (LIA, 165). Yet, she holds on to an idiosyncratic fusion of the classical notion of a maker; the romantic notion of the maker as feeler; and another protofeminist notion—the maker/feeler as woman. As she famously asks, "Also there is why is it that in this epoch the only real literary thinking has been done by a woman" (GHA, 218), and, as famously, answers:

> So then the important literary thinking is being done.
> Who does it.
> I do it.
> Oh yes I do it. (GHA, 222)

III

The tension between Stein's presentation of language as representative and as a self-controlling and self-reflexive system is manageable. David Antin and Marjorie Perloff (Perloff, 67–108) have taught us to regard Stein's literary language as both "pointing" to the "real world" and teasingly pleasing us as a compositional game. It hovers tantalizingly between these capacities.[5]

With such a doubling poetic language, Stein devised her poetics of a doubled, contradictory sense of gender. Between *Tender Buttons*, published in 1914, and *Lucy Church Amiably*, she penned out at least three different strategies that, in varying degrees, juxtapose a reconstitution of patriarchal ideas about gender against the repudiation of those ideas. One strategy prefers reconstitution to repudiation; the second balances them; the third, reversing the first, prefers repudiation to reconstitution. This third maneuver, this preference for repudiation over reconstitution, also tears binary oppositions apart. It allows the disruptions, even the anarchy, of heterogeneity to burst in. Because each strategy differently balances reconstitution and repudiation, they cannot stabilize each other. On the contrary, they destabilize each other—as a triple pun destabilizes the sentence in which it implodes.

That tantalizing hovering of her language then intensifies our sense of destabilization and subversively warns us against accepting the certainty of any text. Covertly arming the guerilla war against certainty is any lack of scaffolding that Stein might have nailed up around her constructions so that we might stand around and measure them. The effect is to dislodge expectations that we can manage the text; that we can gain interpretative mastery without pain. So doing, no matter how remotely, Stein dislodges our trust in the smoothness, regularity, and uniformity of our dominant discourses—including our discourse about gender. Her texts, like nonsense, test what we have construed to be common sense, a way of thinking that "must see the lifeworld as a stable and ordered phenomenon in order to get on with the business at hand" (Stewart, 12). She dislodges our trust even in her residually patriarchal messages about gender.

As she executes her trickle-down theory of subversion, Stein is no ideological feminist, but she does foreshadow the pulsating, lyrical polemic of much contemporary feminist theory. In "The Laugh of the Medusa," to take a familiar example, Hélène Cixous calls for a revolutionary logos that will breed a revolution of the polis: "writing is precisely the *very possibility of change*, the space that can serve as a springboard for subversive thought, the precursory movement of a transformation of social and cultural structures" (879). However, to destabilize is not to eradicate; to dislodge is not to demolish. Traces of patriarchal message remain graven—too wispy to be laws, but chiseled enough to remind us of patriarchal longings.

Let me offer one case study for each of the three poetic strategies that so juxtapose a reconstitution of patriarchal ideas about gender with their repudiation.

(1) *The preference for reconstitution over repudiation.* Stein called the poem "As A Wife Has A Cow: A Love Story" her *Tristan and Isolde* (SW, 541–45). A work of about eighty lines, it is another of Stein's raunchy, tender recollections of her relationship with Toklas. Like most of Stein's poems, it is a block of type. Stein tends to set up one of two blocks: the horizontal rectangles of "As A Wife Has A Cow" or "Tender Buttons," or the vertical columns of portions of "Sacred Emily." Here the word "pale" repeats itself seven times as if it were running off a high-speed press (*Geography and Plays*, 185). Stein's poetry does not blast the page pictorially, race toward the margins, curl up and around, lay down concrete, or aspire to the forms of the ideogram. Edges of type severely border her wild texts, rather as bourgeois ideologies, and her romantic ego can frame her shattering perceptions of the moment.

"As A Wife Has A Cow" is the drama of the husband-author and his two inseparable pleasures, conjugal eros and literature, love and love story, which make each other possible. The poem's first paragraph murmurs:

Nearly all of it to be as a wife has a cow, a love story. All of it to be as a wife has a cow, all of it to be as a wife has a cow, a love story. (543)

In effect, Stein has listed the credits of a verbal movie. The next paragraph moves forward in time to anticipate the cow: "As to be all of it as to be a wife as a wife has a cow, a love story." Then, the third paragraph, in a flashback, shows the cow coming home: "Has made, as it has made as it has made, has made, has to be as a wife has a cow, a love story" (543). In the final paragraph, the cow is present, as if time present was the best, the most gratifying, part of that suspicious sequence: past, present, future. In a rush and climax of open vowels, the husband exclaims: "my wife having a cow as now and having a cow as now and having a cow now, my wife has a cow and now. My wife has a cow" (545).

As Richard Bridgman has shown, Stein chose "cow" as a metaphor for female sexuality and orgasm. "Cow": the sweet-eyed, milk-dripping, warm-breathed, uddered, bell-hung, slow-brained cow! The word that rhymes with wow and now and ow and pow! Its pastoral silliness, a sign of Stein's ludic zaniness, sends up any attempt to straitlace heterosexual marriage in solemnity. Simultaneously, the knowledge, available to even the laziest of Stein's readers, that both "husband" and "wife" might be women severs a sense of the necessity of the putative connections between femaleness and femininity, maleness and masculinity. Despite these repudiations of heterosexual conventions, Stein's sheer repetition of the term "wife" so reinforces the idea of marriage that the reconstitution of those conventions overwrites their sweet mockery.

(2) *The balance of reconstitution and repudiation.* "Patriarchal Poetry," though it moves crisply and briskly, is one of Stein's most intellectually ambitious meditative poems. It, too, explores her relationship with Toklas, her hearth and heart-keeper and muse, as well as the nature of human identity; of grammar; and of differences— between numerical quantities; singularities and collectivities; time periods and tempos; and among persons, places, and things. However, the poem's most insistent concern is "patriarchal poetry," the rubric around which Stein organizes her ideas.

Like a kindly but sardonic analyst, Stein dissects the patriarchs' literary corpus. Patriarchal poetry has had its sins: patriotism; obsession with method; and arrogant, self-reflecting narcissism. Indeed, the speaker even contemplates abolishing it, through refusing to speak of it. "Never to mention patriarchal poetry altogether" (*Yale Gertrude Stein*, 115). However, no literature is wholly evil. Part of a tradition that belongs to her family, to her beloved nephew Allan, patriarchal poetry also provides a foundation on which the speaker can build. She can reject and rejuvenate it. Such a mixture of displeasure and measured praise appears in the poem's first paragraph:

> As long as it took fasten it back to a place where after all he would be carried away, he would be carried away as long as it took fasten it back to a place where he would be carried away as long as it took. (106)

"Fasten it back" and "carry away" seem like a parricidal call for the father's death sentence and burial.[6] However, "carry away" also implies that patriarchal poetry, if properly placed, can write up rapture; can convey ecstasy and the sublime. Later, Stein reiterates her doubled attitude in a series of puns:

> Patriarchal Poetry might be withstood
> Patriarchal Poetry at peace.
> Patriarchal Poetry a piece.
> Patriarchal Poetry in peace.
> Patriarchal Poetry in pieces.
> Patriarchal Poetry at peace to return to Patriarchal Poetry at peace. (133)

Even as she tames the beast, Stein, through that very act, advances the rights of women as authors. Master composers might give way to mater composers. She repeats the imperative sentence, "Let her be," and the substantive, "letter b," until the two collapse; until autonomous female being and language (especially Alice's middle initial) become one. Oscillating between affirmation and negation, she also demands, "Never to let her be what he said." In effect, Stein glides the labial, but phallic, consonant "p" into the labial consonant, and labial, "b." Indeed, some of the more eroticized passages of the poem evoke female genitals. "Wet inside and pink outside. Pink outside and wet inside wet inside and pink outside latterly nearly near near pink" (121). Patriarchal poetry, she will later crack, is "out of pink once in a while" (127).

Eventually, Stein modestly suggests that she might be an author. "Like it can be used in joining gs," she murmurs, putting the initials of Gertrude Stein daintily into the lower case (135). Stein even hints that writing women might cultivate new subjects. A pun on "mint," at once the site of manufacturing money and a sweet herb, implies, in a tantalizing foray into a specifically female territory, that women may abandon a literature based on money and create one based on food, pleasure, and nature. "Patriarchal Poetry obliged as mint to be mint to be mint to be obliged as mint to be," she says judgmentally. But, she promises, "Mint may be come to be as well as cloud and best" (139).[7] Her plants may become, i.e., ornament cloud and best, as well as merging with them.

In the middle of her poem, Stein does up a microcosmic exemplum of her balancing of patriarchal modes and their supplement. A "she" has asked what "patriarchal" is. The speaker has responded, "I know what it is." Having achieved some analytical clarity, she offers "A Sonnet," an example of one of patriarchal poetry's great formal achievements (124). This sonnet is an uxurious tribute from a proud and happy husband to "the wife of my bosom," a woman of transcendent virtues, beauties, and charms. The speaker/husband controls patriarchal tributes to his woman and possesses her body, her "bosom." However, Stein also parodies the sonnet and its earnest sentiments. Her poem, of 18 lines, flows over conventional boundaries. Moreover, the possessive "my" is ambiguous. The husband, too, may have a bosom. To be sure, literature has often granted men bosoms, but both literature and life have tended to feminize them. The sonnet's husband, twisting and tweaking the regulations of sex and gender, may be female.

(3) *The preference for repudiation over reconstitution*. An element of many poems, this strategy announces itself boldly in *Tender Buttons*, the book that established Stein's reputation as an awesome, notorious linguistic rebel. The degendered world of *Tender Buttons* consists of three parts: "Objects," which begins with the naming of a carafe and ends with the naming of a dress and a body; "Food," which starts with a metaphysically charged roast beef and concludes with a linguistically charged table; and "Rooms," a prose poem that analyzes both the interior spaces that contain objects and food and the method of *Tender Buttons* itself.

Even though Stein focuses intensely on domestic things and environments, she does not ground her text in the feminine. For the domestic need not be synonym for the feminine. Cézanne painted apples in a room, but few accuse him of constructing an icon of the feminine. Indeed, Stein audaciously purges *Tender Buttons* of gender, with the aid of English, a language that lacks gender inflections. In the entire text, female pronouns (she/her) appear less than ten times; male less than five. The neutral "it" holds sway. Obviously masculine nouns (man/husband/soldier) march out perhaps eleven times; obviously feminine (ladies/sister) about seven. Proper names sneak in three times: twice as Susan, once as Mildred, the owner of an umbrella. Gender enters only when it is so blatantly a part of biological and social realities that denying its presence—denying, for example, that sisters are not misters—would be distractingly perverse.[8]

Stein's cleansing of gender is a logical part of her larger project: to investigate the particularities of phenomena—be they umbrellas, asparagus spears, or boxes. She wishes to grasp quiddities. To be sure, objects share qualities. Both roses and roast beef can be red. Both carates and eyeglasses are made of glass. To be sure, puns reveal similarities in labels and names. A waist may be a "star glide" or the waste of a "single financial grass greediness" (SW, 471). To be sure, an object may be a code word for something else. Nevertheless, Stein wishes to evade the trap of placing anything or anybody in a class, such as "The Feminine" or "The Masculine," that values the set over the individual member, or that arranges sets in binary opposition to each other. Simultaneously, she hopes to refuse, in an act of epistemological democracy that she learned from Cézanne, to give any single thing priority and power over another in her compositions. The first sentence of "Rooms" reminds author and reader of both desires: "Act so that there is no use in a centre. A wide action is not a width" (498).

Yet, even *Tender Buttons* cannot, will not, wholly erase the heterosexual patterns that Stein and Toklas followed and that helped Stein to write. Because of this, the text is a cautionary fable about two Utopian dreams: an agenda of scarcity that would do away with gender altogether, and an agenda of plenty that would permit everyone to be he, she, or it as one pleased. The last block of words in "Objects" is "This Is The Dress, Aider":

Aider, why aider why whow, whow stop touch, aider whow, aider stop the muncher, muncher munchers.
A jack in kill her, a jack in, makes a meadowed king, makes a to let. (476)

Interpretative possibilities spill from the words—like spirits from Pandora's box. They roil the sinister and the gratifying together, a doubling that reflects Stein's ambivalence about patriarchal heterosexuality. For the block first evokes the image of a male killer, a Jack the Ripper. Someone is shouting for help for the woman, the " 'er," who is his victim. However, far more innocently, someone may be telling someone else to aid a woman with her dress, her toilet. Then the block, fusing death and service, recreates a sexual act, which eating/munching both accompanies and signifies. It may be between the speaker and "Ada," a name into which "Aider" elides, the name that Stein gave Toklas in the first portrait Stein wrote. Adopting a male role from playing cards, the speaker is first a jack, then an even more aristocratic and luscious meadowed king. After "a" (for Alice or Ada?) survives the threat that sexuality embodies (a Victorian belief), she finds release. She lets go (a modern imperative).

IV

Of the modern women poets who wrote in English, only Gertrude Stein had the ability to become, if partially, an encyclopedia of the poetics of the transpositions of gender. Perhaps most women poets, attempting to integrate those two terms, would have felt, more acutely than a man, both the reins of cultural history and the whip of the future, the reign of cultural conventions and the subversive lashings of liberty. However, only a lesbian like Stein, who both parodied and rebelled against heterosexuality, could have acted out and on so many sexual codes. Only an experimental writer could have willfully written out those flexible texts that address both the heterogeneity that is one of gender's most fertile foes and the binarism that is one of its most rock-bound friends.

NOTES

1. I have written about this before, most recently in "Gertrice/Altrude," an essay that also lists my considerable debts to other Stein scholars.

2. Neil Schmitz brilliantly discusses Stein's mockeries (160–259).

3. The lack of explicit pronoun references generalizes the love lyric. Either lover could be the parent, or the baby. Moreover, both parent and baby can have baby "in me"—the parent in sperm, womb, or psyche; the baby in its psyche. Baby can be smiling for parent; parent for baby. The consequence is to destroy binary oppositions between parents and

babies. At worst, this regresses to the recreation of a symbiotic unity between parent and child; at best, it subverts oppositions. I realize how judgmental the previous sentence is.

4. Walker's position disagrees with that of another excellent Stein critic, Susan Stewart, who proposes that Stein's language is "a discourse of infinite perpetuation, a discourse that is both insular and inviolable and, at the same time, able to accommodate everything in the world to the infinite motion of its machinations" (142).

5. To adopt a political metaphor, language serves the same function as a legislator does in a representative system of government. A word both has its own being and responds to a given segment of reality. A legislator has her/his own identity and responds to a given constituency.

6. Schmitz (241–46) compares Stein's treatment of the Dead Father to that of Donald Barthelme.

7. Jerome McGann, in conversation, October 13, 1984, acutely points out that "mint" puns on "meant" as well.

8. In her lecture, "Landscape Is Not Grammar," at the UCLA Symposium, "Considering Gertrude Stein," November 10, 1984, Ulla E. Dydo commented that Stein referred to Toklas as "sister." Once again, Stein's text is autobiographical, a diary.

WORKS CITED

Bridgman, Richard. Gertrude Stein In Pieces. New York: Oxford University Press, 1970.

Cixous, Hélène. "The Laugh of the Medusa." Signs: Journal of Women in Culture and Society (Summer 1976) 1(4):875–94.

Gilbert, Sandra M. "Costumes of the Mind." Writing and Sexual Difference. Ed. Elizabeth Abel. Chicago: University of Chicago Press, 1982.

Jacobus, Mary. "The Difference of View." Women Writing and Writing About Women. Ed. Mary Jacobus. New York: Barnes and Noble Books, 1979.

Perloff, Marjorie. The Poetics of Indeterminacy. Princeton: Princeton University Press, 1981.

Rogers, W. R. When This You See Remember Me. 1948; repr. New York: Avon Discus Books, 1973.

Schmitz, Neil. Huck and Alice: Humorous Writing in America. Minneapolis: University of Minnesota Press, 1983.

Stein, Gertrude. Alphabets and Birthdays. Yale Edition of the Unpublished Writings of Gertrude Stein, vol. 7, with Introduction by Donald Gallup. New Haven: Yale University Press, 1957.

—— Bee Time Vine. Yale Edition of the Unpublished Writings of Gertrude Stein, vol. 3, with Preface and Notes by Virgil Thomson. New Haven: Yale University Press, 1953.

—— *Geographical History of America*. 1935; repr. with New Introduction by William H. Gass, New York: Vintage Books, 1973.

—— *Geography and Plays*. 1922; repr. New York: Something Else Press, 1968.

—— *Lectures in America*. 1936; repr. Boston: Beacon Press, 1957; 3d printing 1967.

—— *Lucy Church Amiably*. 1930; repr. New York: Something Else Press, 1969.

—— "Tender Buttons." *Selected Writings of Gertrude Stein*. Ed. Carl Van Vechten. 1962; repr. New York: Random House (Vintage edition), 1972; pp. 459–97.

—— "What Are Masterpieces and Why Are There So Few Of Them." 1936; repr. New York: Pitman, 1940, 1970.

—— *Yale Gertrude Stein*. Ed. Richard Kostelanetz. New Haven: Yale University Press, 1980.

Stewart, Susan. *Nonsense: Aspects of Intertextuality in Folklore and Literature*. Baltimore: Johns Hopkins University Press, 1979.

Stimpson, Catharine R. "Gertrice/Altrude." *Mothering the Mind*. Ed. Ruth Perry and Martine Watson Brownley. New York: Holmes and Meier, 1984.

Walker, Jayne L. *The Making of a Modernist*. Amherst: University of Massachusetts Press, 1984.

The Mistress
in the Masterpiece

NANCY J. VICKERS

When Virginia Woolf argued that "masterpieces are not single and solitary births" but rather "the outcome of many years of thinking in common, of thinking by the body of the people," she stressed the illusory nature of the old dream of artistic autonomy (68–69). Indeed her usage places the term "masterpiece" in contradiction with its origins—the piece by which one proves one is a master, the single part of a whole (a genre, an author's *corpus*) that silences, by the strength of its voice, all other parts. In the sixteenth century—that period of aggressive/defensive individualism—it was the elusive masterpiece that constituted the obsessive project of self-fashioning patron and self-fashioning artist alike. This essay examines one attempt at mastery, Benvenuto Cellini's bronze relief entitled "The Nymph of Fontainebleau," in order to locate the position of "the body of the people," here a specifically female body, within it. I turn to this "text," on the one hand, because it is characteristic of Fontainebleau—that is to say, French mannerist—style, and, on the other, because "The Nymph of Fontainebleau" took multiple discursive forms. We have, and this is unusual in the world of Renaissance texts, a narrative of its making in the autobiographical mode, two highly detailed descriptions in the ecphrastic mode, and, of course, the relief itself—all by the same hand. Consequently, the analysis of the production and consumption of this "masterpiece," not as isolated product but as process in context, is enhanced by the identifiability of telling gaps, repetitions, and points of convergence between multiple rhetorics.

The "Nymph of Fontainebleau" was commissioned by Francis I to represent a place: "Il Re desiderava d'averci una figura, che figurassi Fontana Beliò" (371).[1] Cellini's figure to figure Fontaine-bleau was destined to articulate a privileged site, to introduce courtier-spectators into the text that was Fontainebleau, to crown the main entrance of a palace that was at once a preferred royal playground and a preferred sign of royal authority. For Francis, the trappings of extravagant pleasure marked extravagant prerogative and power. Be-gun upon his return from a humiliating military defeat at Pavia and a humiliating captivity in Spain, Fontainebleau—the birthplace of French mannerism—emerged, André Chastel maintains, from "the need for prestige" and the "need for caprice" (xiii, translation mine): the failures of the warrior would be supplanted by the successes of the patron. "Having lost Italy," Michelet noted, "Francis created Italy in France" (354, translation mine). Cellini, a Florentine goldsmith turned sculptor, expatriated in 1540, and was charged with conferring upon Francis's place its *genius loci*; he chose to represent a water nymph, for the source of the name—Fontainebleau—was the name of a source in the forest that surrounded the palace.[2]

The narrative of the nymph begins, however, at a point that predates Francis's commission, at a moment in Cellini's career when he was most actively operating the all important conversion from artisan to artist, from craftsman to sculptor. Such a radical professional move required the mastery of new and consecrated me-dia—first casting in bronze and later sculpting in marble. Cellini's first commission from Francis had been the creation of a dozen silver candlesticks, each to be a god or goddess, and each, following royal specification, cut to "exactly the same height as his Majesty himself" (256). Cellini wisely began with the subject that most nearly reflected the King's public self-image, a six-foot Jupiter: "I also felt inclined," he writes in what is arguably the most transitional sentence in the *Vita*, "to cast in bronze the large model I had made for the silver statue of Jupiter. It was the sort of work I had never tackled before" (264). Indeed no matter how monumental, work in silver was still artisan's work: Cellini's chapter on the fashioning of the candlestick appears in his "Treatise on Goldsmithing" not in his "Treatise on Sculpture." In "set-ting his hand" ("messo mano") to new matter, Cellini sought the help of Parisian master founders, but no sooner had the masters begun than Cellini proposed a contest to be won by the novice:

They set their hands ("messon mano") to the project, and when I noticed that they were not going about it in the right way, I hurriedly began work on a head of Julius Caesar, a bust in armor, much larger than life size. I copied it from a little model that I had brought from Rome, that was copied from a splendid ancient head. I also set my hand ("messi mano") to another head of the same size that I copied from a beautiful girl that I kept around for my sexual pleasure ("per mio diletto carnale"). To it/her ("a questa") I gave the name Fontainebleau, which was the place that the King had chosen for his own pleasure ("per sua propria dilettazione"). (365; 264–65)

From this context of artistic rivalry, a first *figura* of Fontainebleau emerges. Cellini's initial bronzes—the pieces with which he outdoes two old masters—form a couple: on the one hand, an armed warrior-ruler imitated from art (the antique model) and, on the other, "Fontainebleau," the head of a woman imitated from nature (the living model). In "Fontainebleau" Francis, the warrior ruler, takes his pleasure ("sua propria dilettazione") and in "Fontainebleau," Cellini, the artist-subject, also takes his ("mio diletto"). This fusing of statue, place, and woman under the name Fontainebleau signals still another rivalry, one that transcends the contest between artists, to reveal a tension between patron and subject that is cast in unavoidably sexual terms.[3] Each is the prideful possessor of Fontainebleau.

But to move from the head of Fontainebleau to the full-bodied nymph, the narrative must continue. Invited with his apprentices to leave Paris for the day, Cellini asks his most trusted employee, Pagolo Miccieri, to stay behind and keep watch over first, his property, and second, that same "beautiful girl," whom, he adds, "I keep around principally for the use of my art" ("per servizio de l'arte mia") "and without whom I could not do it" (384; 279). He goes on to explain that "because he is a man," he has used her for sexual pleasure ("me ne son servito a i mia piaceri carnali") and that he suspects (hopes?) she will give him a son (384; 279). Once out of town, Cellini becomes suspicious, returns home unannounced, and virtually catches Pagolo and the girl, Caterina, in the act. Both are chased from the workshop; there are lawsuits and altercations; and finally Cellini, threatening murder, forces them to marry; this step is but the prerequisite to a carefully plotted and amply described revenge:

Not satisfied with having made Pagolo take such a shameless little whore as his wife, in addition—to round off my revenge—I used to copy from her. . . I made her pose in the nude. . . and then I had my revenge by using her sexually, mocking her and her husband for the various horns ("le diverse corna") I was giving him. I also made her pose in great discomfort for hours at a stretch. Her discomfort annoyed her as much as it pleased me ("me dilettava"), since she was very beautifully made and won me great honor. . . . So, I said to myself, I get two kinds of revenge out of this. First, she's now married, so these are not empty horns ("corna vane") like the horns she gave me when she played the whore with me. Thus I'm taking an excellent revenge against him, and also against her, by making her pose in such discomfort which, beyond the pleasure, wins me credit and profit. What more could I want?

While I was weighing these matters, the slut redoubled her insults, talking about her husband. What she said and did nearly drove me out of my mind, and giving into my rage, I seized her by the hair and dragged her up and down the room, beating and kicking her until I was exhausted. . . . When I had given her a good pummelling, she swore she would never return; so for the first time I realized what a mistake I had made, since I was losing a splendid opportunity to win honor. Besides this, I saw her all torn, bruised, and swollen, and I realized that even if she did come back it would be necessary to have her treated for two weeks before I could use her ("me ne potessi servire"). (396–97; 288–89)

Once Caterina has left, Cellini consults his servant, Ruberta, who scolds him for being so cruel to such a beauty. He excuses himself by recounting the story of her infidelity, which Ruberta dismisses, explaining that infidelity is a French custom, and that in France there is not a husband without his horns ("le sue cornetta") (398; 289). He asks Ruberta to intercede with Caterina, because he "would be pleased to finish his work by using her" ("perché io arei auto a piacere di poter finire quella mia opera, servendomi di lei") (398; 289). Ruberta tells him that he is naive, that the best strategy is to do nothing at all. Caterina will return even sooner if left on her own. And when, for reasons about which we can only speculate—money, the protection of her husband's position, her desire to be the Nymph of Fontaine-bleau—she does, Cellini adds:

Then I began to copy her, and in between times we enjoyed sexual pleasures ("le piaccevolezze carnali") and then, at the same hour as the day
before, she provoked me so much that I had to give her the same beating;
and this went on for several days, always in the same pattern, with little
variation. Meanwhile I, who had won myself great honor and finished my
figure, gave the orders to cast it in bronze.. . . My figure came out beautifully,
and was as finely cast as anything has ever been. (398–99; 290)

The narrative of the making of Fontainebleau stands out in Cellini's
550-page autobiography—by its exceptional length, which I have significantly abbreviated, by the nature of its subject, by its granting of
the only detailed representation we are ever given of modeling (in
both senses of the term) in Cellini's workshop, and—in an autobiography that confesses murders, betrayals, thefts, and emprisonments—
by the fact that it is the only narrative prefaced by an apology. Here,
for once, Cellini acknowledges that he has done something wrong—
although to Pagolo not to Caterina: "If when telling the events of my
life I never admitted to being wrong, I would not be believed when
telling of events in which I know that I was right. I know I made a
mistake in wanting to take such a strange revenge against Pagolo
Miccieri" (288). Caterina's body, then, stands not primarily as the instrument of direct revenge against her—through the discomfort the
artist takes pleasure in inflicting upon her—but, more important, as
the medium of revenge against her husband. Indeed she is not beaten
until she speaks his name. Her flesh becomes simultaneously the
medium of Cellini's artistic accomplishment and the shield that absorbs the blows in a battle between male sexual rivals. " 'To cuckold,' "
notes Eve Kosofsky Sedgwick, "is by definition a sexual act, performed
on a man, by another man" (49). Even Cellini's desire to win favor is
at times obscured by his desire to cuckold Pagolo, to confer horns
upon him (the repeated *corna* and *cornetta*) that will not only equal but
surpass the horns Pagolo conferred upon Cellini. What is most intri-
guing is the telling coincidence of still another tale of sexual rivalry,
here immeasurably more explicit, with still another figuring of Fontainebleau. Out of daily domestic violence emerges a work of art, and
the vocabulary of investment in the violence tellingly repeats the
vocabulary of investment in the art. Caterina's flesh is positioned to
serve *servire*) both sexual and artistic needs; she provides not only

bodily but also visual pleasure (*piacere*) through the "delightful" spectacle of beauty under pressure.

The Nymph was intended to decorate the Porte Dorée of the palace. Above that doorway was a half circle for which the King ordered his figure to represent Fontainebleau. In the 13½ foot lunette Cellini placed an 11½ foot woman ("una femmina" not "una ninfa") reclining in what he calls a beautiful attitude ("in bella attitudine") (372; 270). Her right hand rests on a stag, "one of the King's emblems" (270);[4] her left hand rests on vases from which water seems to flow (see figure 1). On the left there are fauns and boars and on the right, hunting dogs of various kinds. At the sides Cellini designed matching bases and cornices and between them, instead of columns, he placed two 11½ foot satyrs, one of which is shown in figure 2. Each held up the doorway with one arm while in the other he held a weapon—a club or a ball and chains; each looked "fierce" and "aggressive" and was meant "to terrorize" the spectator (270). Although Cellini calls these figures satyrs, he notes that they have nothing of the satyr about them, except for their little horns ("certe piccole cornetta") and their goaty heads; all the rest is in human form (372; 270). Cellini enclosed the whole work in an oblong and for each of the upper angles he designed an angel with a torch in her hand signifying victory (see figure 3). Above them was a salamander, the King's device.

Cellini's never-assembled project, then, was an exceptional full-bronze doorway, an enterprise of virtuoso originality and ambition.[5] Of the scattered, extant fragments of his monumental projects, the nymph is indeed the most monumental; she is, for example, over a foot taller than the Perseus that dominates Florence's Piazza della Signoria. This doorway, moreover, was not understood either by Francis or by Cellini to be empty, albeit impressive, decoration; it communicated meaning[6] both to artist and to patron:

The King began by asking me what was the idea behind the beautiful design [for yet another project], saying that without a word from me he had understood all I had done as regards the doorway. . . . He was well aware that I didn't work like the kind of fool whose art has a certain amount of grace but is completely devoid of significance. (271)

Indeed the door lends itself to ready interpretation. It is clearly a

Figure 1. "The Nymph of Fontainebleau," Benvenuto Cellini.
(Photo: Réunion des Musées Nationaux, Paris)

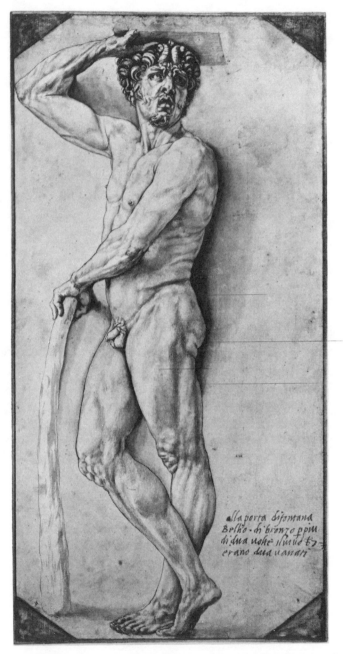

Figure 2. "Satyr," Benvenuto Cellini. (Photo: Ian Woodner Family
Collection, New York)

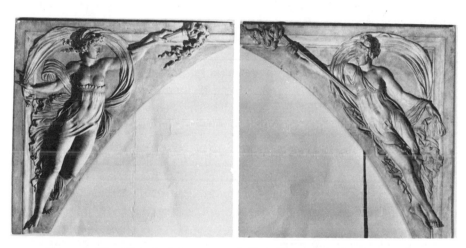

Figure 3. "Two Victories," Benvenuto Cellini. (Photo: Réunion des Musées Nationaux, Paris)

celebration of the Château, that is to say, a celebration of Francis. As a classicizing rendering of woods and waters, the spaces Renaissance reality populated with stags, boars, and hounds, and Renaissance fantasy with nymphs and satyrs, it underlines not only the principle natural features of the forest surrounding Fontainebleau, but also the principal pastimes, hunting and bathing, of the court that frequented it. The stag-king predictably dominates the scene; he is at once possessor of and possessed by Fontainebleau; he is regally crowned by two angels bearing torches to light up his identifying symbol, his salamander amid the flames.

But what, indeed, is the rhetoric of this image? Male figures are vertical; females, horizontal or diagonal. The line that centers the image, its center of power, moves through the nymph's body—note what part of her body—to the stag, and then to the crowning and perhaps crowned salamander. In the imagistic discourses of Francis's power, centering often signals not only dominance, but dominance articulated in sexual terms. Here a lateral, diagonal female gesture serves to underline that centering; the coronation accomplished by the female victories only highlights the central axis. The drama of the lunette thus resides primarily in the stag and the nymph, and secondarily, in the satyrs.[7] For although the latter are fiercely monumental, they are also side-lined. The nymph, none the less, is displayed between two categories of armed male figures: since she traverses the space that separates the horns of the stag from the club or ball and chains of the satyrs, her displayed nakedness constitutes a locus of seemingly inevitable conflict between enemies whose tense opposition is masked only by a strategy of representation that places them momentarily "at rest." Similarly, the low relief on either side of her underlines her median status: on one side, the beasts of the forest and on the other hunting hounds, in short, the opponents of the hunt who, if they are to engage one another, must do so across her body.

Status in the spatial hierarchy, moreover, is reflected in the hierarchy of relief: the angels and the animals are, for the most part, in low relief ("di basso rilievo"); some fauns and boars are in half relief ("di mezzo rilievo"); the satyrs are in more than half relief ("piú che di mezzo rilievo"); the nymph, described initially like the satyrs as in "more than half relief" is later particularized—her head and selected parts of her body stand out in full, while others remain in half; and finally "a great part of the stag's neck" is brought out in "full relief" ("di tutto relievo") (372; 270; see also *Trattoto*, 655).[8] The stag's horns, moreover—tellingly unmentioned in either of the descriptive texts— constitute the lunette's most outstanding and indeed upstanding feature. These horns are so foregrounded as to break out of the architectural frame; they extend above the half circle and thus isolate themselves as the stag's crowning glory. Sixteenth-century hunting treatises indeed term certain stag horns a "couronne" (Du Fouilloux, 20ᵛ); here isolation directly under Francis's device underlines a specifically majestic function.

　　　　Indeed all of the male figures in the doorway program, like all of the male figures in the narrative of its creation, have horns. The "certe piccole cornetta" (372) of the satyrs—the detail that identifies them as satyrs—points us back to Ruberta's characterization of *every* French husband (she includes, I presume, royal ones): "In Francia non era marito che non avessi le sue cornetta" (398). The repeated horns of Cellini's narrative—he gives Pagolo a variety of horns ("diverse corna"), those horns are real horns not empty horns ("corna vane") like the horns Pagolo had given him—repeat themselves in the doorway (398–97). Nowhere else in Cellini's texts are horns even mentioned; nowhere else in his plastic works do we find such a virtuoso display of the artist's ability to horn his subject. A crown of horns, moreover, is an ambivalent signifier: horns speak contradiction. They confer both respect and humiliation; they assert potency and impotence; they convey armed courage as well as flight before the enemy; and they identify the majestic king of the forest as well as the pathetic victim of the hunter, the victim whose horns are mounted as a sign of his having been mastered, whose body is ritually torn to bits and thrown to the dogs. In short, the language of horns is double: it may readily voice the opposite of what it seems to say. The subject-artist's glorification of his King simultaneously speaks an insult—*cornuto*—the insult imposed upon the heads of men when they cannot master women.

　　　　The fate of becoming first a *cornuto*, a horned man, and ultimately a stag is, of course, the fate imposed upon Actaeon by

Diana. While hunting he stumbles upon the goddess and her nymphs bathing in a forest source. Diana, upon seeing him see her (the forbidden nakedness of the divine, but of a female divine) scatters him with drops of water that initiate his metamorphosis. His staglike flight into the woods carries him only to death, to dismemberment by his own hounds, as he pathetically attempts to articulate his identity; the words "Know your master" are, according to Ovid, the words he cannot utter (*Metamorphoses*, 3.230, translation mine). This tale of the hunter hunted, of the master mastered by a woman he cannot control, is clearly inscribed by Cellini in his personification of Fontainebleau. A female nude in a source accompanied by a stag would connote Diana to any sixteenth-century spectator-reader. Indeed, after Francis's death, Henri II gave Cellini's lunette to his mistress, Diane de Poitiers, to decorate her chateau at Anet.[9] When, in the nineteenth century, the original was moved to the Louvre, catalogues referred to it as "the Diana."[10] Rosso's "Nymph of Fontainebleau," a strikingly similar image, which—if indeed by Rosso—must predate that of Cellini, notably does not include a stag; it is Cellini who inscribes the stag within the embrace of the figure that figures Fontainebleau.

A stag's head in this position—that is to say viewed full front—is called in the heraldic code "a stag at gaze," and I would like to take my cue from that heraldic notation in analyzing what this stag's gaze accomplishes. It is, in the doorway complex, an isolated gaze: the victories look up to the salamander; the animals look horizontally into and out of the frame; the nymph looks down and to the side, perhaps at one of the hounds;[11] the satyrs, it seems, turn slightly up and toward the center, in the direction of the nymph and the stag they are supporting. The stag, however, looks straight ahead; his stare directly engages his spectator. The nymph was, of course, created to be viewed by any number of people—in short an entire court, men and women, as well as its visitors—but its lesson to them was, I would argue, the privileged status of its principle, its inscribed, viewer. In the stag's gaze, the King as viewer mirrors himself. He, as well as everyone else, reads his control of his possession, his mastery of a graciously consenting Fontainebleau.

Representations of the Diana-Actaeon story play a special role in the visual arts in that they dramatize the act of seeing, they self-reflexively figure the voyeuristic pleasure of a male gaze riveted on female nakedness.[12] The casting of the royal gaze in these terms communicates once again a double message: on the one hand, the stag-king is an Actaeon who, for the duration of this representation, is not dismembered; he is a voyeur embraced by the object of a previous, forbidden gaze, a voyeur permitted the pleasure of viewing a Diana whose threat has obviously been neutralized. On the other, the freeze frame represented is a moment lifted out of a narrative, leaving its viewer to wonder if plot has been permanently halted by royal prerogative or whether it is to be resumed. Let me compare two Fontainebleau images, clearly done in the 1540s, as elaboration: the first, most probably a tapestry design, is entitled "Francis I and the Nymphs of Fontainebleau" (see figure 4). In the background we see the Château and in the foreground the fountain itself populated by naked nymphs striking a variety of poses. The "bathers' convention" is, of course, a traditional test of artistic virtuosity, a proof of mastery of that ultimate challenge to the figurative artist, the human body. Display of multiple nudes viewed from multiple perspectives is, first and foremost, ostentatious display of the master's control of his medium. To the left, Francis and his court stand at the edge of the spectacle, and yet no one but Francis looks at it. The gazes of his courtiers all turn in upon each other; only he enjoys the privilege, the pleasure of looking. It is his gaze, a royal gaze—and in a nation under Salic law— a male gaze, that dominates the scene.

Turning next to an engraving by Jean Mignon after Luca Penni (figure 5), the Diana-Actaeon story is transposed into a typically bellifontaine setting; the natural pool has become a classicizing bath. From it, Diana, protected by her nymphs, scatters water on a hunter who has already assumed his stag head. His pose, moreover, virtually repeats that of the King in the previous sketch: the turn of the head, the disposition of the *contraposto*; the angle of the armed arm; the movement of the hand toward the naked woman; even the cut of the garment. Centered above the engraving is the previously cited imperative from Ovid's *Metamorphoses*: "Dominum Cognoscite Vestrum," "Know your (masculine) master." The citation, tellingly, is from the scene that this engraving has specifically written out of the story; in the background we see Actaeon in flight but nowhere do we see him

Figure 4. "Francis I and the Nymphs of Fontainebleau," Claude Badouyn (?).
(Photo: Réunion des Musées Nationaux, Paris)

Figure 5. "The Metamorphosis of Actaeon," Jean Mignon after Luca Penni. (Photo: Graphische Sammlung Albertina, Vienna)

torn to bits by his dogs, nowhere do we see him attempt to speak his mastery of them. What then does "Know your master" mean? Who speaks it? Does Diana assert, in the masculine, a control that has been neutralized by the engraving's erasure, or rather is the revised master a regally posed Actaeon? For in any neutralizing representation of Diana with a stag, either the stag tames Diana or Diana tames the stag.

To carry neutralization one step further we need only return to Cellini's lunette, to a Diana who embraces her Actaeon. However, this Actaeon does not encounter Diana's gaze; he—as a mark of possession—displays her to view: "The very act of rendering visible," writes Sharon Willis, "expresses a capture, and a power relation" (96). I would like to dwell momentarily on the notion of "display" since it reveals, I think, one of the defining strategies of this image. "To display"—from the Latin *displicare*, "to scatter, to disperse, and, in late Latin, to unfold—as in unfolding a banner to view"—is "to spread something out, to open it up, to exhibit it to be seen, and, by extension, to exhibit it ostentatiously."[13] In the "Display of Heraldry" it signifies "to lay or place a human or animal form with the limbs extended"; in the "display of rhetoric," "to set forth in representation, to depict, to describe." Consider, for example, the "Nymph of Fontainebleau" attributed to Rosso (figure 6), who is posed so much like Cellini's and yet with a difference. As veil, her legs bend up and turn sideways; her right arm crosses her body; her head is only seen in profile. When we shift to Cellini (figure 1), the entire body is tipped forward to a point of precarious imbalance; the front leg drops and both legs are elongated; both shoulders (not just the left) are thrown back to open up the chest, both arms extend; and the head twists away from the center to permit a mixed profile and frontal view. The left leg, for example, strikes an impossible pose, flatly frontal at the foot while in profile at the knee. Even the mannered gesture that ostensibly asserts the nymph's power, her possessive embrace of a subdued stag/king, reveals through the discomfort implicit in its taut flatness the uneasiness provoked by such an assertion. Cellini's staging of gracious consent and control through easy repose reveals on close examination a calculated con-

Figure 6. "The Nymph of Fontainebleau," Pierre Milan after Rosso (?). (Photo: Bibliothèque Nationale, Paris)

tortion aimed at enhancing voyeuristic pleasure: "I made her pose in great discomfort" ("con gran disagio") "for hours at a stretch. And in that discomfort" ("questo disagio") "she was as much annoyed as I was delighted" ("me dilettava"), "since she was very beautiful and won me great honor"; and again, "so I'm also taking revenge against her . . . by making her pose in such discomfort" ("con tanto disagio") "which, beyond the pleasure" ("oltra al piacere"), "wins me credit and profit" (396–97; 288–89). It is, in this exchange between male artist and female model, her *disagio* which permits his *piacere*, his *diletazzione*. It should be noted that Cellini virtually never describes working from an adult male model and that his female models are typically bound to him through a triple power relation: they are servants within his household; they serve his sexual needs; and they serve the requirements of his art. The very vocabulary of heterosexual hierarchies that unites male artist, male patron, and male viewer, then, in sexual/aesthetic pleasure articulates, as its corollary, the discomfort of its female subject. A female viewer's response, determined as it is by a displacement of the structuring identification away from the seer and onto the object seen, then reenacts *disagio*. This response, too, as Lillian Robinson and Lise Vogel have argued in a related context, is part of what the image means.[14]

        The label "mannerist" as applied to works of art derives from the Italian *maniera* ("style"), which derives in turn from the Latin *manus* (hand). It is commonly held that mannerist art is about style. As such it places subject matter (*materia*) in the background in order to highlight skill (*maniera*), to call attention to the original touch of the individual who manipulates the subject. "Manner," writes Claude-Gilbert Dubois, "is the opposite of matter. One would have to invent 'matterism' to stand as complement to 'mannerism.' The matterist would have something substantial to say, for the mannerist there is no substance. The mannerist has nothing to say, except the manner of saying nothing" (15, translation mine). Dubois goes on to argue that in the relationship between the mannerist artist and the figure his art would ostensibly represent, it is the mark of the hand of the artist rather than the mimetic representation of the model that is structured to command attention. It is only logical, then, that mannerist art has prompted stylistic analysis, analysis of manner at the expense of analysis of matter. But the rhetoric of mannerist art does indeed say something, at the very least something about the ability of certain matter to move to the background while being positioned in the foreground.[15] What matter—if we can postulate a subject matter, a matter not subjected but acting as subject—would in fact lend itself to (consent to? submit to?) its own neutralization, would offer up its body to serve (*servire*) the "profit and credit" of the master mannerist. When Cellini sets his hand to his matter, that application takes three forms: the caressing of the "piacevolezze carnali," the pummeling of the rage, and the modeling of the masterpiece. And each manipulation is to leave *his* mark: he would, after all, give himself a son through Caterina, that is, imprint male form on formless female matter through the gesture of insemination; he would beat her to vent his rage against Pagolo, to take revenge in the tears and bruises of her flesh; and finally, he would win favor from Francis by privileging royal pleasure, by displaying Fontainebleau to view at the cost of (indeed because of) Caterina's bodily discomfort. In each case, Caterina's flesh is positioned as medium in the articulation of a relationship between men. Between the horned satyrs and the horned stag—potent or impotent, but in either case marked as male—lies Fontainebleau. Through her a complex hierarchy of male rivalries is played out: through the ostentatious display of Fontainebleau, Francis outdoes his rival sovereigns; through the subversive possession of Fontainebleau, the subject rivals the monarch; through the artistic mastery displayed in Fontainebleau, Cellini not only equals but surpasses rival masters; through intercourse with and abuse of Fontainebleau, Cellini makes clear who is master of the house.[16]

But the story of Fontainebleau is not quite this straightforward: there is indeed another woman in this text and she, too, at some level, is its source. Cellini recounts as follows one of the King's visits to his workshop:

And because he had with him *his* Madame d'Etampes [his mistress], they
began to talk about Fontainebleau. Madame d'Etampes said to his Majesty
that he ought to have me make something beautiful to decorate *his* Fontainebleau. (268, italics mine)

"His Fontainebleau" can, of course, be read two ways in Madame
d'Etampes's mediating sentence: *his* palace or *his* source. Francis opted
for the second, enthusiastically turning to Cellini, to ask him how he
would go about making a fountain, how he would convert a natural
source into a work of art. So Cellini set his hand ("messi mano") to a
model of Fontainebleau (371; 268). A month and a half later, when
Francis returned, the master craftsman had produced *two* models: on
seeing the first, that of "The Nymph of Fontainebleau," the King was
delighted; on seeing the second, that of the fountain itself, the King's
pleasure became even greater. Cellini's fountain was a square and in
each of its four corners sat a female figure, each figuring one of those
virtù which the King protected and in which he took delight ("si diletta")
(374): one figured literature, another figured the arts of design (sculpture, painting, architecture); still another, music; and the last liberal-
ity—that is, patronly support, money—which made possible the existence of all of the *virtù*. For Cellini, Francis's "fathering of the arts"
was literal; Jupiterlike, he inseminated them with a shower of gold.
Through them he took his pleasure; through them he left his mark on
French culture. In the center of Fontainebleau, Cellini planned a ped-
estal taller than the basin of the fountain itself, upon which a fifty-
four-foot nude figure to represent Francis, a Mars, was to be constructed: "In very truth," said the King, calling his treasurers, "I've found
a man after my own heart" (271).

      Fontainebleau may well be a place where, as Malherbe
later wrote, "Nature submitted to the miracle of Art" (82, translation
mine),[17] but it is also a place where art submitted to the early modern
monarch. And yet irony, here, belongs to the realm of individual history
and not official image making. For it was, Cellini maintains, that
aristocratic mistress who outmaneuvered the master artist by out-
smarting, and ultimately outliving, the master monarch. Indeed the
risk of medium turned unruly, of matter turned subject, is the consti-
tution of an obstacle. Moving in the space between the King and the
"man after his own heart"—acting as woman and as aristocrat—this

mistress it seems horned them both by finding sexual/political pleasure in bodies other than that of her master and by plotting to scatter the frustrated, consumed, fragmented *corpus* of a Renaissance Actaeon named Cellini.

NOTES

1. Quotations from Cellini's *Vita* in Italian are from the Bruno Maier edition; English translations are my adaptations of the George Bull translation. My modifications of Bull are generally directed at achieving a more literal rendering of Cellini's prose. All references are in parentheses in the text: if only Italian appears, the page reference is to Maier's edition; if only English appears, the page reference is to Bull's translation; if both Italian and English appear, the first reference is to Maier and the second to Bull.

2. On the origins of the myth of a "Nymph of Fontainebleau" and on her various representations, see Pressouyre (88–89).

3. On Cellini's awareness of the type of patrons for whom he worked and of their uses of his art, see Avery (206–8).

4. On Cellini's identification of the stag as an emblem of the King, see Pressouyre (88).

5. See Grodecki (62); and Pope-Hennessy (409 and 411).

6. See Pope-Hennessy (411); and Pressouyre (89).

7. My reading here differs from that of Pope-Hennessy, who considers the two monumental satyrs the "dominant feature" of the doorway (406).

8. Laura Mulvey's distinction between the flat spatial disposition of the "woman as icon" in film and the "three dimensional space" of the "active male figure" may be suggestively related to the generally heightened relief of the stag and satyrs in contrast to the generally imbedded relief of the nymph. See Mulvey (12–13).

9. On the history of the identification of the "Nymph of Fontainebleau" with Diana, see Pressouyre (89–90).

10. See Pressouyre (89–90).

11. See Pressouyre (88).

12. See my "Diana Described." Bardon characterizes Cellini's stag as a prisoner of beauty and virtue, as an "Actéon royal figé dans sa profanatoire admiration" (56).

13. Definitions are adapted from the Oxford English Dictionary.

14. The analysis of Robinson and Vogel emerges from an anecdote recounting a female spectator's reactions to Boucher's *Reclining Girl*, a portrait of a mistress of Louis XV (280 and 298). See also Mulvey on male visual pleasure.

15. On the ways in which the privileging of "manner" tends to neutralize "matter," see Suleiman.

16. My theoretical framework clearly suggests the triangulated construct of mimetic desire outlined by René Girard, but as recast in the work of such feminist critics as

Mary Jacobus, Patricia Klindienst Joplin, and Eve Kosofsky Sedgwick, whose analyses are attentive to the role played by gender in the positioning of individuals upon that triangle.
    17. Cited by Cahn (78).

WORKS CITED

Avery, Charles. *Florentine Renaissance Sculpture.* New York: Harper and Row, 1970.

Bardon, François. *Diane de Poitiers et le mythe de Diane.* Paris: Presses Universitaires de France, 1963.

Cahn, Walter. *Masterpieces: Chapters in the History of an Idea.* Princeton: Princeton University Press, 1979.

Cellini, Benvenuto. *The Autobiography of Benvenuto Cellini.* Trans. George Bull. Harmondsworth and New York: Penguin, 1956.

—— *Trattato della scultura.* In *La Vita, con l'aggiunta di: trattato dell'oreficeria, trattato della scultura, discorsi sopra l'arte, lettere e suppliche, poesie.* Milano: Longanesi, 1958.

—— *La Vita.* Ed. Bruno Maier. Novara: Istituto geografico de Agostini, 1962.

Chastel, André. "Fontainebleau, formes et symboles." L'*Ecole de Fontainebleau.* Paris: Editions des Musées Nationaux, 1972; pp. xiii–xxviii.

Dubois, Claude-Gilbert. *Le Maniérisme.* Paris: Presses Universitaires de France, 1979.

Du Fouilloux, Jacques. *La Vénerie.* 1585; repr. Angers: Charles Lebosse, 1849.

Grodecki, Catherine. "Le Séjour de Benvenuto Cellini à L'Hôtel de Nesle et la fonte de la Nymphe de Fontainebleau d'après les actes des notaires parisiens." *Bulletin de la Société de l'Histoire de Paris et de l'Ile-de-France* (1971); 98:45–80.

Jacobus, Mary. "Is There a Woman in This Text?" *New Literary History* (1982); 14:117–41.

Joplin, Patricia Klindienst. "The Voice of the Shuttle is Ours." *Stanford Literature Review* (1984); 1:25–53.

Malherbe, François. *Oeuvres.* Ed. Antoine Adam. Paris: Gallimard, 1971.

Michelet, Jules. *Histoire de France.* Paris: Bonnot, 1978. Vol. 10.

Mulvey, Laura. "Visual Pleasure and Narrative Cinema." *Screen* (1975), 16(3):6–18.

Ovid. *Metamorphoses.* Trans. and ed. Frank J. Miller. 2 vols. London: Heinemann, 1916. Vol. 1.

Pope-Hennessy, John. "A Bronze Satyr by Cellini." *The Burlington Magazine* (1982), 124:406–12.

Pressouyre, Sylvia. "Note additionnelle sur la Nymphe de Fontainebleau." *Bulletin de la Société de l'Histoire de Paris et de l'Ile-de-France* (1971), 98:81–92.

Robinson, Lillian S., and Lise Vogel. "Modernism and History." *New Literary History* (1971), 3:177–97. Repr. in *Images of Women in Fiction: Feminist Perspectives.* Ed. Susan

Koppelman Cornillon. Bowling Green: Bowling Green University Popular Press, 1972; pp. 278–307.

Sedgwick, Eve Kosofsky. "Homophobia, Misogyny, and Capital: The Example of *Our Mutual Friend*." *Rariian* (1983), 2(3):126–51. Repr. in *Between Men: English Literature and Male Homosocial Desire*. New York: Columbia University Press, 1985.

—— "Sexualism and the Citizen of the World: Wycherley, Sterne, and Male Homosocial Desire." *Critical Inquiry* (1984), 11:226–45.

Suleiman, Susan. "Reading Robbe-Grillet: Sadism and Text in *Projet pour une révolution à New York*." *Romanic Review* (1977), 68:43–62.

Vickers, Nancy J. "Diana Described: Scattered Woman and Scattered Rhyme." *Critical Inquiry* (1981), 8:265–79. Repr. in *Writing and Sexual Difference*. Ed. Elizabeth Abel. Chicago: University of Chicago Press, 1982; pp. 95–109.

Willis, Sharon. "Lettre sur des taches aveugles: A l'usage de celles qui voient." *L'Esprit créateur* (1984), 24:85–98.

Woolf, Virginia. *A Room of One's Own*. New York and Burlingame: Harcourt, Brace & World, 1929.

The Conception of Engendering
The Erotics of Editing

MARY ANN CAWS

> And for my part I will try to punctuate this book to make it easy for you to read, and to break it up, with spaces for a pause, as the publisher has asked me to do. But this I find very extremely difficult.
>
> For this book is the talking voice that runs on, and the thoughts that come, the way I said, and the people come too, and come and go, to illustrate the thoughts, to point the moral, to adorn the tale.
>
> Oh talking voice that is so sweet, how hold you alive in captivity, how point you with commas, semi-colons, dashes, pauses and paragraphs?
>
> Foot-on-the-ground person will have his grave grave doubts, and if he is also a smug-pug he will not keep his doubts to himself; he will say: It is not, and it cannot come to good. And I shall say, Yes it is and shall. And he will say: So you think you can do this, so you do, do you?
>
> Yes I *do*, I *do*.
>
> —Stevie Smith, *Novel on Yellow Paper*

SELF-PRESENTATIONS

"**A** Society," Virginia Woolf's devastating critique of the male in his patriotic, paternal, and prideful plumage, sets up a gender contrast between the book-producing male and the child-producing female, unable to understand each other: "True, they console themselves with stars of all shapes, ribbons of all shades, and incomes of all sizes—but what is to console us?" (in Marcus, 84). Later, her woman member of the Outsiders' society in the equally devastating *Three Guineas* reveals the same amazement in front of masculine insignia as do Montesquieu's Persian travelers confronting Parisian society two centuries earlier: the splendor of male public attire causes the non-insigniaed female to marvel at distinctions and difference:

Some have the right to wear plain buttons only; others rosettes; some may wear a single stripe; others three, four or five. And each curl or stripe is sewn on at precisely the right distance apart—it may be one inch for one man, one inch and a quarter for another. Rules again regulate the gold wire on the shoulders, the braid on the trousers, the cockades on the hats . . . Even stranger, however, than the symbolic splendour of your clothes are the ceremonies that take place when your wear them. . . . And whatever these ceremonies may mean you perform them always together, always in step, always in the uniform proper to the man and the occasion. (TG, 19–20)[1]

Two radically opposed conceptions of self-presentation are illustrated by a contemporary newspaper anecdote about a hero and a less recent series of anecdotes about a literary heroine of modest stature.

It was reported in the New York Times recently that a Marine Commandant presented his own insignia to a wounded corporal who had indicated his faithfulness with a written note. The corporal—his leg broken, his lungs collapsed, his arm crushed, his skull fractured, and his eyes full of concrete dust—had scribbled on a piece of paper for the general the two words "Semper fi," the abbreviated form of Semper Fidelis, the motto of the always faithful marines. This moving anecdote is not so much about how you really can always tell it to the marines, in no matter what state, and tell it seriously; but rather, how the marine could tell it was the general. What criteria of verifiability does a wounded and blinded man employ to tell a general from a just plain guy? Here it is the general who tells us: " 'I told him I was the Marine Commandant', said General Kelley, 'and before he believed me, he reached up and touched my four stars to make sure it was me' " (NYT, November 16, 1983). Now I grant the marine had his eyes full of dust, but they were full of stars anyway. The point (beyond the pathos of the anecdote, which is real enough) is this: *he* knew it was *him* (in fact they both knew), because of the stars and stripes, stuck on, sewed on, or pinned on.

The proper show of fidelity to the general in uniform was indeed to notice his stars and to express allegiance to them, for they had become the man who wore them. Both men then played their roles correctly, and correctly figured out who they were. So the insignia were passed on, the faith kept, and the story told in the papers.

The second anecdote is in direct contrast to the one above. In the preface to an edition of Emily Dickinson's poems, Thomas Wentworth Higginson tells us that when she sent him her first communication, together with her poems unsigned in a larger envelope, her name was penciled on a small card in a small envelope included in the other. No insignia and no permanence, not even ink to mark the signature and keep the trace. "I could not weigh myself, myself. My size felt small to me" (ED, 8). The faint pencil outline, like a bird track, he remarked, was in keeping with what she called "my barefoot rank" (ED, 9). And yet this unpretentious self-presentation and these bare feet are allied with a sure-footed and clear-eyed evaluation of the genuine ground she covers. "Perhaps you smile at me. I could not stop for that. My business is circumference" (ED, 10). What she brings to bear is quite simply everything: even in a moment of despair, incapable of transmitting and conveying the majesty of nature, she is nevertheless laden with what many of us would find quite inconceivable: "the mountains I could not hold now, so I brought but the Gods" (ED, 13).

Of these two self-conceptions or self-presentations, the first is entirely clothed in clothing, totally entrapped in costume, and the second is minimal in all outer traces and majestic in inner bearing. How do I know when it is myself, and how can the others tell? Can the general tell it is himself because he is recognized by the touch system? Emily Dickinson knew all along, and it was for others to marvel at the self-effacement allied with such certain majesty.

How we sign or designate ourselves,[2] then, comes sooner or later to bear on whatever it is we think of ourselves as bringing forth. Our bearing is surely at least double: what we look like and write like and speak like depends on how we know, and whether we know, and how long we have known it is us. Not always, but often, male and female knowledge differ in kind and result. My extreme cases bear witness to that, insofar as it would be difficult to imagine the roles reversed. But I am making no promise to play fair.[3]

WHO ENGENDERS?

The problem is how we are to learn what our bearing might be, in finding out who we are. It is not always permitted to engender one's own voice and text. Yeats in his telling of A *Vision*, his own of course, describes how the communicator who spoke to him through his wife's automatic writing came to his attention, this event dated on the afternoon of October 24, 1917, four days after their marriage. He persuaded her to give the unknown writer an hour or two every day, and the communicator proved his good taste by taking his first theme from Yeats's own and just published *Per Amica Silentia Lunae.* So the wife, as medium, gave her writing favors to another, and obligingly did not interfere in the process:

My wife's interests are musical, literary, practical, she seldom comments upon what I can dictate except upon the turn of a phrase; she can no more correct it than she could her automatic script at a time when a slight error brought her new fatigue. But the communicator, as independent of her ignorance as of her knowledge, had no tolerance for error. (YV, 21)

The writing wife's role, it seems, consisted of letting the writing pass through her transparently, of not getting in the way. The symbolists had particular designs on the transparent woman, who served up the sign, conveying it with fidelity, patience, and absolute personal silence. She herself is patiently ruled out. To Mallarmé, for example, the ballerina as she danced was neither woman nor dancer, she was the conveyor of the sign. Rather than dance, she enacts "by the marvel of shortcuts and leaps, by a corporal writing. . . a poem disengaged from any scribe's apparatus" (I, 192). She is only emblem, unindividualized metaphor. Something about her action might signify a part of general beauty—some flower or cloud or jewel or wave—which could be appropriated by the symbolist's own (male) spiritual nudity. She has the ornament, even in her undress, while he, in full evening dress, has the bareness; she offers up the allegory in her full impersonality, "between her feminine appearance and some mimed object, for a certain union: she stabs it with a sure-pointed toe, and places it" (I, 181). But the observer knows that in this performance is nothing real, that it is exterior to the true action on the true stage inside the mind.

That is perfect performance, with the performer performing nothing for nothing, but delicately engendering the conception of ideal conception: "Before taking one step she invites us, with two fingers, with a pleated quiver of her skirt, simulating an impatience of feathers toward the idea" (I, 195). She is but a soul dizzy "as if placed in the air by an artifice" (I, 198), an untutored, unlettered ballerina as dizzy dame playing out her profession; what she is supposed to do, she does: "she exposes the nudity of your concepts and silently will write your vision like a Sign—that she is" (I, 197). The verb Mallarmé applies to her performance is double-pronged: "délivrer," at once to set free and to hand over; in short, she really delivers and then she really and tactfully disappears. She may be named: Loie Fuller, that "fountain of herself never running dry" is a hieroglyph (I, 202), but is not herself when dancing. She is the direct instrument of the idea, her legs doing the idea's writing, not her own. She isn't given the real to act in or out.

This conception of an idea engendered by the one who neither chooses it nor understands it, who simply passes it on for the gentleman to ogle, cherish, and write about, is a far cry from the gentleman editor of a female writer, whether married to her or not. For the writer both chooses and understands, sees and listens, writes and gives birth. And yet, he the other may have the last word.

ENGENDERING MODE

I want to forge ahead, on my own lines.
—Virginia Woolf, VWD, 5:56

The two meanings to which one crucial word in this context can give birth will necessarily find themselves on the lying-in and delivery tables at the same time, all the more so since the meanings are of and at the origin. "Matrix," in its sense of womb, the place or situation in which something is conceived and is developed, meets with the printing matrix, or the metal plate for typefaces. What is born, then, is born to reading. Now, giving birth in print to somebody's brainchild, one's own or the child of bitextual love, does not just require long gestating patience, is not just fraught with dangers of loss and suffering, but is beset, at least in some readings of the postmatrix or printed situation, with misunderstandings, mundane, readable, and lively.

Partly, these can be attributed to the simplistic tradition of the male model of fathering or giving birth to the text. This is, often even in the case of a female creator, thought of as properly men's business, particularly in the case of a marriage conceived of along patriarchal lines—not "my own lines," as in Woolf's diary, but those others, established by tradition. The vocabulary of hospital life is instructive here: as interns and residents prepare in medical training, one of the most eulogistic recommendations is said to be "strong work." The expression stresses not the compassionate or healing nature of the profession but the macho-dominant culture. Strong work and strong natures prevail. Strong work is exactly what Virginia Woolf sets out to do by writing.[4] She proves to her "own conviction" that she can write "with fury, with rapture, with absorption still" (VWD, 5:64). Of her angularity, she speaks with an insider's knowledge, even as she would take an "outsider's" stance in regard to the world of the establishment and so must always write "against the current"; so the bringing of her books into the world for their reception by others she explicitly compares to giving birth—sometimes difficult, sometimes less so (of *Three Guineas*, "This is the mildest childbirth I have ever had," VWD, 5:148).

All the metaphors associated with writing for her are indicative of *strong* work, along her own lines. If she is not rowing against the current she is riding against it, preferably at top pace: "and having got astride my saddle the whole world falls in shape, it is this writing that gives me my proportions" (VWD, 3:343). For this she may, as she says, "harness" not just the steed but also, and more particularly, herself (VWD, 5:67), strenuously, for her extreme dash. In her diary, Woolf notes with admiration the gait of Lord Byron's style and its gender:

The springy random haphazard galloping nature of its method. . . an elastic shape which will hold whatever you choose to put into it. . . . He writes cantos without once flogging his flanks. He had, evidently, the able witty mind of what my father Sir Leslie would have called a thoroughly masculine nature. (VWD, 1:181)

In her turn, when she is writing at top speed, fully harnessed to her work, the joint effort of horse and rider is exemplary and no less male in its virtue than that of Lord Byron: "Oh how violently I have been galloping through these mornings!" she exclaims about the writing of the controversial tract *Three Guineas*. "It has pressed & spurted out of me, if that's any proof of virtue, like a physical volcano. And my brain feels cool & quiet after the expulsion. I've had it sizzling now since— Well, I was thinking of it at Delphi I remember" (VWD, 5:112). A note sends us back to a reflection on "the male virtues" (VWD, 4:95), a passage she marks as "thinking of the book again."

At less exalted moments, her ride over textual terrain is compared, in her diary entries, to a less strenuous gait: "After a most dismal hacking got a little canter, & hope now to spin ahead" (VWD, 5:61). Itching under the literary cult of personality she sees about her, she wants to run "full tilt" always, never "trickling and teasing in this irritating way" in the wake of "Edith and Gertrude and Tom and Joyce and Virginia" herself, longing to "come out in the open again, when everything has been restarted, and runs full tilt" (L, 209). Only that quality which she calls the remorseless severity of her mind at its ceaseless labors is able to subvert, by reading, the "forces of dominance and power" endemic to strong writing. So reading acts to "eliminate the ego: and it's the ego that erects itself like another part of the body I don't dare to name" (in RN, 25).

The ego in that highly eroticized sense remains inseparable from what happens at the inception of a new book; she writes of couching her novel portrait of Vita as *Orlando* "automatically on a clean sheet: Orlando: A Biography. No sooner had I done this than my body was flooded with rapture and my brain with ideas" (October 9, 1927; L, 428). But such excitement leads to letdown: she is assailed by doubt after all the intensity of the birth-giving act of writing. "The question now is, will my feelings for you be changed? I've lived in you all these months—coming out, what are you really like? Do you exist? Have I made you up?" (L, 474). And as the doubt continues, and the dryness of vocabulary and thought with it, the mind dry in the dust after the raptures of the initial tumescence ("In October my mind was dripping: That is the only life," 477), she now detests her own "volubility" and wonders if Vita was not, as she has begun to think of all her friends, a myth. This she will implicitly admit, after completing her book on Roger Fry and suffering her usual "after book gloom," resembling nothing so much as a postpartum depression.

At such moments, despair dries up the fluid energy which was hers in the "full flood" of composing *Three Guineas*, when she was plunged into the swollen and excited current, when another novel might "swim up" at any moment. Gone are the former gallop and the spurting power of her occasional hard rides when she was equipped with "my old spurs and my old flanks" (VWD, 5:232), when "work, work, work" was her final prescription, and fighting her surest instinct (VWD, 5:50–54). Her major strength seemed to be a fruitful opposition, a will to againstness, as she figuratively and repeatedly swam and rode and produced against the currents and the moments. We recognize the fighting Virginia especially in her despair of feeling the moments "flying, flying" and sensing her own senses too vivid, until she longs "to invent any way of dimming my own eyes, which are, sometimes, too bright, aren't they? Couldn't we drop something into time to make it thick and dull?" (L, 561; December 2, 1928). "And I find myself in the old driving whirlwind of writing against time. Have I ever written with it?" (VWD, 3:180).

The explicit love affair with Vita, of which *Orlando* is the engendered text, is matched by an odd and partly posthumous relationship with Roger, of which Virginia's *Roger Fry* is the late fruit.

What a curious relation is mine with Roger at this moment—I who have given him a kind of shape after his death—was he like that? I feel very much in his presence at the moment: as if I were intimately connected with him; as if we together had given birth to this vision of him: a child born of us. Yet he had no power to alter it. And yet for some years it will represent him. (VWD, 5:305–7)

That must be what two-parent engendering is like, bearing to the world a resemblance. That Virginia did in fact elide any reference to Roger's prolific love affairs in the book, including that major one with Vanessa, works against any complete resemblance, in this work about which she was always hesitant—about both undertaking it and the result. The "intimate connection" is no guarantee of completeness. Virginia's relation to Leonard was of course quite other, and in this her masculine virtues, her full-speeded gallop, met a resistance of the sort that we recognize with a jolt, literary and personal. Here is the text, from the last volume of the diaries, concerning Virginia's portrait of Roger:

One Sunday. . . L. gave me a very severe lecture on the first half. We walked in the meadows. It was like being pecked by a very hard strong beak. The more he pecked the deeper, as always happens.. . . It was a curious example of L. at his most rational & impersonal: rather impressive; yet so definite, so emphatic, that I felt convinced. I mean of failure, save for one odd gleam, that he was himself on the wrong track, & persisting for some deep reason—dissympathy with R.? lack of interest in personality? Lord knows. I note this plaited strand in my mind; & even while we walked & the beak struck deeper deeper had this completely detached interest in L.'s character. (VWD, 5:271)

We cannot help remembering, as we read this, the extraordinary passage in *To the Lighthouse* when Mr. Ramsay plunges repeatedly his sharply self-pitying demands into the calm of Mrs. Ramsay's dreamy and more silent nature. For all the eternity of any text, her madonna figure sits by the window knitting an Auerbachian sock[5] for the lighthouse keeper's son and measuring it against little James's leg, as the philosopher makes his own demands for sympathy, utters his own laments of inadequacy. It is after Virginia's mother's early death that Sir Leslie bewails her not having known how much he loved her, and after Mrs. Ramsay's death that Mr. Ramsay acts in similar fashion, self-pity equaling belated compassion. And it is after Virginia's death that Leonard edits her diaries, bearing what witness he could to his love and to her energies spent and genius surviving.

　　　　A slightly later passage than the one just quoted shows us Leonard in what we might imagine to be the same mood of emphasis and definiteness, of neatness and impersonal convincing tidiness: "And L. is lecturing & arranging the room. Are these the things that are interesting? that recall; that say Stop you are so fair? Well, all life is so fair, at my age. I mean, without much more of it I suppose to follow" (VWD, 5:352). There was indeed not much more before her suicide. The last journal entry concludes with Leonard seeing to his rhododendrons, and that is all we have of her.

AS PRESENTED AND POSSESSED

Now the arrangement or tidying of rooms and flowers and texts is of course an act of love. Not an act like any other, but unique. Virginia writing of Roger felt she gave birth with him, to him. Is that what Leonard felt when editing Virginia's A *Writer's Diary*? Is that what Ted Hughes felt when editing Sylvia Plath's journals and stories, burning up the bits that their children should not see?

Let us listen to his judgment on the work—his work—and in fact on hers. Ted Hughes is speaking, as he says, "as an editor" of her unpublished writings, and he is speaking, as he does not say, of his wife after her presumed suicide. "What she really coveted," says the editor husband, "was a natural and colloquial style. It was the arithmetical, sophisticated syntax of her earlier poetry, 'imagey and static' (her words), that laid the dead hand on her narratives, and her vain efforts to throw it off were a big part of her labor." But it is not, I would contend, Sylvia's dead hand editing and passing judgment here, writing of her "helplessness," of the "weakness of her weaker stories," of her lack of objectivity and of her "limitation" as a prose writer. And it is not her dead hand either that cuts out parts of her private journal and publishes the rest for the living eye. Ted lays his judgment before us, saying these private things shouldn't be published, and I lay it before you, thinking perhaps they should.

The logical thing, no doubt, would be to publish this more private side of her journal complete. It seems probable that her real creation was her own image, so that all her writings appear like notes and jottings directing attention towards that central problem—herself. Whether this is right or wrong, with some personalities it simply happens. As an editor of Sylvia Plath's unpublished writings, watching this happen to her, I am more and more inclined to think that any bit of evidence which corrects and clarifies our idea of what she really was, is important, insofar as her writings persuade us of her importance. But living people figure everywhere, even in her most private discussions with herself, and—an editor has to face it—some things are more important than revelations about writers. The vivid, cruel words she could use to pin down her acquaintances and even her close friends were nothing she would want published and would be no joke to the recipients, still less so now that she is internationally famous and admired for her gift of phrase. This shouldn't need to be said. (8)

A few terminological ironies pervade his text: can we really forget that this self-termed "editor having to face it" is also in some sense still her husband, who does not have to face his wife's suffering through him, since she committed suicide? If the editor-husband's excisions are necessary because the readership would find the full version "no joke," that is not much of a joke either. None of this is really a side-splitting subject, and the language of the editor's preface makes, I think, a bit light of the whole matter.

The picture yielded up by the pages selected from Sylvia's journals by the husband is wonderful indeed. A neighbor comes into the playroom where Sylvia and Ted are "typing opposite each other in piles of sprawled paper over the dull pewter pot of steaming tea" (JP, 70). Ted and Sylvia hug each other while little Frieda looks on "peacefully from her lunch, her big blue eyes untroubled and clear" (JP, 71). Ted and Sylvia are picking daffodils in the early evening (JP, 71). And since the diaries are quoted backwards in time, this entry Sylvia made follows upon those idyllic ones, as if in retrospection instead of prediction:

I deserve that, don't I, some sort of blazing love that I can live with. My God, I'd love to cook and make a house, and surge force into a man's dreams, and write, if he could talk and walk and work and passionately want to do his career. I can't bear to think of this potential for loving and giving going brown and sere in me. Yet the choice is so important, it frightens me a little. A lot. (JP, 260)

She made, then, her choice, and he did indeed passionately want to do his career, as she did hers, and finally he did hers too, did it over a bit by editing. He helped her engender, by his live hand, her text—backwards, making it presentable.

The question really is double; how do we present ourselves, and how are we presented?

In Charlotte Brontë's *Villette*, Lucy Snowe, urged to wear male raiment in order to play her part in the school play, begs to be allowed to dress herself. She simply wears women's garb, and supplements it with a few little things, all marked as little in the text. She puts over the dress "a little vest, a collar, a cravat, and a paletot of small dimensions" (V, 288). And so she neither replaces what she has and wants to wear, nor shocks the custom: she simply learns to supplement. Mostly she spends her time withdrawing to a quiet nook, and knowing that the man she loves will always keep, in his mind and heart, "one little closet, over the door of which was written 'Lucy's Room'" (V, 555). It is a matter of just asking for a little, in order to play the role right. She has to know, and knows, her little place. Of course, we hope, times have changed. We wear what we like and speak as we choose, writing a text we think will come through it all untouched, unscathed, and in our own voice and garb.

But then at the beginning of our own century, in our own classic American memory, Alice James, said Henry, did it not quite right. About the possible publication of his sister's diary in May 1894, he told William he was "intensely nervous and almost sick with terror about possible publicity" even with a private printing. The Concord newspaper might get hold of it, people might read what he had said of them for Alice's own shut-in entertainment, and worst of all, Katherine Loring, the editor, seemed to feel no discretion about using proper names. Here is James:

I feel very unhappy, & wonder about the strangeness of destiny. I used to say everything to Alice (on system), that would *égayer* her bedside & many things in utter confidence. I didn't dream she wrote them down. It is the printing of these precious *telles-quelles* that disturbs me when a very few merely superficial (leaving her *text* sacredly, really untouched) wd. have made all the difference. (AJ, 354)

Editing, then, as excising or exercising the right of the seigneur to make a few little discriminatory omissions, is really and sacredly to leave the ladies' text untouched. For James, though, the sacred text is nevertheless eminently treatable and touchable if that touch and treatment serve to protect bedside talk.

Considering Henry's objection to Alice's correct transcription of his voice and to her all-too-correct lady editor's failure to edit it out of Alice's journal, an anecdote Woolf recounts is particularly and bitterly ironic. For if the woman editing Alice did not sufficiently protect Henry James by excision and coverup, the man editing Virginia Woolf's article on James in 1921 fully made up for it by his efficacious defense of the Master against the pen, no less masterly than his own, which would have pricked him. The anecdote which she quotes at length, amusing as it is, cuts deep to reveal just what current she is having to write against, and just how powerful it is. Bruce Richmond, the editor, goes about his suppressive task, of course, with tact and scissors, toward a predictable result:

> And now you use the word "lewd." Of course, I don't wish you to change it, but surely that is rather a strong expression to apply to anything by Henry James. I haven't read the story lately of course—but still my impression is—
> Well, I thought that when I read it: one has to go by one's impressions at the time.
> But you know the usual meaning of the word? It is—ah—*dirty*. Now poor dear old Henry James—At anyrate, think it over, & ring me up in 20 minutes.
> So I thought it over & came to the required conclusion in twelve minutes & a half.
> But what is one to do about it? He made it sufficiently clear not only that he wouldn't stand "lewd" but that he didn't much like anything else. I feel that this becomes more often the case, & wonder whether to break off, with an explanation, or to pander, or to go on writing against the current. (VWD, 2:151–52)

She knew the meaning of the word, we think, and was quite a good reader of poor dear old Henry James and of the current too; about self-editing she knew also. So she went on writing, as we know, and fighting too. A *Writer's Diary* is Leonard's editing homage to her after her death, a hands-on job if there ever was, but it is the first transmission of her writing voice as it worked itself out and for which we are therefore grateful: "I get back into my working fighting mood, which is natural to me. I don't see myself a success. I like the sense of effort better" (WD, 83). What she was engendering, after all, and against the current, was her writing self. "One always harnesses oneself by instinct, & can't live without the strain" (VWD, 5:65).

John Middleton Murry, editing the journals and papers of his former wife Katherine Mansfield, which he was supposed to have destroyed, increased both his own wealth and the opprobrium of their entwined life, personal and textual. A footnote in the last volume of Woolf's diaries recounts the Bibesco affair, involving Murry, who had abandoned his wife at home in misery, pain, and near to death. The most recent editor of Mansfield relates, also in a footnote, the story of Murry's finding, with his new wife, "the house of his dreams," bidding for it a sum he did not have, and receiving by a great stroke of fortune just over that sum in royalties from Katherine's books. "I felt Katherine's blessing was on our marriage," he wrote grandly (KM, 11). Regardless of her dying wishes, he transcribed and published almost everything, in a patchwork of his making. And then, in a crowning irony, through this text of his, by publishing more and more of his wife's private papers revealing tensions in the marriage, Murry cast himself publicly in the role of the husband who had failed her (KM, 11).

These footnotes to literary history, its editorial and personal betrayals are of course not the whole story about who conceives of what and how texts are engendered. They leave out, among other things, what we might call the wonderful authorial self-possessedness of possession by the text. Katherine Mansfield describes it with a certain absence of charm but an equally convincing presence and simplicity: this is, we feel, true and unelaborated possession and, above all, self-possession:

I *am writing*—do you know the feeling and until this story is finished I am engulfed. It's not a tragic story either—but there you are. It seizes me—swallows me completely. I am Jonah in the whale and . . . we're thrashing through deep water. I fully realize it. It's the price we have to pay—we writers. I'm lost—gone—possessed and everybody who comes near is my enemy. (KM, 198)

There are other quite wonderful possessions besides this sort, and other possessional engendering relations to be written of. Surely one of the oddest and most appealing of gender writing relations, tragic to the point of suicide, is that of the artist Dora Carrington. So attached to Lytton Strachey was she that four months after his death from intestinal cancer, she shot herself, unable to see any reason to continue living without him. A diary entry reads: "What point is there now in what I see every day, in conversation, jokes, beautiful visions, pains, even nightmares? Who can I tell them to, who will understand?" (C, 620). Another, six days later: "What can I do. For no future interests me. I do not care about anything now," and her dreadful realization *"that everyday for the rest of my life you will be away"* (C, 627). The general attitude has been to deplore her inability to pull up her socks, so to speak, and just get on with living and with art.

Sandwiched forever, whenever she is read (and that is all too rarely), between a preface by David Garnett, who edited *Selected Letters and Extracts from Her Diaries*, and an epilogue by her brother Noel Carrington, her sad plight is explained as her act is explained away. For David Garnett insists repeatedly on her hatred of femaleness; in each of her relationships, he says, "it was the hatred of being a woman which poisoned it" (C, xi). Never did she overcome, according to him, "her shame at being a woman" (C, xi). And, graver still, he links this (repeating it at least as often as she does), her hatred of femaleness, to what he calls her misfortune in loving the homosexual Strachey, who did her the disservice of dying on her: "on Carrington's side her intense dislike of being a woman . . . gave her a feeling of inferiority so that a normal and joyful relationship was next to impossible." Then he continues, drawing what is surely a rather fine distinction: "Yet for many years they were happy together" (C, x). The trouble, he repeats, is that she hated being a woman (who wouldn't, we hear him thinking), although it is also too bad Lytton was basically, well, just not suited. So they had happiness, but not joy, the latter obviously implying what it obviously implies.

Now I mean to defend neither suicide nor unsuitability, but it certainly seems to me that their being happy all those years is not to be so lightly discounted; on the contrary, even if the union did not produce anything other than text. We cannot fail to remember one of Woolf's suicide notes to Leonard, even if some have wondered if it was not written more for him than for her: "No two people have ever been so happy together." My own view is that a naive perspective is not always to be distrusted, nor are statements about happiness. It might well, after all, have been so.

Carrington, no more a mother than Woolf, had an attitude to maternity which her brother takes with a seriousness sufficient to have him end her book upon it, finishing his epilogue on her tragedy and thus rather finishing her off a second time. "As her own friends in turn came to marry she was apt to treat it as a lapse from grace, with maternity an inevitable but none the less deplorable sequel for a person of intelligence" (C, 639). This is in any case a highly peculiar ending for a volume of 639 pages, a sort of flat and anticlimactic note which has its importance only in relation to two things: to Garnett's preface about her joylessness with Lytton and to that "normality" rejected by the female artist figure ending her life over love.

Carrington's abnormality was most obvious, it seems, when she cut her hair, because no one at Bedford believed in such a thing: "For a long while our mother," says Noel, "continued to lament the loss of 'such beautiful hair' as if it were a family rather than a personal possession.... From that moment her mother began to treat her with a trace of caution in reprimands, even though she could not restrain her inquisitiveness or gestures of pained disapproval" (C, 639). But the pained disapproval is that also of the editors. David Garnett rather strangely telescopes her end with her love, beginning: "Though her end was tragic, for she was totally committed to Lytton," as if that very commitment were the tragic thing. It was at the very least the real thing, and inescapably reads as such.

Garnett rightly points out that those around her should have considered her art important, going on to lament that she had no Duncan Grant to work with her, as Vanessa Bell did. It always helps a woman artist to have a man around to work things through and out with her, because it is surely—as we are told three times Carrington thought—a terrible thing to be a woman. With hair short or long.

While I am convinced it is not the business of anyone at all to discredit her final act, her choice after a great deal of consideration, her own attitude toward her grief is itself, for me, the tragic point. She had enough trouble hanging on to her own talents: witness, for example, her submission to the *Weekend Review* of an obituary of Lytton to a contest asking for obituaries of famous writers, to be written in their own style. Of this celebrated piece of parody, which took first place, she confesses her fear that everyone will say Lytton wrote it for her, and, she continues, "I am terrified when I send my address the editor will refuse me my prize" (C, 620). And, as if one of Lytton's elongated fingers were reaching from the grave to reprimand her, quite like the realization Woolf so hated about the patriarchal leavings of religion ("God's got a finger in my mind"), Carrington refuses to herself the one thing that would give her comfort, for it would be, as a child's misbehavior would be, "bad":

That craving for death which I know he disapproved of and would have disliked. If I could sit here alone just holding his clothes in my arms on the sofa with that handkerchief over my face I feel I would get comfort, but I know these feelings are bad. And if I became bad then I should feel he would disapprove and all would be worse. So I must and cannot go backwards to his grave. (C, 624)

Lest we be tempted to find only childishness and weakness in her very heartbreak, we should look at the other side of her attitude, where she pored over Hume's thoughts on suicide, which Lytton had read her, and with which they both agreed ("A man who retires from life does no harm to society"), questioning her friends, "Can you refute Mr Hume?" (C, 631). This is not the question of a child, although here too there is present the longing for an authoritative father figure by a daughter who had been deserted, in fact, by her father. Significantly, of all those whose signs of friendship she valued after her loss, Virginia Woolf was the one who seemed most to matter: "Your letter most of all because you understand" (C, 631), wrote Carrington to Virginia, who probably did best understand.

OUR TEXTUAL VOICE

None of the voices I am invoking here resembles another, or engenders its same. None exactly matches in tone any of ours. Yet what if all of these voices, of the madonna-mother and of the sisterhood, the insistent and the hesitating, the strident and the submissive, the poetic and the neatly formed, what if they were all so many costumes like those about which Mrs. Swithin asks her timeless question, knitting and knitting so many things together toward the conclusion of Woolf's *Between the Acts*: is it that "we act different parts but are the same?" (BA, 215). We are acting still, each of us even here and now, an "unacted part" conferred by our different clothes and costumes.

We wonder, is beauty on us too, as Woolf's narrator saw it to be on each of the actors between those acts? *Between the Acts* ends with an opening closure whose frame stretches to include the universe, as the former act of knitting or knitting together yields its place to that of sewing, itself dropped in its turn for a wider and more primitive scene, reaching back to the beginning before any play at all, reframing the whole and each of the acted and unacted parts until the universe is reengendered by the word:

Isa let her sewing drop. The great hooded chairs had become enormous. And Giles too. And Isa too against the window. The window was all sky without colour. The house had lost its shelter. It was night before roads were made, or houses. It was the night that dwellers in caves had watched from some high place among rocks.

Then the curtain rose. They spoke. (BA, 219)

Why would not each reader ask herself the question included in this text, about speaking in our roles and in and through those of others, the essential question as I hear it now?

Was this voice ourselves? (BA, 189)

It is the original *conception* that should not be altered, and the original voice—our own, for and from all of us—that should be coming to the light of day.

The voice of all women adjusting our memory to our truth is an *engendering voice*. Zora Neale Hurston's eulogy of women as she makes her origin and truth besides, speaks of black memory and the suffering we all engender from: "Now, women forget all those things they don't want to remember, and remember everything they don't want to forget" (TWG, 9). And Woolf's moving, brief incantation: "what we must remember, what we would forget" (BA, 155), ambivalent as it is, is in our memory always.

I want to end on a tale about choosing and remembering, where the quest for a true saying and true staying power works its way through the voice, life, and text of another. Christa Wolf's *Quest for Christa T.* is the story of a girl who can blow a trumpet, change the lives about her, be endlessly unlike all others, and yet who—unaware of the effect she has—can be seen and heard only through the narrator of the text, through whom she must then find herself, even after her death to everything but this text of memory. Fiction is completely overcome by presence, and the paths taken or not taken here seem somehow, in spite of distance of countries and tone, to be our own.

The paths we really took are overlaid with paths we did not take. I can now hear words that we never spoke. Now I can see her as she was, Christa T.,

when no witnesses were present. Could it be possible?—The years that
re-ascend are no longer the years they were. Light and shadow fall once
more over our field of vision: but the field is ready. Should that not amaze
us? (CT, 23)

The goal of this account, says the narrator, was both to find Christa T.,
and to lose her again, to know and accept both: "To set about it and
write the first sentence: the quest for her—in the thought of her";
then, as she comes, "to send her away again" (CT, 99). The greater part,
we read in the center of the tale, is done. For by now we have understood that the tale is ours because it is about becoming "*oneself, with
all one's strength*" (CT, 149), about *originating* and never letting anything
become "something finished" (CT, 167). It is really, if I may borrow a
term from Plato, about *generativity*, about that kind of permanent engendering which undoes the editing hand, surprises the explaining
mind, and unsettles forever such questions as: "but who is this about?
what did she do in the tale, and why did she die? and why, above all,
do we care?"

　　　　　Christa T., as I read the tale, is really about our own tales
and the tales of our own final engendering of ourselves through our
dealing with the texts of others, as they deal with themselves. It is
about our learning to celebrate the peculiar vibrancy that may come
through another voice, to our own. "When, if not now?": this refrain
echoing throughout the book stays to haunt us, until we tell our own
tales and those of others we care about. If we conceive them well, if
we invent them generously, we are faithful to them and to what we can
become by our conceptions. This is what is truest about them, and
about us. We have to deal with loss now and all the time, of others
and of ourselves, but we have to find now, and all the time, a real
keeping power. We have to engender some *staying promise*.

　　　　　If, says the narrator of *Christa* T., I could have invented her,

I'd have let her live.

So that I could sit, as I did that morning, again and again at her table. For
Justus who's bringing the coffee pot in, for the children who are speechless
with joy because their favorite pastries are on their plates.

Then the sun rose, red and cold. There was snow on the ground. We took
our time over breakfast. Stay a while, Christa T. said; but we drove off.

If I'd been allowed to invent us, I'd have given us time to stay. (CT, 175)

And this tale was really about being allowed to invent us, all of us, all over again, finding our several voices through our metaphors, and with enough time to stay.

NOTES

1. Initials refer to the corresponding ones in the list of works cited.

2. See Goffman for an intelligent analysis of how we go about presentation.

3. About the metaphor, and the text itself, my conversations with Carolyn Heilbrun have helped me clarify what I wanted to bring to bear.

4. The chapter on Virginia Woolf in my book, *Reading Frames in Modern Fiction*, (Princeton: Princeton University Press, 1985), pp. 237–61, develops some of the ideas here.

5. The reference is to Eric Auerbach's discussion of Mrs. Ramsay knitting James's cock, by which the story itself is measured. See "The Brown Stocking," in Auerbach, 463–88.

WORKS CITED

Abel, Elizabeth E., ed. *Writing and Sexual Difference*. Chicago: University of Chicago Press, 1982. (WSD)

Auerbach, Eric. *Mimesis: The Representation of Reality in Western Literature*. New York: Doubleday Anchor, 1957.

Brontë, Charlotte. *Villette*. Harmondsworth: Penguin Books, 1979. (V)

Carrington, Dora. *Selected Letters and Extracts from Her Diaries*. Ed. David Garnett. New York: Ballantine, 1970. (C)

Dickinson, Emily. *Selected Poems and Letters*. Ed. Robert N. Linscott. New York: Anchor Books, 1959. (ED)

Goffman, Erving. *The Presentation of Self in Everyday Life*. New York: Doubleday Anchor, 1959.

Hurston, Zora Neale. *Their Eyes Were Watching God*. Urbana: University of Illinois Press, 1978. (TWG)

Mallarmé, Stéphane. *Igitur, Divations*. Paris: Poésie /Gallimard, 1976. (I)

Mansfield, Katherine. *Letters and Journals*. Ed. C.K. Stead. Harmondsworth: Penguin, 1977. (KM)

Marcus, Jane, "Liberty, Sorority, Misogyny." In *The Representation of Women in Fiction*. Selected Papers from the English Institute, 1981. Ed. Carolyn G. Heilbrun and Margaret R. Higonnet. Baltimore: Johns Hopkins University Press, 1983.

Plath, Sylvia. *Johnny Panic and the Bible of Dreams: Short Stories, Prose, and Diary Excerpts*. Ed. Ted Hughes. New York: Harper, 1980. (JP)

—— *The Journals of Sylvia Plath*. Ed. Ted Hughes and Frances McCullough. New York: Ballantine Books, 1982. (JSP)

Smith, Stevie. *Novel on Yellow Paper*. London: Virago Press, 1981. (SNY)

Strouse, Jean. *Alice James: A Biography*. New York: Bantam, 1980. (AJ)

Wolf, Christa. *The Quest for Christa* T. Trans. Christopher Middleton. London: Virago Press, 1982. (CT)

Woolf, Virginia. *Between the Acts*. New York: Harcourt Brace, 1969. (BA)

—— *The Diary of Virginia Woolf*. Ed. Anne Oliver Bell. 5 vols. New York: Harcourt Brace, 1977–1984. (VWD)

—— *Letters*. Ed. Nigel Nicolson and Joanne Trautman. 6 vols. New York, Harcourt Brace, 1975. (L)

—— *Reading Notebooks*. Ed. Brenda Silver. Princeton: Princeton University Press, 1983. (RN)

—— *Three Guineas*. New York: Harcourt Brace, 1966. (TG)

—— *A Writer's Diary*. Ed. Leonard Woolf. St. Albans: Triad/Panther, 1978. (WD)

Yeats, William Butler. *A Vision*. New York: Collier, 1965. (YV)

The Mark of Gender

MONIQUE WITTIG

I

The mark of gender, according to grammarians, concerns substantives. They talk about it in terms of function. If they question its meaning, they may joke about it, calling gender a "fictive sex." It is thus that English when compared to French has the reputation of being almost genderless, while French passes for a very gendered language. It is true that, strictly speaking, English does not apply the mark of gender to inanimate objects, to things or nonhuman beings. But as far as the categories of the person are concerned, both languages are bearers of gender to the same extent. Both indeed give way to a primitive ontological concept that enforces in language a division of beings into sexes. The "fictive sex" of nouns or their neuter gender are only accidental developments of this first principle and as such they are relatively harmless.

The manifestation of gender that is identical in English and in French takes place in the dimension of the person. It does not concern only grammarians, although it is a lexical manifestation. As an ontological concept that deals with the nature of Being, along with a whole nebula of other primitive concepts belonging to the same line of thought, gender seems to belong primarily to philosophy. Its raison d'être is never questioned in grammar, whose role is to describe forms and functions, not to find a justification for them. It is no longer questioned in philosophy, though, because it belongs to that body of self-evident concepts without which philosophers believe they cannot develop a line of reasoning and which for them go without saying, for they exist prior to any thought, any social order, in nature. So they call gender the lexical delegation of "natural beings," their symbol. Being aware that the notion of gender is not as innocuous as it appears, American feminists use gender as a sociological category, making clear that there is nothing natural about this notion, as sexes have been artificially constructed into political categories—categories of oppression. They have extrapolated the term *gender* from grammar and they tend to superpose it on the notion of sex. And they are right insofar as gender is the linguistic index of the political opposition between the sexes and of the domination of women. In the same way as sex, man and woman, gender, as a concept, is instrumental in the political discourse of the social contract as heterosexual.

In modern theory, even in the assumptions of disciplines exclusively concerned with language, one remains within the classical division of the concrete world on the one hand, and the abstract one on the other. Physical or social reality and language are disconnected. Abstraction, symbols, signs do not belong to the real. There is on one side the real, the referent, and on the other side language. It is as though the relation to language were a relation of function only and not one of transformation. There is sometimes a confusion between signified and referent, so that they are even used indifferently in certain critical works. Or there is a reduction of the signified to a series of messages, with relays of the referent remaining the only support of the meaning. Among linguists, the Russian Bakhtin, a contemporary of the Russian formalists whose work has at last been translated, is the only one who seems to me to have a strictly materialist approach to language. In sociolinguistics, there are several developments in this direction, mostly among feminists.[1]

I say that even abstract philosophical categories act upon the real as social. Language casts sheaves of reality upon the social body, stamping it and violently shaping it. For example, the bodies of social actors are fashioned by abstract language as well as by non-abstract language. For there is a plasticity of the real to language: language has a plastic action upon the real.

About gender, then, it is not only important to dislodge

from grammar and linguistics a sociological category that does not speak its name. It is also very important to consider how gender works in language, how gender works upon language, before considering how it works from there upon its users.

Gender takes place in a category of language that is totally unlike any other and which is called the personal pronoun. Personal pronouns are the only linguistic instances that designate the locutors in discourse and their different and successive situations in relationship to that discourse. As such, they are also the pathways and the means of entrance into language. And it is in this sense—that they represent persons—that they interest us here. It is without justification of any kind, without questioning, that personal pronouns somehow engineer gender all through language, taking it along with them quite naturally, so to speak, in any kind of talk, parley, or philosophical treatise. And although they are instrumental in activating the notion of gender, they pass unnoticed. Not being gender-marked themselves in their subjective form (except in one case), they can support the notion of gender while they seem to fulfill another function. In principle, pronouns mark the opposition of gender only in the third person and are not gender bearers, per se, in the other persons. Thus, it is as though gender does not affect them, is not part of their structure, but only a detail in their associated form. But, in reality, as soon as there is a locutor in discourse, as soon as there is an 'I', gender manifests itself. There is a kind of suspension of the grammatical form. A direct interpellation of the locutor occurs. The locutor is called upon in person. The locutor intervenes, in the order of the pronouns, without mediation, in *its proper sex*—that is, when the locutor is a sociological woman. One knows that, in French, with *je* ('I'), one must mark the gender as soon as one uses it in relation to past participles and adjectives. In English, where the same kind of obligation does not exist, a locutor, when a sociological woman, must in one way or another, that is, with a certain number of clauses, make her sex public. For gender is the enforcement of sex in language, working in the same way as the declaration of sex in civil status. Gender is not confined within the third person and the mention of sex in language is not a treatment reserved for the third person. Sex, under the name of gender, permeates the whole body of language and forces every locutor, if she belongs to the oppressed sex, to proclaim it in her speech, that is, to appear in language under her proper physical form and not under the abstract form, which every male locutor has the unquestioned right to use. The abstract form, the general, the universal, this is what the so-called masculine gender means, for the class of men have appropriated the universal for themselves. One must understand that men are not born with a faculty for the universal and that women are not reduced at birth to the particular. The universal has been, and is continually, at every moment, appropriated by men. It does not happen by magic, it must be done. It is an act, a criminal act, perpetrated by one class against another. It is an act carried out at the level of concepts, philosophy, politics. And gender by enforcing upon women a particular category represents a measure of domination. Gender is very harmful to women in the exercise of language. But there is more. Gender is ontologically a total impossibility. For when one becomes a locutor, when one says 'I' and, in so doing, reappropriates language as a whole,[2] proceeding from oneself alone, with the tremendous power to use all language, it is then and there, according to linguists and philosophers, that there occurs the supreme act of subjectivity, the advent of subjectivity into consciousness. It is when starting to speak that one becomes 'I'. This act—the becoming of *the* subject through the exercise of language and through locution—in order to be real, implies that the locutor be an absolute subject. For a relative subject is inconceivable, a relative subject could not speak at all. I mean that in spite of the harsh law of gender and its enforcement upon women, no woman can say 'I' without being for herself a total subject—that is, ungendered, universal, whole. Or, failing this, she is condemned to what I call parrot speech (slaves echoing their masters' talk). Language as a whole gives everyone the same power of becoming an absolute subject through its exercise. But gender, an element of language, works upon this ontological fact to annul it as far as women are concerned and corresponds to a constant attempt to strip them of the most precious thing for a human being—subjectivity. Gender is an ontological impossibility because it tries to accomplish the division of Being. But Being as being is not divided. God or Man as being are One and whole. So what is this divided Being introduced into language through gender? It is an impossible Being, it is a Being that does not exist, an ontological joke, a conceptual maneuver to wrest from women what belongs to them by right: conceiving of oneself as a total subject through the exercise of language. The result of the imposition of gender, acting as a denial at the very moment when one speaks, is to deprive women of the authority of speech, and to force them to make their entrance in a crablike way, particularizing themselves and apologizing profusely. The result is to deny them any claim to the abstract, philosophical, political discourses that give shape to the social body. Gender then must be destroyed. The possibility of its destruction is given through the very exercise of language. For each time I say 'I', I reorganize the world from my point of view and through abstraction I lay claim to universality. This fact holds true for every locutor.

II

To destroy the categories of sex in politics and in philosophy, to destroy gender in language (at least to modify its use) is therefore part of my work in writing, as a writer. An important part, since a modification as central as this cannot happen without a transformation of language as a whole. It concerns (touches) words whose meanings and forms are close to, and associated with, gender. But it also concerns (touches) words whose meanings and forms are the furthest away. For once the dimension of the person, around which all others are organized, is brought into play, nothing is left intact. Words, their disposition, their arrangement, their relation to each other, the whole nebula of their constellations shift, are displaced, engulfed or reoriented, put sideways. And when they reappear, the structural change in language makes them look different. They are hit in their meaning and also in their form. Their music sounds different, their coloration is affected. For what is really in question here is a structural change in language, in its nerves, its framing. But language does not allow itself to be worked upon, without a parallel work in philosophy and politics, as well as in economics, because as women are marked in language by gender, they are marked in society as sex. I said that personal pronouns engineer gender through language, and personal pronouns are, if I may say so, the subject matter of each one of my books—except for *Lesbian Peoples Material For a Dictionary*, written with

Sande Zeig. They are the motors for which functioning parts had to be designed, and as such they create the necessity of the form.

The project of *The Opoponax*, my first book, was to work on the subject, the speaking subject, the subject of discourse—subjectivity, generally speaking. I wanted to restore an undivided 'I,' to universalize the point of view of a group condemned to being particular, relegated in language to a metaandric category. I chose childhood as an element of form open to history (it is what a narrative theme is for me), the formation of the ego around language. A massive effort was needed to break the spell of the captured subject. I needed a strong device, something that would immediately be beyond sexes, that the division by sexes would be powerless against, and that could not be coopted. There is in French, as there is in English, a munificent pronoun that is called the indefinite, which means that it is not marked by gender, a pronoun that you are taught in school to systematically avoid. It is *on* in French—*one* in English. Indeed it is so systematically taught that it should not be used that the translator of *The Opoponax* managed never to use it in English. One must say in the translator's favor that it sounds and looks very heavy in English, but no less so in French.

With this pronoun, that is neither gendered nor numbered, I could locate the characters outside of the social division by sexes and annul it for the duration of the book. In French, the masculine form—so the grammarians say—used when a past participle or an adjective is associated with the subject *on*, is in fact neuter. This incidental question of the neuter is in fact very interesting, for even when it is about terms like *l'homme*, like *Man*, grammarians do not speak of neuter in the same sense as they do for *Good* or *Evil*, but of masculine gender. For they have appropriated *l'homme*, *homo*, whose first meaning is not *male* but *mankind*. For *homo sum*. Man as male is only a derivative and second meaning.[3] To come back to *one*, *on*, here is a subject pronoun which is very tractable and accommodating since it can be bent in several directions at the same time. First, as already mentioned, it is indefinite, as far as gender is concerned. It can represent a certain number of people successively or all at once—everybody, we, they, I, you, people, a small or a large number of persons—and still stay singular. It lends itself to all kinds of substitutions of persons. In the case of *The Opoponax*, it was a delegate of a whole class of people, of everybody, of a few persons, of I (the 'I' of the main character, the 'I' of the narrator, and the 'I' of the reader). One, *on* has been for me the key to the undisturbed use of language, as it is in childhood when words are magic, when words are set bright and colorful in the kaleidoscope of the world, with its many revolutions in the consciousness as one shakes it. One, *on* has been the pathway to the description of the apprenticeship, through words, of everything important to consciousness, apprenticeship in writing being the first, even before the apprenticeship in the use of speech. One, *on*, lends itself to the unique experience of all locutors who, when saying I, can reappropriate the whole language and reorganize the world from their point of view. I did not hide the female characters under male patronyms to make them look more universal, and nevertheless, if I believe what Claude Simon wrote, the attempt at universalization succeeded. He wrote, speaking about what happened to the main character in *The Opoponax*, a little girl: "I see, I breathe, I chew, I feel through her eyes, her mouth, her hands, her skin. . . . I become childhood."[4]

Before speaking of the pronoun which is the axis of *Les Guérillères*, I would like to recall what Marx and Engels said in *The German Ideology* about class interests. They said that each new class that fights for power must, to reach its goal, represent its interest as the common interest of all the members of the society, and that in the philosophical domain this class must give the form of universality to its thought, to present it as the only reasonable one, the only universally valid one.

As for *Les Guérillères*, there is a personal pronoun used very little in French which does not exist in English—the collective plural *elles* (*they* in English)—while *ils* (*they*) often stands for the general: *they say*, meaning *people say*. This general *ils* does not include *elles*, no more, I suspect, than *they* includes any *she* in its assumption. One could say that it is a pity that in English there is not even a hypothetical plural feminine pronoun to try to make up for the absence of *she* in the general *they*. But what is the good of it, since when it exists, it is not used. The rare times that it is, *elles* never stands for a general and is never bearer of a universal point of view.[5] An *elles* therefore that would be able to support a universal point of view would be a novelty in literature or elsewhere. In *Les Guérillères*, I try to universalize the point of view of *elles*. The goal of this approach is not to feminize the world but to make the categories of sex obsolete in language. I, therefore, set up *elles* in the text as the absolute subject of the world. To succeed textually, I needed to adopt some very draconian measures, such as to eliminate, at least in the first two parts, *he*, or *they-he*. I had to provide a shock for the reader entering a text in which *elles* by its unique presence constitutes an assault, yes, even for female readers. Here again the adoption of a pronoun as my subject matter dictated the form of the book. Although the theme of the text was total war, led by *elles* on *ils*, in order for this new person to take effect, two-thirds of the text had to be totally inhabited, haunted, by *elles*. Word by word, *elles* establishes itself as a sovereign subject. Only then could *il(s)*, *they-he* appear, reduced and truncated out of language. This *elles* in order to become real also imposed an epic form, where it is not only the complete subject of the world but its conqueror. Another consequence derived from the sovereign presence of *elles* was that the chronological beginning of the narrative—that is, the total war—found itself in the third part of the book, and the textual beginning was in fact the end of the narrative. From there comes the circular form of the book, its *gesta*, which the geometrical form of a circle indicates as a modus operandi. Now in English the translator, lacking the lexical equivalent for *elles*, found himself compelled to make a change, which for me destroys the effect of the attempt. When *elles* is turned into *the women* the process of universalization is destroyed. All of a sudden, *elles* stopped being *mankind*. When one says "the women," one connotes a number of individual women, thus transforming the point of view entirely, by particularizing what I intended as a universal. Not only was my undertaking with the collective pronoun *elles* lost, but another word was introduced, the word *women* appearing obsessively throughout the text, and it is one of those gender-marked words mentioned earlier which I never use in French. For me it is the equivalent of *slave*, and, in fact, I have actively opposed its use whenever possible. To patch it up with the use of a *y* or an *i* (as in *womyn* or *wimmin*) does not alter the political reality of the word. If one tries to imagine *nogger* or *niggir*, instead of *nigger*, one may realize the futility of the attempt. It is not that there is no solution to translating *elles*. There is a solution although it was difficult for me to find at the time. I am aware that the question is a grammatical one, therefore a textual one, and not a question of translation.[6] The solution for the English translation then is to reappropriate the collective pronoun *they* which rightfully belongs to the feminine as well as to the masculine gender. *They* is not only a collective pronoun but it also immediately develops a degree of universality which is not immediate with *elles*. Indeed, to obtain it with *elles*, one must produce a work of transformation that involves a whole pageant of other words and that touches the imagination. *They* does not partake of the naturalistic, hysterical bent that accompanies the feminine gender. *They* helps to go beyond the catgories of sex. But *they* can be efficient in my design only when it stands by itself, like its French counterpart. Only with the use of *they* will the text regain its strength and strangeness. The fact that the book begins with the end and that the end is the chronological beginning will be textually justified by the unexpected identity of *they*. In the third part, the war section, *they* cannot be shared by the category to be eliminated from the general. In a new version the masculine gender must be more systematically particularized than it is in the actual form of the book. The masculine must not appear under *they* but only under *man, he, his*, in analogy with what has been done for so long to the feminine gender (*woman, she, her*). It seems to me that the English solution will take us even a step further in making the categories of sex obsolete in language.

Talking about the key pronoun of *The Lesbian Body* is a very difficult task for me, and sometimes I have considered this text a reverie about the beautiful analysis of the pronouns *je* and *tu* by the linguist Emile Benveniste. The bar in the *j/e* of *The Lesbian Body* is a sign of excess. A sign that helps to imagine an excess of 'I,' an 'I' exalted. 'I' has become so powerful in *The Lesbian Body* that it can attack the order of heterosexuality in texts and assault the so-called love, the heroes of love, and lesbianize them, lesbianize the symbols, lesbianize the gods and the goddesses, lesbianize the men and the women. This 'I' can be destroyed in the attempt and resuscitated. Nothing resists this 'I' (or this *tu*, which is its name, its love), which spreads itself in the whole world of the book, like a lava flow that nothing can stop.

To understand my undertaking in this text, one must go

back to *The Opoponax*, in which the only appearance of the narrator comes with a *je*, 'I,' located at the end of the book in a small sentence untranslated[7] in English, a verse of Maurice Scève, in *La Délie*: "*Tant je l'aimais qu'en elle encore je vis*" (I loved her so that in her I live still). This sentence is the key to the text and pours its ultimate light upon the whole of it, demystifying the meaning of the opoponax and establishing a lesbian subject as the absolute subject while lesbian love is the absolute love. *On*, the opoponax, and the *je*, 'I' of the end have narrow links. They function by relays. First *on* completely coincides with the character Catherine Legrand as well as with the others. Then the opoponax appears as a talisman, a sesame to the opening of the world, as a word that compels both words and world to make sense, as a metaphor for the lesbian subject. After the repeated assertions of Catherine Legrand that I *am the opoponax* the narrator can at the end of the book take the relay and affirm in her name: "I loved her so that in her I live still." The chain of permutations from the *on* to the *je*, 'I,' of *The Opoponax* has created a context for the 'I' in *The Lesbian Body*. This understanding both global and particular, both universal and unique, brought from within a perspective given in homosexuality, is the object of some extraordinary pages by Proust.

To close my discussion of the notion of gender in language, I will say that it is a mark unique of its kind, the unique lexical symbol that refers to an oppressed group. No other has left its trace within language to such a degree that to eradicate it would not only modify language at the lexical level but would upset the structure itself and its functioning. Furthermore, it would change the relations of words at the metaphorical level far beyond the very few concepts and notions that are touched upon by this transformation. It would change the coloration of words in relation to each other and their tonality. It is a transformation that would affect the conceptual-philosophical level and the political one as well as the poetic one.

NOTES

This essay appears, in somewhat different form, in *Feminist Issues* (Fall 1985), 5(2).

1. See Colette Guillaumin, "The Practice of Power and Belief in Nature," *Feminist Issues* (Summer 1981), 1(2): 3–28 and (Summer 1983), 1(3): 87–109; "The Question of Difference," *Feminist Issues* (Spring 1982), 2(1): 33–52; "The Masculine: Denotations/Connotations,"

Feminist Issues (Spring 1985), 5(1): 65–73; Nicole-Claude Mathieu, "Masculinity/Femininity," *Feminist Issues* (Summer 1980), 1(1): 51–69; "Biological Paternity, Social Maternity," *Feminist Issues* (Spring 1984), 4(1): 63–71.

2. Cf. Emile Benveniste, *Problems in General Linguistics* (Coral Gables, Fla.: University of Miami Press, 1971).

3. The first demonstration of the women's liberation movement in France took place at the Arch of Triumph, where the grave of the unknown soldier is located. Among the mottos on the banners, one read: "*Un homme sur deux est une femme*" (One man in two is a woman). The purpose of the demonstration was to lay a wreath in honor of the wife of the unknown soldier (more unknown even than the soldier), and it took place in support of the American women's demonstration of August 1970.

4. In *L'Express* at the time of the publication of *L'Opoponax* in 1964.

5. Nathalie Sarraute uses *elles* very often throughout her work. But it is not to make it stand for a universal, her work being of another nature. I am convinced that, without her use, *elles* would not have imposed itself upon me with such force. It is an example of what Kristeva calls intertextuality.

6. Indeed David Le Vay's translation is a beautiful one, particularly for the rhythm of the sentences and the choice of the vocabulary.

7. *The Opoponax* in English is deprived of the complete body of poetry which in French was incorporated into the text as an organic element. It was not differentiated by italics or quotation marks. In English this complete body of poetry stands out untranslated and has no operative virtue whatsoever.

Surprising Fame:
Renaissance Gender Ideologies
and Women's Lyric

ANN ROSALIND JONES

In Renaissance iconography, fame is a woman: a winged figure heralding present and future reknown. Ronsard, in his 1555 *Hymne* to Henri II, writes of "La Fame qui vole et parle librement,/ et qui sujette n'est à nul commandement" (ll. 341–42). But in Renaissance gender ideology, fame was not *for* women. Ronsard's figure of free-speaking liberty is diametrically opposed to the social ideal of woman as it was constructed by early modern writers on feminine conduct. In the discourses of humanism and bourgeois family theory, the proper woman is an absence: legally, she vanishes under the name and authority of her father and her husband; as daughter and wife, she is enclosed in the private household. She is silent and invisible: she does not speak, and she is not spoken about.

I am going to analyze this ideological climate in some detail, in order to suggest how problematic the notion of literary fame was for women writing in the Renaissance. I might call what I am doing the study of pre-poetics: of the conditions necessary for writing at all, and of the ways those conditions shape the lyrics of sixteenth-century women writers. In this period, when public eloquence was becoming the central requirement for masculine careers, when training in oration and written argument was essential for men managing cities, for ambassadors and advisors to princes, for courtiers and poets, prohibitions against women's speech seem to have intensified. Ruth Kelso, a historian of Renaissance gender doctrines, conjectures that women may have been on the receiving end of a cultural guilt complex: as men turned more and more to secular, civic ambitions, the residual Christian virtues of humility and retirement from the world were displaced onto women (25, 26).[1] Two writers on education provide an illustrative contrast. Juan Luis Vives, writing for the teachers of men in De Tradendis Disciplinis (1516), celebrates rhetoric as a training system for all mental capacities and professional positions:

Rhetoric is of the greatest influence and weight. It is necessary for all positions in life. For in man the highest law and government are at the disposal of will. To the will, reason and judgment are assigned as counsellors, and the emotions are its torches. Further, the emotions of the mind are enflamed by the sparks of speech. So, too, the reason is impelled and moved by speech. Hence it comes to pass that, in the whole kingdom of the activities of man, speech holds in its possession a mighty strength, which it continually manifests. (181)

Lionardo Bruni, some years earlier, wrote a letter-essay to a noblewoman, defining what an elite education for a woman should be: De Studiis et literis (c. 1405). Bruni was more liberal than many men who wrote on education, but he expressly prohibited the study of rhetoric to women. He wrote to Baptista di Montefeltro, the about-to-be-married countess to whom he directed his tract:

subtleties of Arithmetic and Geometry are not worthy to absorb a cultivated mind. . . and the great and complex art of Rhetoric should be placed in the same category. My chief reason is the obvious one, that I have in view the cultivation most fitting to a woman. To her neither the intricacies of debate nor the oratorical artifices of action and delivery are of the least practical use, if indeed they are not positively unbecoming. Rhetoric in all its forms—public discussion, forensic argument, logical fencing, and the like—lies absolutely outside the province of woman. (126)

Bruni excludes rhetoric because it belongs to the public realm, the sphere of law, politics, and diplomacy, which was firmly defined as off-limits to women. Certain women of the high nobility, such as Anne de Beaujeu, recognized that the wives of princes played highly visible and articulate roles, but exceptions of this kind were not acknowledged by humanists reinforcing the long-standing public/private dichotomy in their writing on contemporary sex roles. Writers aiming advice at fathers and husbands in lower ranks limited women's exposure to language and learning even further. They opposed the frivolous and potentially dangerous pleasures of poetry and philosophy to the sober, useful work assigned to the daughters and wives of the petty gentry and urban merchant class. Giovanni Bruto typifies this counteraristocratic move in his L'*Institutione di una fanciulla nata nobilmente*, published in a French translation in Anvers in 1555. Bruto dedicated this tract to the daughter of a Genoese shipping magnate, whom he clearly wanted to prevent from aspiring to the courtly accomplishments and the elite cultural training of women above her station. He opposes domestic virtue to public ambition; he links literary fame to lascivious self-indulgence. He begins with a transvaluation of historical categories, rewriting the reputations of classical heroines such as Sappho and Diotima:

They, I say, never got so much fame by their learning as they did defame, for their unhonest and loose living. And I suppose there is no man of reason and understanding, but had rather love a Mayden unlearned and chaste, than one suspected of dishonest life, though never so famous and well learned in philosophy.[2] (B8ᵛ)

He goes on to set up a pair of antithetical images that appear throughout Renaissance attacks and defenses of women who write:

how far more convenient the Distaffe and Spindle, Needle and Thimble, |are| for |maids| with a good and honest reputation, then the skill of well using a pen or writing a lofty verse with diffame dishonor, if in the same there be more erudition than virtue. (C2ʳ)

The spindle and distaff versus the pen, private decency versus infamous verse: these oppositions aren't self-evident. Why should learning and writing be equated with immorality and dishonor? Bruto's assumption that learning and chastity are mutually exclusive points to the concern—the obsession, in fact—that underlies the great majority of Renaissance pronouncements on women's speech and fame: female sexual purity. The link between loose language and loose living arises from a basic association of women's bodies with their speech: a woman's accessibility to the social world beyond the household through speech was seen as intimately connected to the scandalous openness of her body. By leaving the confines of domestic privacy, a woman exposed herself to dangers of both visual and verbal kinds. To be seen and to be engaged in conversation were equally potentially transgressive.

An early instance of this body/speech analogy appears in Francesco Barbaro's 1513 essay on *The Duties of a Wife*. Barbaro repeats a Roman anecdote about a noble matron who withdrew her bare arm from the sight of a man who had praised it: "Ah, but it is not public," she said. Like most Italian humanists who cited Roman texts, Barbaro approves of this one; and he goes on to make its implicit assumptions explicit: "It is proper that the speech of women never be made public; for the speech of a noblewoman can be no less dangerous than the nakedness of her limbs" (205). This equation between women's bodies and women's speech depends upon a further assumption: women's onlookers and hearers are always men. The threat envisioned by male social theorists comes from an audience that is always presumed to be masculine. The body-speech link is made more bluntly in a popular tag quoted by the English translator of an Italian treatise on jealousy, (Benedetto Varchi, *The Blazon of Iealousie*, 1615). Richard Toste's summing up of marital common sense suggests that racy speech in a woman is worse than an actual sexual lapse:

Maides must be seene, not heard, or selde, or never,
O may I one such wed, if I wed ever.
A Maid that hath a lewd Tongue in her head,
Worse than if she were found with a Man in bed. (Stallybrass, fn. 18)

It is clear in Shakespearean comedy that verbal challenges from women were perceived as sexual challenges as well (see, on this subject, the witty coda to Lisa Jardine's chapter on the representation of shrews in Elizabethan and Jacobean drama, "Scolding or Shrewing Around?").[3] And the equation between women's chat and women's sexuality also surfaces in etiquette books such as Stefano Guazzo's *Civil Conversation* (1574; English trans. 1581). When the leading speaker in Guazzo's dialogue announces that he will now discuss "la conversatione delle donne," his listener assumes that he means men's sexual relationships with prostitutes, with the kind of women who play at "the game of embraces" ("con le quali si giuoca alle braccia" [1:290]). The confusion is symptomatic: the man takes "conversation," like the-modern word "intercourse," to have two meanings. Among men it is civil, that is, public, civilizing; between men and women, it is carnal.

At court, where women were habitually seen and heard, as the onlookers and the admiring chorus for men's self-display, the tension between public accessibility and private chastity was acute. Even in the idealizing atmosphere of Castiglione's *Courtier*, the speeches of male characters register the strain arising from the contradictory requirements imposed on the court lady, or *donna di palazzo*: to demonstrate courteous affability but also to be pure in manners and body. Giuliano de' Medici recommends that feminine speech balance a "ready livelieness of wit" against "sober and quiet manners"; the female courtier must compensate for being entertainingly witty (*arguta*) by also being unfailingly modest (*discreta*). She must, Giuliano says, "keepe a certain mean very hard, and come just to certain limits" (343). The admitted delicacy of this balance confirms that, in a woman, verbal fluency and bodily purity are understood to be contrary conditions.

By the early seventeenth century, remarks on women's speech suggest that an intensification of prohibitions was underway, particularly in England, where the Protestant focus on marital duties intensified surveillance over daughters and wives. Richard Brathwaite, in *The English Gentlewoman* (1631), hints at a certain frustration at the difficulty of controlling his countrywomen's speech:

To enter into much discourse. . . with strangers argues lightness or indiscretion: what is said of maids may properly be applied to all women: *They should be seen and not heard*. . . . women's tongues are held their defensive armor, but in no particular detract they more from their honor than by giving too much scope to that glibbery member. (78)

He expands the classical *topos* of the teeth as a natural fence for the tongue into an elaborate image of repression and containment:

What restraint is required in respect of the tongue may appear by that ivory guard or garrison with which it is impaled. See how it is doubly warded, that it may with more reservancy and better security be restrained! (88)

The belief that women's speech opened them to irresistible sexual temptation, that articulateness led to promiscuity, produced a related set of prohibitions against women's being spoken *about*. Men's eyes and men's tongues were assumed to share the power to define and possess a feminine object. Wives especially were warned of the indecency of worldly fame. Orazio Lombardelli, writing to his young wife in 1574, declared, "Being known to many men is not a sign of moral health. And acquiring a nickname, . . . like being sung about in songs, are signs of too much desire to be seen" (*Dell 'Uffizio della Donna Maritata*, 27–28). Robert Greene attributes similar ideas to two classical authors to the same effect (*Penelope's Web*, 1601):

The wise and learned man Euboides, whose sayings have ever been counted as oracle, was of this opinion, that the greatest virtue in a woman is to be knowne of none but her husband: alleging the saying of Argius, that the praise of a woman in a strange mouth is nothing else but a secret blame. (E4^r)

The injunction to silence and invisibility was laid upon all women, married or not. Thucydides was much quoted: "The most praiseworthy woman is she whose praises are kept within the walls of the private house" (in Tasso, 2)[4] and Aristotle's distinction between the sexes—"Silence is the virtue of woman as eloquence is of the man" (in Tasso, 3)—was used as a basis for paradoxical commands. Barbaro concludes his commentary on women's speech by declaring, "Women should believe that they have achieved the glory of eloquence if they will honor themselves with the outstanding ornament of silence" (*De Re Uxoria*, 206). This sounds like nonsense; it is. But it is also a logical outcome of the reasoning through which Renaissance gender theory produced the ideal woman. She was distinguished by what she did not do, or, equally important, by what men did not do to her: she was unseen, unheard, untouched, unknown—at the same time that she was obsessively observed. This must be what is meant by saying that women occupy a negative position in culture.

More precisely, I have been describing the *assignment* to women of a negative position in culture. But there is a difference between being the subject *of* discourse and being a subject *in* discourse. No system of sexual opposition allows its participants to speak freely, but the poetic collections of Renaissance women show that they did not simply accede to the silencing logic of their culture. Those who submitted entirely, of course, are not available for reading; those who wrote did so through a range of responses to the interdiction against going public. None of the three poets I am going to discuss rebelled outright against the idealization of the silent woman. Rather, they carried out a sort of *bricolage* with social dictates, enacted a partial obedience toward them, earned the right to fame through a series of subtle appropriations and reshufflings of prevailing notions of feminine virtue. A pose of deference and of self-effacement before the masculine right to fame could act as a scaffolding for various countermoves: a woman poet could promote her own reputation; she could weave a class-based model of the good bourgeois daughter into a defense for women's poetic practice; she could disarm and surround potential male critics by drawing them into a system of cooperative or dialogic authorship. More open challenges to the exclusion of women from humanist claims to fame occurred during the sixteenth century, but I am concerned less with heroines here than with canny compromisers, whose responses to their male contemporaries reveal how *situational* women's writing was, and to what extent it needs to be understood as an adaptation to the gender ideologies reigning in the *pre*-texts of literary culture. Renaissance women poets, given their enforced location outside public discourse, worked their ways into them more often by indirection than by confrontation.

It is important not to overestimate the room for maneuver available to women. One thing that sets their anxiety of authorship[5] apart from the anxiety of later women writers is the absolute centrality of men as writers and as readers in the sixteenth-century literary system. Every woman poet recognized the necessity of winning men over to her side as mentors and as critics. The enormous feminine audiences for romances and novels of the eighteenth and nineteenth centuries did not exist in the 1500s: women were advised to read religious and moral tracts rather than contemporary poetry, which was considered trivial or risky for them. And although women poets occasionally open or close their collections with appeals to women readers, it is very rare to find them acknowledging or taking encouragement from other women poets. Their models and their judges are men, and they do not count on a sympathetic reading. Two Ovidian heroines appear throughout the love poetry of Italian women writing in the Cinquecento: Philomel and Echo, figures of feminine speech-lessness that might be taken as emblems of the isolated woman poet in an era of literary prohibitions. Philomel, whose tongue was cut out by the rapist Tereus, nonetheless wove her story into a tapestry of her own devising; Echo, made mute in punishment for her connivance with Jove, could only repeat the tag ends of phrases uttered by the ever-elusive Narcissus.[6]

PERNETTE DU GUILLET:
SELFLESSNESS AS SELF-SERVICE,
OR FAME THROUGH DEMURRAL

It may be better to be Echo than to be entirely inaudible, however. And the case of Pernette du Guillet shows that echoing may be a cover for forays into new verbal territory. Pernette, writing in Lyon in the early 1540s, adopted a stance of selfless discipleship to Maurice Scève. The publishing circumstances of her *Rymes* suggest that she avoided acting on any public ambition herself; it was left to her husband to publish her poems after her death in 1545. She claims in several poems that her one goal is to lose herself entirely by being transformed into her model and mentor. In her fifth epigram, for example (in which she writes "CE VICE MUERAS" as an anagram of Scève's name), she promises him, "Je tascheray faire en moy ce bien croitre,/ Qui seul en toy me pourra transmuer" (I shall try to increase in myself that good/ Which alone will be capable of transforming me into you) (Epigram 5, ll. 3–4). Imitation here is metamorphosis into the Other. Pernette continues to deny any desire for an independent poetic voice; in Epigram 6 she announces that she is incapable even of contributing to Scève's fame, that is, of reciprocating the poems he has composed in praise of her, unless he lends her the skill to write exactly as he does: "Preste moy donc ton eloquent sçavoir/ Pour te louer ainsi que tu me loues" (ll. 9–10). The echo-writing she envisions here sounds less like imitation than ventriloquism: the disciple hopes to become her master's voice.

But there is a subtle ploy of fame-claiming and fame-bargaining going on here. In that last line, "So that I may praise you as you praise me," Pernette points to her own fame as the topic of

Scève's massive poetic output; it has been his poems in her praise
that set this exchange of compliments in motion. Thus fame leads to
fame: being spoken about obliges Pernette to speak in return. The
praises of the master poet are invoked as a justification for the responses of the disciple. By appealing to a notion of gender-free reciprocity, the woman poet makes her writing look like the fulfillment
of a courteous obligation rather than a transgression of gender boundaries. Pernette's enactment of selfless modesty is actually a strategy
of self-defense.

      In a later poem, the pose of self-effacement before the
male poet's reputation frames an extraordinary fantasy of gender
transgression. Pernette's *Elégie* 2 is a rewriting of the Actaeon myth, in
which the woman poet takes on the death-dealing powers of the
goddess Diana and directs them toward the erotic and verbal domination of the male poet.[7] Pernette imagines herself bathing naked in
a fountain. Singing a poem and playing the lute, she would lure her
lover toward her, but she would deflect his embrace by splashing him
with "l'eau pure de la clere fontaine," turning him not into a "Cerf"
(deer) but a "serf," (slave) a "serviteur" acknowledging her total "puis-
sance" over him. The narrative ends with Pernette's renunciation of
this divine power to transfix the man. She sacrifices her desire to
enslave him, "à l'asservir," in a gesture of homage to his fame. She
defers to Apollo, the Muses and his public audience, taking on the
role of one reader among many:

> Laissez le aller les neuf Muses servir,
> Sans le vouloir dessoubz moy asservir. . .
> Laissez le aller, qu'Apollo je n'irrite,
> Le remplissant de Deité profonde,
> Pour contre moy susciter tout le Monde,
> Lequel un jour par ses escriptz s'attend
> D'estre avec moy et heureux, et content.
>   (ll. 47–54, 59–60)

> Let him go, to serve the nine Muses,
> Without wanting to enslave him to myself. . .
> Let him go, let me not anger Apollo,
> Filling him full of deep godly power,
> To stir up the entire world against me,

That world which hopes one day through his writing
To be, along with me, both fortunate and happy.

But her performance throughout the elegy is far less humble than this expiatory final gesture. *She* represents and controls the scene of seduction, *she* invents the pun that turns the poet into a deer and into her slave, she attributes to *herself* the power of sending the poet back to his vocation. After thirty-eight lines of erotic aquatics, she cannot finally disappear into the anonymous group identity that she claims at the end of the poem. The movement of the elegy toward this apparently modest conclusion, however, may make possible the surfacing, the de-repression, of its central fantasy. Pernette finally neutralizes her transgression of gender laws—her role as seductress and literalizer of Neoplatonic metaphors of devoted service—through a ritual of self-sacrifice or self-erasure. But the elegy's framework of socially endorsed modesty simultaneously supports an experimental vision of sexually and verbally active femininity.

CATHERINE DES ROCHES:
HOUSEHOLD BARGAINS, OR CLASS LOYALTY
AS THE RIGHT TO WRITE

The enabling fiction of self-abnegation before a male mentor has something in common with a broader tactic adopted by another French woman, writing in Poitiers twenty years after Pernette: Catherine Des Roches, the daughter in a mother-daughter pair who published joint collections of poems in 1578 and 1583. Catherine Des Roches appropriated a class-based definition of feminine virtue as a support for her writing: she aligned herself with bourgeois writers celebrating the practical activity of the domestic woman against the frivolous and presumably decadent dilettantism of the aristocratic lady. This was a line of argument that had begun as early as Leon Battista Alberti's *Della Famiglia* (1433–34) and was extended in a careful distinction made by Jacques Du Bosc in his L'*Honneste Femme* (1632). Du Bosc is sympathetic to many womanly refinements, but he limits them to the childless noblewoman: "It should not be thought that in this portrait of the accomplished lady we intend to paint a mother of a family who is expert in giving orders to her servants and who has the duty of caring for her children. Music, history, philosophy and other such exercises are more appropriate to our picture than those of a good housewife" (178). Des Roches, by identifying herself with solidly useful household work, with the spinning that was the constant task of the poor and middle-class family woman, applies for a compensatory license to write.

A first instance of this identification with antiaristocratic class ideals comes in her paraphrase of a popular Renaissance text, the Old Testament portrait of the virtuous woman, whose "price is far above rubies" (*Proverbs*, 31). Des Roches's "La femme forte descritte par Salomon" is a fascinating modernization of the Hebrew ideal of the hard-working, all-providing wife and mother. This was an active and a practical ideal, and Des Roches emphasizes both these qualities in her expansion of the Biblical text. The Old Testament basis for the eight-line passage below is a mere two lines in the King James version: "She girdeth her loins with strength, and strengtheneth her arms." Des Roches enlarges this statement into a critique of the physical inactivity of aristocratic women by praising the active force of the housewife. In common with writers such as Alberti, she eroticizes domestic energy: the housewife is beautiful in her strength:

> Vous la verriez parfois r'accourcir sa vesture,
> Troussée proprement d'une forte ceinture,
> Et revirer apres ses manches sur les bras
> Qui paroissent charnus, poupins, douïllets et gras:
> Car il ne faut penser que la delicatesse
> Se trouve seulement avecques la paresse.
>
> (Oeuvres, 149)

> You'd see her at times pin up her gown,
> Neatly bound in with a sturdy belt,
> And then roll up her sleeves on her arms,
> Which look plump and rosy, tender and full:
> For it's wrong to believe that delicacy
> Co-exists only with laziness.

Her concluding couplet has a combative, critical ring:

> La femme ménagère est plus belle cent fois
> Que ne sont ces Echo qui n'ont rien que la voix.

> The housewifely woman is a hundred times lovelier
> Than these mere Echos who have only a voice.

It is clear here that Des Roches is asserting class independence from aristocratic notions of feminine beauty and reticence in feminine discourse. By speaking as the good bourgeois daughter, she claims and celebrates a counteridentity in the process of being formed against the presumed self-indulgence of higher-ranking women. She demonstrates her loyalty to two histories simultaneously: she appears to serve the men of her class, as she serves the marital theory of the Old Testament by translating it into French.

But the confidence, even the aggressiveness, of this paraphrase takes on a different cast in a sonnet, "A ma quenoille" (To my distaff), in which Des Roches balances concessions to domestic imagery against a claim to public space as a writer. This is a complicated poem, full of repetitions and retractions, because it carries out a complicated strategy. Des Roches is so hesitant to admit any desire for fame that she speaks *around* its possibility. The first quatrain of the sonnet depends upon negation and periphrasis. The desire for a literary reputation is dismissed as a vain search after ephemera:

> Quenoille, mon souci, je vous promets et jure
> De vous aimer tousjours, et jamais ne changer
> Vostre honneur domestic pour un bien etranger,
> Qui erre constamment et fort peu de temps dure.

> Distaff, my care, I promise and swear
> I'll love you forever, and never forswear
> Your homely glory for an outside desire,
> Which wanders forever and lasts but a day.

But this dismissal of a poetic career goes hand in hand with two emblems of the writer's trade. Des Roches appeals to the distaff for permission and protection; she transforms the conventional household emblem into a shelter against insult and infamy, the criticism that she assumes will follow upon her use of ink and paper:

> Vous ayant au costé, je suis beaucoup plus seure
> Que si encre et papier se venoient à ranger
> Tout à l'entour de moy, car pour me revanger
> Vous pouvez bien plustost repousser une injure.

> With you by my side, I am safer by far
> Than if ink and paper joined in a circle
> In my defense; for, to protect me,
> You are abler by far to push back an attack.

This is highly defensive vocabulary. If fame is only indirectly named in the poem, the necessity of combatting hostile responses is not; "revanger" means to protect oneself through counterattack, and "repousser" has equally military connotations. Des Roches writes with a clear eye to the resistance her role as a poet is certain to stir up.

In the sestet, she protects herself by setting up an elaborate equilibrium between the male-defined symbol of feminine industry and her counteremblem of woman as writer. The cajoling intimacy in her appeal to the distaff foregrounds the difficulty of reconciling sixteenth-century demands for housewifely modesty with the guilty desire to write:

> Mais quenoille m'amie il ne faut pas pourtant
> Que pour vous estimer, et pour vous aimer tant
> Je delaisse du tout cest'honneste coustume
> D'escrire quelque fois; en escrivant ainsi
> J'escris de vos valeurs, quenoille mon souci,
> Ayant dans la main le fuzeau, et la plume. (152)

> But distaff, my love, it's surely not the case
> That because I admire you and love you so much,
> I must leave off entirely my virtuous habit
> Of writing at times; for when I do write,
> I write of your value, distaff, my care,
> With the spindle and the pen together in my hand.

Des Roches's promise of unfailing loyalty to womanly virtues is, then, the first step in a propitiatory maneuver. This spinner wants to write, so she disguises her ambition as homage to the ideologically sanctified spindle, the "fuzeau" of her final line. The coordinating conjunction of her last line supports the balancing act toward which she has been working all along: the spindle *and* the pen, not either/or but both/and. This is Des Roches's way past the enforced choice between domestic virtue or writerly publicity. Her love poem to the emblem of housewifely routine earns her access to a feminine pen, which acquires a new respectability through its juxtaposition with the unimpeachable "quenoille." Tight class loyalty (and a certain complicity with masculine fantasy) makes possible a loosening of gender rules. This daughter of the bourgeoisie expands those rules to include herself as writer.

TULLIA D'ARAGONA: NEGOTIATING CELEBRITY, OR FAME AS A MULTI-PARTY CONTRACT

The ingratiating compromise worked out by Catherine Des Roches takes on a more dramatic and expanded form in the collected poems of an Italian courtesan, Tullia d'Aragona. I offer her as a final instance of women's claims to fame because her collection of *Rime* (Venice, 1547) exposes the structure and the processes of fame in a way that few Renaissance texts, by women or by men, do. As a courtesan, Tullia d'Aragona was an admittedly public woman, a sexual professional whose capital consisted in successfully manipulated display: spectacular appearances in processions and at banquets, a high intellectual style. Her reputation, on which she based the high fees that distinguished the courtesan from the common prostitute, depended on a male clientele, the Venetian and Florentine literati and courtiers with whom she traded sexual favors in return for literary recognition. Her set of poems reveals rather than conceals the negotiations and exchanges through which Renaissance writers—perhaps all writers—construct a reputation for themselves.

Throughout the *Rime* Tullia collects and preserves poetic praise in the form of verse epistles, the letters of recommendation through which she and her interlocutors build up a group identity assembled through laudatory dialogues. The *Rime* are composed of 105 poems. Forty-nine are by Tullia; thirty-nine of these are sonnets addressed to men whom she names both in her titles and in the poems themselves. The middle section of the collection is a long eclogue written for Tullia by her old ally, Girolamo Muzio: "La Tirrhenia," in which the nymph of the title is given charisma through the enumeration of her admirers, recognizable as contemporary writers, professionals and noblemen, encoded in Muzio's pastoral pseudonyms. The third section of the book consists of fifty-five poems by men, addressed to Tullia by acquaintances she had cultivated throughout fifteen years of elite literary coteries in Rome, Ferrara, and Venice. What is going on in this multiauthored collection? It is clearly not the product of a unique, originary voice; it is, rather, a carefully organized collaboration, designed as a set of testimonials to Tullia's beauty and eloquence.

How did she acquire this dossier, and why did her contributors oblige? Many of her sonnets are transparent requests for *laude*, poems of praise, and although she regularly deprecates her own lyric competence, she often promises a praise-poem in return. A case in point: writing to Benedetto Varchi, she begins with a eulogy of his "high, immortal worth" and complains that her melancholy and bad fortune prevent her from rising to his "high knowledge and sweet song." But she suggests, in her conclusion, that even dying of grief would be bearable if Varchi wrote a poem in her honor:

> Ma s'a me pur così convien finire
> La penna vostra al men levi il mio nome
> Fuor degli artigli d'importuna morte.

> But if I must die in this way,
> Let your pen [wing] at least raise my name
> Above the weapons of relentless death. (Sonnet 22, p. 8a)

In her sixth sonnet, written to Cosimo de' Medici (who had saved her from prosecution for breaking the sumptuary laws of Florence, which required that courtesans wear a yellow-bordered veil), she makes a similar shift: her posture of helplessness again gives way to a strategy of self-commemoration. Claiming that Cosimo's virtues surpass her ability to praise him, she asks the Muses to produce a eulogy in her stead. But this self-effacement suddenly turns into a claim of authorship, after all. In her final line, Tullia adopts a literary-historical perspective on her own performance, naming herself and her setting in place and time from the third-person perspective of a posthumous biographer: "Cosi dicea la Tullia in riva d'Arno" (Sonnet 6, p. 4a: "Thus spake Tullia, on the banks of the Arno").

Tullia's determination to textualize her own name, to be the subject as well as the author of her poems, orchestrates many of the echo poems in the first section of the *Rime*. These paired *proposte/ risposte* sonnets share the same rhyme scheme: one by a man to Tullia, one by her in return (or one by her, followed by a man's response). Typically, the topic of these duets is fame itself. One pair opens with a sonnet by Antonio Grazzini ("Il Lasca"); he describes Tullia as a figure of international renown in order to argue that only she can formulate compliments worthy of her reputation. In response, she tells him that his celebration has revived and rejuvenated her, to the extent that she can now praise him in return. The stakes in this exchange are new: they are not the claim to private passion through which a male poet wins public fame. What circulates in the dialogue is not desire or even flirtation but a familiar lexicon of literary terms: sheets of paper, styluses and style, the penning of praise. Tullia, the woman poet, is addressed, precisely, *as* a woman poet by "Il Lasca"; and in spite of the intimacy suggested by the juxtaposition of the two poems, the exchange foregrounds the reputation-swapping that is the real business of Tullia's *Rime*, romanticized in gestures toward erotic pairing—gestures which also serve the reputation-building of men in Tullia's sociotextual circuit.

IL LASCA

Se'l vostro valor Donna gentile
Esser lodato pur dovresse in parte,
Vopo sarebbe al fin vergar le carte
Col vostro altero, et glorioso stile.
Dunque voi sola a voi stessa simile,
A cui s'inchina la natura, et l'arte
Fate di voi cantando in ogni parte
TULLIA, TULLIA suonar da Gange a Thile.
Si vedrem poi di gioia et maraviglia
Et di gloria, et d'honore il mondo pieno
Drizzare al vostro nome altare, et tempi.
Cosa che mai con l'ardenti sue ciglia
Non vide il Sole rotando il Ciel sereno.
O ne gli antichi, o ne moderni tempi.

LA TULLIA

Io, che fin qui quasi alga ingrata, et vile
Sprezzava in me cosi l'interna parte,
Come un fior che tosto invecchia, et parte
Da noi ben spesso nel piu bello Aprile.

Hoggi, LASCA gentil non pur a vile
Non mi tengo (merce de le tue carte)
Ma movo anchor la penna ad honorarte,
Fatta in tutto a me stessa dissimile.
Et, come pianta, che suggendo piglia
Novo licor da l'humido terreno,
Manda fuor frutti, e fior, benche s'attempi,
Tal'io potrei, si nuovo mi bisbiglia
Pensier nel cor di non venir mai meno,
Dar forse anchor di me non bassi essempi.

[LASCA]

If your high worth, gentle lady,
Had to be praised, if only in part,
Yours would be the task of covering paper
With your lofty and famous style (stylus).
Thus you alone equal to yourself,
To whom nature and art bow down,
You yourself make, singing everywhere,
TULLIA, TULLIA echo from the Ganges to Thule.
Then we will see the world, filled with
Joy and wonder, with your glory and honor,
Raise up altars and temples to your name—
Something the sun, with his burning brows,
Has never seen as he wheels through the calm sky,
Either in ancient or in modern times.

[TULLIA]

I, who till now, like a weak and lowly weed
Have scorned my inner self,
Like a flower, which suddenly ages and leaves
Us in the midst of the loveliest April,
Today, gentle LASCA, I no longer
See myself as vile, thanks to your poem,
But I raise my pen again, to honor you,
Transformed entirely from my former self.
And, as a plant, drawing up new moisture
From the dampened earth,
Sends forth fruits and blossoms, even though it grows older,
So may I, since a new thought whispers
In my heart that I need never decay,

Produce again, perhaps, not unworthy
Examples of what I can do.

> "Sonetti di diversi alla signora Tullia
> con le risposte di lei," pair 5, p. 18a

Most Renaissance lyric collections included poems writ-
ten in praise of their author, but Tullia's *Rime* take this representation
of mutual admiration to an extreme: of 105 poems, only 49 are hers.
She was not interested in assembling a self-enclosed oeuvre, but in
gathering distinguished men into an affirmative chorus. Their willingness to participate in this "polylogue" calls for analysis. I would argue
that Tullia's collection substitutes an improving fiction for the realities
of a courtesan's life and the rivalry among her clients. In the *Rime*,
potential rivals are transformed into flattering mirrors for each other;
Tullia is a channel through which her interlocutors emerge as members
of a masculine elite constructed within the group text. She makes
herself the medium through which each man takes on some of the
luster of his fellows. This idealized version of male bonding becomes
explicit in Muzio's eclogue, in which he lists Tirrhenia's admirers and
their accomplishments one after another. As the list gets longer, each
of its members takes on greater and greater éclat. The process ends
when the shepherd Dametas crowns Tirrhenia with a garland woven
of the famous "souls" who have sung her praises (ll. 211–15). The
gesture records for posterity both the woman and the men who attest
to her desirability—and to each other's erotic connoisseurship. Rather
than denying her desire for fame, or disarming male readers with a
display of class solidarity, Tullia absorbs her critics into her text and
fixes them in postures of admiration.

Fame of this kind, the erotic starring role in a cast of many
men, was certainly not permissible to a married noblewoman like
Pernette or to a middle-gentry daughter like Catherine Des Roches.
Tullia's assembling of a group portrait was a consequence of her
position as a socially saturated, public figure. She did not challenge
the assumption that verbal forwardness in a woman went hand in
hand with sexual forwardness; she profited from it. (The *Rime* were
published four times in her lifetime, and they won her publishers for
a later philosophical dialogue and a verse romance.) And precisely by

going after fame so single-mindedly, she demystified the whole issue of poetic reputation. Fame is never the simple result of independent merit or aesthetic autonomy. The solitary poet goes unread; the famous poet is socially constituted, invented through the gaze, the commentary, the assessment of others. It is no accident that two of the best known women poets of the Renaissance, Louise Labé and Veronica Franco, were notorious before they were famous. For a woman who entered the realm of poetic publicity inevitably had to break the rules of gender decorum.

But I hope I have shown that the rules could be bent as well as broken. Prohibitions on women's intercourse with the literary world were not as paralyzing as they were intended to be. Their effect was not to silence women but to provoke them into complex forms of negotiation and compromise. I would characterize Pernette, Catherine Des Roches, and Tullia d'Aragona as subversive conformists; without directly opposing social interdictions, they nonetheless took oblique paths toward fame. Pernette backed into it. Her denial of her own ambition and her deference toward her mentor increased the likelihood that her poems would be published. (Good girls sometimes get away with surprisingly gross disobedience.) Des Roches, more positively, made an alliance with the men of her class, an alliance through which she earned more than they perhaps bargained for. As an expert in calculated concession, she proved that a woman can be loyal to more than one cause at a time. Tullia, finally, affirmed the sexual suspicion that underlay Renaissance gender ideology: the woman of many words may indeed be a woman of little chastity. But she refused the double standard. Men are equally involved, she demonstrated, in the group exchange of poetic reputation-building. Altogether, this trio suggests that women's writing in the Renaissance needs to be read for resistance and invention as well as sociotextual constraint. For men and women, fame was not the same. Women claimed it in intricate and indirect ways: they spun safety nets for themselves from the loose ends of masculine discourse, they composed poems that record rather than harmonize the tensions they confronted in a cultural context that demanded women's silence. Reading such poets consequently requires an ear open to the half-said, the quickly withdrawn, the manipulation of masculine rituals of self-eternalization.

"Fame," in English, comes from the Greek root *phanei*, to speak and to be spoken about. The two were linked through prohibition in the ideologies aimed at women in early modern Europe. How, then, do we now read a woman who could be condemned in 1550 as unworthy of hearing precisely because she wanted to be heard? Pre-poetically, by necessity. Women are spoken of; they speak to. The "of" and the "to," the context and the audience, must be the starting-points for any understanding of sixteenth-century women writing.

NOTES

1. For a general argument that the Renaissance disempowered women, with a focus on courtly love as ideology in Italy, see Kelly-Gadol (139–64). A more optimistic view, stressing class differentials, urban flexibility, and reformed religion as benefits for women, is Davis (65–95). See also the introduction to Ferguson et al. for an overview of economic and ideological changes, especially as they affected Englishwomen.

2. Compare the remark of Thomas Powell, aiming at the upwardly mobile fathers of merchant and professional families in London. In *The Art of Thriving*, he writes of middle-class daughters: "Instead of Song and Musick, let them learne Cookery and Laundry. And in steade of reading Sir Philip Sidney's Arcadia, let them read the grounds of good Huswifery. I like not a Female Poëtesse at any hand" (114–15).

3. Lisa Jardine (121–40).

4. Torquato Tasso quotes but also, atypically, questions Thucydides in his *Discorso della virtù femminile, e donnesca*.

5. I borrow this term, which I use less psychologically but similarly as a way of describing women writers' confrontation with the cultural restriction of writing to men, from Sandra Gilbert and Susan Gubar, *The Madwoman in the Attic*.

6. Gaspara Stampa calls on Philomel (and her sister Procne) in her *Rime* (Venice, 1554), Sonnet 173. Veronica Franco mentions both in her *Terze Rime* (Venice, 1575), 3, ll. 25–27. Tullia d'Aragona aligns herself with the Ovidian victim in one of her best-known sonnets, "Qual vaga Philomela" ("Like the Longing Philomel"), *Rime*, 28. References to Echo occur in Stampa (*Rime*, 152) and in Franco (*Terze Rime*, 3, ll. 16–18). The conduct-book writer, Robert Cleaver, appeals to the Echo myth with very different intentions: "as the echo answereth but one word for many, which are spoken to her, so a Maid's answer should be in a single word" (*A Godly Forme of Houshold Government* [London, 1588], p. 94).

7. For an early analysis of this elegy, see Perry, 259–71. I am indebted to Lawrence Lipking for his observation that Pernette further reverses gender roles in this poem by making herself the agent through whom Apollo is filled with divinity—in contrast to the Sybil, who was traditionally on the receiving end in this process (Poetics of Gender colloquium, Columbia University, November 1984).

WORKS CITED

Alberti, Leon Battista. *Della Famiglia (Libro Secondo)*. Turin: Einaudi, 1972.

Aragona, Tullia d'. *Rime della Signora Tullia d'Aragona, et di diversi a lui*. Ed. Enrico Celani. Venice, 1547; repr. Bologna: Romagnoli Dall'Acqua, 1891, 1968.

Barbaro, Giovanni. *De Re Uxoria*. Paris, 1513, 1533. Trans. in *The Earthly Republic: Italian Humanists on Government and Society*. Ed. Benjamin Kohl et al. Philadelphia: University of Pennsylvania Press, 1978.

Brathwaite, Richard. *The English Gentlewoman*. London, 1631.

Bruni d'Arezzo, Lionardo. "Concerning the Study of Literature: A Letter Addressed to the Illustrious Lady, Baptista Malatesta." In *Vittorino da Feltre and Other Humanist Educators*. Ed. William Harrison Woodward. New York: Columbia University, Teachers College Press (Classics in Education, no. 18), 1963.

Bruto, Giovanni. *L'Institutione di una Fanciulla nata nobilmente*. Anvers, 1553. Trans. Thomas Salter, as *A Mirrhor mete for all Mothers, Matrones and Maidens, intituled the Mirrhor of Modestie*. London, 1579.

Castiglione, Baldessar. *Il Libro del Cortigiano*. Venice, 1528; repr. Turin: UTET, 1964. Ed. Bruno Maier. Trans. Sir Thomas Hoby, *The Book of the Courtier*. London, 1561; repr. London: H. M. Dent, 1974.

Cleaver, Robert. *A Godly Forme of Houshold Government*. London, 1588.

Davis, Natalie Zemon. "City Women and Religious Change." In *Society and Culture in Early Modern France*. Stanford: Stanford University Press, 1975.

Du Bosc, Jacques. *L'Honneste Femme*. Paris, 1632.

Du Guillet, Pernette. *Rymes*. Ed. Victor Graham. Geneva: Droz, 1968.

Des Roches, Madeleine and Catherine. *Les Oeuvres de Mes-Dames des Roches de Poetiers, mère et fille*. Paris, 1578.

Ferguson, Margaret; Quilligan, Maureen; and Vickers, Nancy, eds. *Rewriting the Renaissance: The Discourses of Sexual Difference in Early Modern Europe*. Chicago: Chicago University Press, 1986.

Gilbert, Sandra M., and Gubar, Susan. *The Madwoman in the Attic: The Woman Writer and the Nineteenth-Century Literary Imagination*. New Haven: Yale University Press, 1979.

Greene, Robert. *Penelope's Web*. London, 1587; 2nd ed., 1601.

Guazzo, Stefano. *La Civil conversatione del signor Stefano Guazzo*. Venice, 1575. London, 1581. (Trans. George Pettie). Repr. London: Constable, 1925. Ed. Edward Sullivan.

Jardine, Lisa. *Still Harping on Daughters: Women and Drama in the Age of Shakespeare*. Totowa, N. J.: Barnes and Noble, 1983.

Kelly-Gadol, Joan. "Did Women Have a Renaissance?" In *Becoming Visible: Women in European History*. Ed. Renate Bridenthal and Claudia Koonz. Boston: Houghton Mifflin, 1977; repr. in *Women, History, and Theory: The Essays of Joan Kelly*. Chicago: University of Chicago Press, 1985.

Kelso, Ruth. *Doctrine for the Lady of the Renaissance*. Urbana and Chicago: University of Illinois Press, 1956, 1978.

Lombardelli, Orazio. *Dell'Uffizio della Donna Maritata: Capi Centottanta*. Florence, 1585.

Perry, T. A. "Pernette du Guillet's Poetry of Love and Desire." *Bibliothèque d'humanisme et Renaissance* (1973), vol. 35.

Powell, Thomas. *The Art of Thriving, or the plaine Path-way to preferment*. London, 1635.

Ronsard, Pierre de. "Hymne du treschrestien Roy de France Henry II de ce nom." *Les Hymnes de 1555, Oeuvres complètes*. Ed. Paul Laumonier. Paris: Droz, 1935, vol. 8.

Tasso, Torquato. *Discorso della virtù femminile, e donnesca*. Venice, 1582.

Toste, Richard, trans., *The Blazon of Jealousie*. London, 1615. Quoted by Peter Stallybrass in "The Body Enclosed," fn. 18, in Ferguson et al., eds., *Rewriting the Renaissance*.

Vives, Jean Luis. *De Tradendis Disciplinis (The Transmission of Knowledge)*. Trans. Foster Watson. Totowa, N J.: Rowman and Littlefield, 1971.

Opaque Texts and Transparent Contexts: The Political Difference of Julia Kristeva

ALICE JARDINE

I will begin with a quotation: "Furthermore, I do not know if it is to a change in representation that we should entrust the future." I appropriate for myself the pronoun "I" in this reflection of Jacques Derrida's and, having thoroughly renounced the task of figuring out who the "we" is in his sentence, I hereby claim it as feminist: "I (now and here) truly *do not know* if it is to a change in representation that we—as feminists—should entrust the future."

It is from this site of uncertainty—of not-knowing—that I speak with you here on the pre-text (so to speak) of some texts, some contexts, politics, and differences, and Julia Kristeva.[1] There is a certain transparency to all of this: somewhere between a set of texts and contexts, I am here to speak of a difference which is somehow political and which will be represented by Kristeva. But then one notes that the *texts* of which I am to speak would be *opaque*, from *opacus*: darkened, shady, impermeable to light; and that the *contexts* would be *transparent*, from *trans* + *parens*: to appear through, to show completely, to be free from deceit or deception. Of course, in a certain contemporary French thought, neither of these things in the first part of my title are possible. A *text* is not a text if it is totally opaque, refusing to be brought to light, completely impervious to the hermeneutic gesture; and a *context* is never totally transparent, appearing in some kind of referential purity. Now, somewhere in between these two readings— the clear, fast, so-called spontaneous, more transparent one, and the unclear, slower, so-called reflexive, more opaque one—between the first reading and the second reading (first and second only by virtue of our intellectual habits), is a certain kind of difference which is *political*: a difference in attitude toward *interpretation* which I will be talking about here with reference to Kristeva and with reference to possibilities for a strategical feminist ethics.

The difference I am alluding to between reading texts and contexts transparently or opaquely is one that represents a familiar dichotomy. Roughly speaking, "*Anything worth saying can be said simply and clearly*" is our Anglo-American motto par excellence, while much of continental and especially French philosophy and criticism over the past twenty-five years has unveiled the presuppositions of that "simple clarity" with admirable lucidity.[2] To choose an attitude toward interpretation—and therefore toward language—these days is to choose more than just an attitude: it is to choose a *politics* of reading, it is to choose an *ethics* of reading, whose risks and stakes for feminism are what interest me.

As you know, "ethics" is the framework used historically in the West for thinking about the possible faces of morality. *Ethikos*, so very Greek, is that which in its dictionary usage (and here I use a most reliable source, a Cambridge University Student Handbook for Moral Philosophy) refers to "the Study of the Ultimate Good for Man." It is, here in the West, our science of *oughtness*. Traditionally, it has been either distinguished from or ruled by, according to the era: *theology* (the Study of the Ultimate Good for God and the Universe) and *Politics* (the Study of the Ultimate Good for the State). *Today*, Ethics—the possibility of having an Ethic, a Message—seems, indeed, to be in as much trouble as are Man, the State, God—and, now, perhaps, even our "Universe."

The Ethic of Feminism has been and continues to be: the "Study of the Ultimate Good for Woman." We can change the terms of what is Good, True, or Right; Bad, Untrue, or Wrong for Women; one can say, in fact, that morality has only been decided for the good of Man—and that now we will decide it for Woman and eventually, benevolently, for Man as well. But, in so doing, feminism does not change its "Frame of Reference" (as Barbara Johnson might say). It remains, as has been pointed out so loudly in Paris, but another Humanism. The *ethos* of feminism—where it is at home, where it is most comfortable—to the extent that it continues to share the conceptual apparatus of traditional E*thics*, could, therefore, get in trouble as well.

Now the extreme uncertainty and oscillation I experience faced with texts and contexts—the transparency and opaqueness, ethics and politics of both—is compounded by my very stubborn, indigenously American feminist "I" and "we." I refuse to give them up; at times I hesitate to use them. I want to share some components of that oscillation with you because I think I am not alone in finding that a new kind of *ethicity*, a completely different kind of ethicity, is today being mapped out at the crossroads of a certain modernity and a certain feminism. We will not try to decide here and now whether this will be ultimately "good" or "bad" for women.

First, what do I mean by modernity? I'm not absolutely sure that the way in which I'm using the word can or should be defined. But it might be helpful to indicate briefly a few parameters of the question. For example, while I do not primarily use the term in the sense of the "modern"—as in "the ancients vs. the moderns," or as used by Baudelaire, Mallarmé, and Nietzsche—the history of the word cannot help but determine our use of it. While the "avant-garde" is fraught with difficulties of definition, both politically and conceptually, in both the United States and Europe, many of those writers qualified as avant-garde at one point or another since the turn of the century interest me as participants in the project of modernity. My use of the term should not be confused (as it most often is) with "modernism"— the generic label commonly attached to the general literary and artistic movement of the first half of the twentieth century. With the term "modernism," however, we are closest—at least in terms of the so-called literary text—to what concerns me. It is the word "postmodern," as commonly used in the United States, that perhaps most accurately corresponds to what the French name *la modernité*, and that most directly applies to the set of writers I will be valorizing here: those writing self-consciously from within the (intellectual, scientific, philosophical, religious, literary) *epistemological* crisis specific to the postwar period. To put it very clearly, I am most concerned with those writers, whom we may call our contemporaries, who do not try in their writing to pretend that the first half of the twentieth century didn't happen.

For example, in a discussion of the term "postmodern," John Barth puts it this way:

It *did* happen: Freud and Einstein and two World Wars and the Russian and sexual revolutions and automobiles and airplanes and telephones and radios and movies and urbanization and now nuclear weaponry and television and microchip technology and feminism and the rest and there's no going back to Tolstoy and Dickens and Co. except on nostalgia trips. (70)

While Barth's reference is to "fiction writers," I would extend his definition of the ideal "postmodern" writer today to theorists as well, to those theorists who have understood the stakes involved in the intensified search for new modes of conceptuality able to account for, and perhaps change, the course of the twentieth century. What I shall be calling modernity here thus designates a particular attitude, a certain *posture* toward thinking about the human and speaking subject, signification, language, and writing that is of interest to me in relationship to feminist thought.

It is in France where I think the condition of modernity has received the attention it deserves. It is there where a generation of intellectuals (many of them far from patriotically French, a fact often forgotten here)[3] has rejected parts or all of the conceptual apparatus we inherited from nineteenth-century Europe; including, necessarily, certain elements and logics of the conceptual apparatuses based in traditional movements of human liberation; including, of course, feminism. Why this rejection? The reasons have been painstakingly laid out in their texts over the past twenty-five years: our ways of understanding in the West have been and continue to be complicitous with our ways of oppressing. They have laid bare the vicious circles of intellectual imperialism, of the do-Good morality of humanist ideology; they have elaborated at length how that ideology is based on reified, naturalized categories or concepts like "experience," the "natural," the "empirical," or, in another mode, like the "Ethical," the "Right," the "Good," and the "True."[4] Perhaps the clearest way to contain in one word the gesture they have performed on the texts and contexts of humanist ideology would be to focus on one of the key words of semiotics, the word "denaturalization": these writers have denaturalized a world humanism naturalized, a world whose anthrocentrism no longer makes sense. It is a strange new world they have invented—a world *unheimlich*. It appears that the Judeo-Christian philosophies, especially humanism, can no longer contain that world.

Lyotard says modernity is thus about the lack of consensus, the default of democracy and its reigning notions of representation and the intellectual. For him, in a world of mass media, of microchip and satellite technology, the denotative category of what is True and False has become impossible to maintain and pulls down with it the prescriptive, "ought-to" categories of what is just and unjust, right and wrong—just like a row of dominoes. Gilles Deleuze and Jacques Derrida would say, if in different ways, that the image upon which our Western Identity and Ethics is founded—the *visage*, the human face—the one that has been heretofore White, European, and Male—is cracking apart. All that remain are simulacra and masks. For Foucault, modernity began "when words ceased to intersect with representations and to provide a spontaneous grid for the knowledge of things" (304).

Modernity is, in all of these cases, about the loss of narrative. Our stories in the West—their so-called form and content (but especially their form)—have not provided innocent pleasures and, today, their massification or breakdown have rendered them, for some of us, completely illegitimate.

Modernity seems to be about not knowing, about not being sure, about having no story to tell. It also seems to be about loss: loss of identity, loss of truth, legitimacy, knowledge, power—loss of control.

Some of the responses to this loss have been nostalgic, cynical, usually reactionary, sometimes frantic—trying to place the bricks back in the wall just as quickly as it crumbles. We know those responses. They are sometimes perhaps our own. But, in France, the reactions to that loss, on the part of the several writers most concerned here, have been to *affirm* and *valorize* the loss itself. They have been exploring new conceptual tools capable of accounting for new factors beyond the control of the Western/White/Male all-too-Human Subject. They have turned, for help, to those thinkers of the nineteenth century who were already speaking that loss of control: Freud, Nietzsche, Marx, in order to better elaborate this strange condition called modernity.

In order to think in new ways, it has become necessary to speak and write in new ways, and of primary interest to me over the past few years has been the way in which this has necessitated churning up the ancient dichotomies, and especially genders frozen in the Greek foundations of our thinking, and how these genders have been taking on new configurations. *Gynesis*—from the Greek *gyn*—signifying woman and *-sis* designating process—is the word I invented some time ago to designate the process of putting into discourse and indeed valorizing the feminine, woman, and her historical connotations, as somehow intrinsic to new and necessary modes of thinking, speaking, and writing in the twentieth century—not only in France, and not only in literary studies.[5]

Finally, I would just add (and here I am not oscillating, but taking a position) that for me, these discourses in France attempting to take into account the modes of transdisciplinary conceptuality attuned to modernity are the only contemporary Western discourses I have discovered thus far that seem able to account for the new texts and contexts of the world as it appears to us, or to imagine other worlds whether they are possible or not.

Now, I'd like to switch registers a bit and speak even more transparently (if that is possible) as a feminist, trained in the Anglo-American tradition, who relies very heavily on concepts like experience and right/wrong/true/false—and who decided to live in Paris awhile. This is not to indulge in banal personal anecdotes, but to balance the rather opaquely textual sketches of modernity that I have been evoking thus far, with what often appears to their critics, especially their American critics, as fairly transparent contexts: those of Paris—there where a postphenomenological, post-Marxist Parisian intelligentsia has been finding it necessary to think about / talk about / write about woman. I was encouraged by this new attention to the feminine until I realized that there seemed to be an almost existentially arbitrary gap between *woman* and *women*—a problem of enunciation, at least where the men were concerned. When the women were speaking and writing, it became more complicated . . .

Many of the women in France who without hesitation refer
to themselves as feminists, that is, those whose lives and work are
devoted to feminism in an almost Anglo-American way, have been very
suspicious of and, indeed, ultimately have wanted little to do with
these theories and texts of modernity. Articulate, well-read, and angry,
they have declared war on the female members of the Parisian intelligentsia who feel that feminism, *as an -ism* is: at the very least,
problematic—its political unconscious not having been sufficiently
analyzed; at the most, that feminism is already too advanced in its
recuperation by the dominant ideology and its institutions, especially
the media, to be of any more radical political use. For example, women
in the group "Psychoanalysis and Politics" have declared their post-
feminism in writing and their antifeminism in Hélène Cixous's semi-
nars and elsewhere. Other women theoreticians have made their positions clear less flamboyantly but just as firmly: traditional feminism
has been an historically determined and limited phenomenon that
has served its time; feminism, in the Anglo-American vein, is embraced
only by the daughters of the fathers in love with and dependent upon
patriarchal institutions—they are the Athenas of today. We must move
on to more important things, they have said. . .

Faced with this context, my American brand of optimism
changed rather rapidly to defensiveness and pessimism:

But, then, maybe this is just French? I thought.

Maybe it's just a fashion?

Maybe, this is all being caused by a simple generation
gap?

But no. I was beginning to sound like a French caricature
of an American academic. The seeds of the West's modernity—the
death of the Cartesian subject, the dislocation of dialectical progression, the loss of assurance of truth through the authority of the father—
were implanted at the turn of the century. The beginnings of the ends
of Man—of the great European Master discourses—cannot be explained away by nationality, fashion, or generation gaps.

But, even so, is it not possible that this valorization of the
female—almost as if in timely opposition to the newborn feminist
subject—*is* but a new ruse of reason?

It was easiest, of course, to think about the *men* participating in gynesis: is this not a new way for men to counter their fear and indeed paranoia as women's voices have grown stronger? After all, male paranoia *is* about the fear of loss. President Schreber provides the classic example. Like the men of modernity, he too became obsessed by a great world catastrophe, the end of our world as we know it. He alone could restore it to its lost bliss, but only by transforming himself into a woman . . .

Is that why all of these guys want to be wom*en*? or was it wom*an*? And *what about* the women participating in gynesis? Valorizing, each in her own way, the "female parts" denied by Western philosophy?

This brings me to what I sometimes refer to as my Atlantis syndrome—inevitably experienced, it seems, by many of those attempting to think through what I am in shorthand referring to as a certain French textual modernity and a certain Anglo-American contextual feminism.

For there is a "we" here; shaky but insistent: if one is convinced that it is henceforth anachronistic, even impossible, to retain the conceptual apparatus in which feminism as classical philosophy is rooted, how can a *we* nevertheless continue with *our* feminism? How can we (ought we?) continue? How can I/we/you—one—think seriously about modernity without woman rendering women beside the point? I and those who share my concerns would seem to be caught between a set of feminist conceptual *assumptions* proven incompatible with the very premises of our modernity and which are controlling our ways of knowing, and a modernity whose inflationary discursive dependence on the "feminine" risks challenging what women have come to know, the hard way, through historical experience.

Traditional philosophers of Ethics would probably throw up their hands in despair at this point and say that I am but experiencing, here, a *moral/ethical* dilemma—and that I'm acting (as it were) "just like a woman." As outlined by Carol Gilligan in her book *In a Different Voice*, the male developmental psychologists (in this instance, Professor L. Kohlberg) might say that I am stuck at what we can call "The Stage 3 Moral Position"—that I am split between a masculine attitude and a feminine attitude; between thinking and feeling; between hypothetical dilemmas and real life. According to Kohlberg, that's as far as women ever get—the Stage 3 Moral Position—and that's *bad*. Carol Gilligan says it is *good*. Frankly, I have no idea whether it is good or bad. But as a strategic position, it does seem to generate questions and some anger along the way. (So perhaps it can't be all bad?) In any case, I personally have felt compelled to call upon this so-called "feminine" strategy of the either/or, neither/nor, a logic of the in-between, in order to *illuminate* not *invalidate* those discourses attuned to modernity where they make contact with feminist thinking and vice versa. I, again personally, try to do that in different ways depending on where I'm at. In France, I'm more "American" Feminist—whittling away at the accepted currency of feminine metaphors. Here, I try to be more "French"—and shake up, whenever I can, our so-called "ident-ities" so intent on procuring an idea named "equality." This is not to transcendentalize—to imply that one body—anybody—has a right to change positions for each occasion. On the contrary. A few existen-tial years ago, it would have been called "thinking against yourself."

I have stolen this so-called female strategy of the in-between—what in America must be called Moral Position #3—not from Jacques Derrida or, in another mode, from Gilles Deleuze, but from those women writers working in France at the crossroads of modernity and feminism; those participating more or less explicitly in gynesis; those most insistent on the feminine while exploring modernity—in particular, Hélène Cixous, Luce Irigaray, and Julia Kristeva.

The differences between these female-written and the male-written texts of modernity I have predominantly evoked up to this point are not in their "content"; in fact, these women seem at times to be almost miming the masters of modernity (a strategy in itself). No, those differences are in their enunciation; in their modes of discourse; in their twisting of female obligatory connotations; in their haste or refusal to use the pronouns "I" and "we"; in their degree of willingness to gender those pronouns as female; in their adherence to or dissidence from feminism as a movement; in the tension between their desire to remain radical and yet be taken seriously in what remains a male intellectual community; in the extent of their desire to prescribe what posture women should adopt toward the new fem-inine configurations of modernity; in the degree of their desire, indeed, to privilege *women* as subjects of modernity.

And what of the differences *among* these three women participating in gynesis? They have all recognized that modernity entails a certain valorization of the feminine; they all insist on the ways in which the mother has been silenced and indeed mutilated in order for our Western culture to exist; on the need for the maternal to be henceforth signified in new ways. They have all insisted on various aspects of the male and female libidinal economies and their complex links to the outworn occidental modes and habits of our minds. And yet, the paths they have taken are very different. Each would insist that her work is completely different from that of the other two. In fact, each often perceives the other two as intellectual and political enemies.

So what are the possible borderlines between *their* conceptualizations of modernity and woman—let alone women? If, as I have basically concluded, the male text participating in gynesis *is* rooted in male paranoia, what happens when women take over this discourse—especially in the name of woman? Must we then necessarily speak of female paranoia? or is some other configuration of modernity/gynesis/feminism possible, no longer based in paranoia, when practiced by women?

I pose these questions, as yet without answers, very much here in the United States, in the margins of a dialogue between a feminism which, in the name of modernity (and indeed, at times, of epistemological purity) insists upon renouncing its identity; and a pragmatic feminism, attuned to origins and goals, which still yearns to sign its name. The only thing I *am* certain of, at this moment and in these margins, is that the questions raised by this dialogue must not be de-politicized—rendered academic, neutral, and therefore acceptable . . . untroubling. This is why I have proposed, in the second part of my perhaps by now less transparent title, to concentrate on one version of this still politicized strategy located at Moral Position #3—a strategy announced by the phrase "the political difference of Julia Kristeva."

I think that one of the most difficult things to remember, here in the United States, is that the various people we designate by the phrase "contemporary French thought" not only represent a particular set of *epistemological* questions (questions upon which most of those people can agree)—but that they also represent a set of highly politicized conceptual systems offered as working responses to those questions—and that *there* ends the agreement among them. Anecdotes about how none of these people can talk to each other in Paris may be amusing to *us* here, but the disagreements which led to those estrangments are more deeply rooted in fundamental political issues than they are in squabbles among personalities. The clearest example of what I mean by this is perhaps the ways in which the French intellectuals most well known here have taken, at one point or another, a rigorously anti-Marxist, or at the very least para-post-Marxist stance—to the extent that Marxism has remained bound to traditional conceptualizations of dialectics, the human subject, the function, even existence of something called literature, etc. Foucault's archeologies, Lacan's unconscious, Althusser's ideology, Deleuze and Guattari's machines, Lyotard's figurations, Derrida's deconstructions, Irigaray's and Cixous's feminine, etc.—*are* their individual logics as responses to that Marxist thought. They are highly politicized elements of interpretive systems brought to bear not only upon narrow textual questions, but upon some of the most difficult larger epistemological questions facing the West today. Through those responses, each of these writers has created his or her own *ethos*, that conceptual place where they are most at home. And those places are very different.

Let us briefly recall some of the unchanging coordinates of Kristeva's ethos—by now, probably overfamiliar to some of you, but nevertheless important to situate continually with regard to the most pressing questions of our current historical moment. My situating of what is ultimately a complex and constantly evolving conceptual apparatus is necessarily biased. Kristeva's thought is peculiar: it is transparent enough that it tends to be reduced very quickly to a set of bipolar opposites by her critics (and thereby criticized as being everything from ultraanarchistic to ultraconservative); but at the same time, it is opaque enough to be uncritically idealized by her most fervent admirers. I will try to avoid both extremes.

There are, in a sense, three Kristevas—and for the sake of brevity, I will refer to them as the Kristevas of the 1960s, 70s and 80s. (I am sure there are more Kristevas to come.)

The Kristeva of the 1960s was the Kristeva of *Tel Quel* and semanalysis. Semanalysis was the term first proposed in $\Sigma\eta\mu\epsilon\iota\omega\tau\iota\kappa\dot{\eta}$ (*Semeiotike / Recherches pour une sémanalyse*, published in 1969) to describe what she called then a new materialist theory of signification whose own internal logic would remain isomorphic to its privileged object: poetic language. While rarely used in her subsequent work, the term designates both the terrain and process through which Kristeva has contributed to a reformulation of the speaking subject and its text over a period of now almost two decades.

The new science of semanalysis, announced in the blissful aftermath of 1968, was, first of all, an effort to take account of and valorize those radical signifying practices excluded from or assigned to the margins of official mass culture in the West. It was addressed to what she and others would later call "limit-texts," with special emphasis on those texts written since the late nineteenth century and in dialogue with twentieth-century crises in Western thought. It was to analyze the epistemological and ideological ruptures signaled or already realized by these limit-texts as well as to set the ground for a new, general theory of writing and subjectivity. It was in this early work that Kristeva emphasized—as did other members of *Tel Quel*—the most radical moments of Marx's theory of production, Freud's analysis of dreams, Saussure's work on anagrams, and Althusser's on ideology, in order, as she put it, to reconceptualize the figurability of history and the history of figurability.

By the early 1970s, Kristeva had thoroughly formalized the most important components of semanalysis and they became part of a system: a non-Cartesian theory of the subject, not dependent on the ideology of language only as a transparent communication system, but as reverberated through the Freudian and Lacanian unconscious. Her vocabulary was refined and signed: the semiotic and symbolic; the phenotext and genotext, etc.—and all was elaborately developed in the style of the first half of *La Révolution du langage poétique*. It was, in fact, with the Kristeva of *La Révolution* that the Kristeva of the 70s took form. There, Mallarmé and Lautréamont served as examples of how semanalyzing poetic language could help us to shed our stubborn Cartesian and Humanist skins—and begin to look beyond the so-called "message" or "ethic" of a text to its form, its networks of phantasies; to a sentence's rhythm, articulation, and its style—how it could help us to understand how those elements *are* the message, bound up in a conceptuality that we cannot hope to change only at the level of the utterance. For her, it is the economy *of* language and sexuality— not the history of ideas *on* language and sexuality—that articulates social relationships in the West.

It was in 1974, the year of *La Révolution*, that there appeared, in all of its explicitness, on Kristeva's intellectual horizon, the two limits which continue to mean the most to her: the two political extremes of our century and its responses to the crises of monological Western thought: Fascism and Stalinism, and thus inevitably anti-Semitism. According to Kristeva, those two limits—besides being historical, political phenomena, rooted in concrete historical and economic contexts as well as personalities—are also rooted in the psychic mechanisms of the human subject and are laid bare in the psychic traces of the radically poetic text. For her, fascism is the return of the repressed (of what she calls the feminine-connoted semiotic) into rigid religious or political structures. Instead of being socialized, the semiotic is unchained. From this point of view, Stalinism is but the default of Fascism: the barbarous other side of the human face.

I might just remind you here that Kristeva is Bulgarian and that through the biographemic texture of her writing can be traced a certain *fear*, a fear not unlike that which many of us are experiencing today with regard to the larger political climate in which we are living; a climate which we often qualify in shorthand as a "backlash," but which is much more than that. It is a climate of sustained, popularly supported—and, indeed, massively desired—paranoia, particularly with regard to the relationship between production and reproduction, the *regulation* of the mother's body once again serving as ground for a monolithic, nationalistic ideology. Here, Kristeva's insistent return to the 1930s—what *were* those intellectuals and writers doing?—can provide food for thought. For me, her work intervenes at the tense intersection between this actively informed *fear* and our naively passive *belief* that Fascism or Stalinism cannot possibly return.

Kristeva's one basic question became increasingly more insistent and explicit. How can we give a sign, a discourse, to that which is and has been repressed throughout Western history? How can we find a subject for what has been repressed while avoiding these two extremes: psychic explosion and psychic censorship? What can be new modalities for reshaping the monological and monotheistic laws at the foundations of our Western culture without inviting the return of the repressed in its potentially monstrous and apocalyptic reality?

It was in *La Révolution* that Kristeva first talked about ethics: an increasingly important element in her work of the 1970s, for her, ethics can no longer be the observation of laws, moralistic or normative judgment, scientific or otherwise. But the question of ethics must not be scorned or rejected (as with Lacan, for example); left in perpetual suspension (as in Deleuze and Guattari); or deferred (sometimes rather guiltily, as in Derrida). Ethics can no longer be "a coercive, customary manner of ensuring the cohesiveness of a particular group through the repetition of a code," but, rather, must come up "wherever a code (mores, social contract) must be shattered in order to give way to the free play of negativity, need, desire, pleasure, and jouissance, before being put together again, although temporarily and with full knowledge of what is involved." And, in her words, "Fascism and Stalinism stand for the barriers that the new adjustment between a law and its transgression comes against" ("The Ethics of Linguistics," 28). For Kristeva, the only possible ethicity for the late twentieth century in the West is what she terms the negativization of narcissism within a practice. In other words, what is ethical is a practice which dissolves narcissistic fixations—dissolving them before they become rigidified as sociosymbolic structures. And that is the ethical—hence political— function of an artistic and theoretical practice which ruptures the representations of even the most liberal and progressive discourse.

It goes without saying that this includes the discourse of feminism. It was during the 1970s that Kristeva wrote the most explicitly about the feminine, and sketched the outlines of her own participation in gynesis—a participation which like that of the other two women theorists I have privileged here rings differently from its male versions. That is, when taken up by female voices, gynesis becomes strangely subversive, promising, at the very least, new kinds of questions unburdened by the repetition of the dialectics of master/slave oppression. On the other hand, Kristeva's participation in gynesis is unlike that of these two other women theorists in that she does not include the category of "women as subjects" within its boundaries. She began her concentration on the feminine by analyzing it only as a kind of "glue" that has held our patriarchal history and its conceptual systems together. She began to analyze the ways in which the feminine has been sublimated or fetishized in different cultures and at different points in history. She began emphasizing how this feminine is linked to the Mother within the classical Western oedipal structure. But she refused to definitively untangle the woman subject from the feminine. Except for scattered comments on women's need for maternity (often rather shocking to the American feminist's ears), she broke with Irigaray and Cixous completely when it came to prescribing what women's relationship today should be to that feminine—or at least, has always approached that topic with extreme caution. She has consistently rejected the notion that women should either valorize or negate this feminine whose function in Western culture is still changing with the evolution of our modernity.

It became increasingly clear through the 1970s that Kristeva was not going to participate in hypothetical descriptions of the female subject's potential liberation from patriarchy. In fact, her writing took a decisive turn. By the mid-70s, it was obvious that it was the Male-Subject-Creative-of-Our-Dominant-*and*-Marginal Culture that Kristeva was going to x-ray—building a sort of inventory of possible male libidinal economies. One may regret and criticize her lack of attention to women subjects and their texts—I certainly do—but there can be no doubt that this was a calculated political decision on her part.

What Kristeva did do was continue her search for a conceptuality which would provide space for her definition of ethics: an understanding of that which pulverizes the truths of our age before they become too rigid, but one that does not lose sight of those truths, thereby descending into an esoteric, mystical, or even—*à la limite*—psychotic discourse. For example, *La traversée des signes*, a collection of essays on Chinese, Indian, and other sign systems, was not just a result of Kristeva's involvement with *Tel Quel* and its 70-ish Maoism, as is often charged—but was, rather, fully consistent with her project of x-raying other forms of intelligibility, mapping their promises and limits for changing Western culture. *Polylogue*—a collection of essays all written in the 1970s—treats everything from Giovanni Bellini to film theory. But what unites the essays is Kristeva's backing away from *explicating* her theoretical apparatus toward looking at individual signifying practices by men in terms of two other limits: language *before* it signifies and communicates meaning; and language at the point where it is losing or has *lost* meaning: that is, at language acquisition and at psychosis. Her emphasis shifted even more radically toward an understanding of the place of the archaic mother and father, or more precisely, of the fantasies engendered by them. This intensification of focus on the two limits of language—its *before* and *after*, if you like—continued Kristeva's ethical project: not the condensation or solidification of meaning, but an understanding of meaning's doubleness, its unnamable, its unspeakable—its grounding in the unsignifiable.

The importance of one particular event in Kristeva's personal trajectory during the 1970s cannot be overestimated. She decided to become a psychoanalyst, and, in my opinion, what came out of Kristeva's practice as an analyst and, in particular, out of her extreme attention to the mechanisms of transference, was a return, with renewed fascination, to her main, most consistent concern—political extremes—but this time, as someone more independent and sure of her critical voice.[6] She assumed fully her place as a cultural critic, someone attuned to the epistemological and psychic logics underwriting today's more overtly moral or political dilemmas. She struck out on a somewhat singular, at times lonely intellectual path in Paris—and, in fact, even in terms of the Paris/U.S. connection. Refusing both the positivism of American interpretive systems and what she sees as the interminability of new French philosophies, she turned to what, in clinical language, is termed "the borderline patient," and to the problems of interpretation intrinsic to this new kind of human subject—more specifically, the male writing subject of Western culture in the late twentieth century. Kristeva delved, head first, into our turn-of-the-century *mal du siècle*, looking for what is specific to it—and for what can be done about it, if anything.

The Kristeva of the 1980s began, in my opinion, with the publication of *Folle vérité* in 1979. She writes there of the *vréel*—the kind of new "truth" modern men seem to be desperately searching for and can't seem to find, a truth which has "massively left behind the secure terrain of logic and ontology" ("Le vréel," 11). She attacked the questions of how to render this *vréel vraisemblable*, signifiable, before it might explode in what we call "reality." The word *vréel* is composed, of course, of three words: the true (*vrai*), the real (in Lacan's sense), and the feminine pronoun *elle*. From an analysis of the resurgence of mysticism in our time to readings of sophistic thought, these essays bear witness to our time as one of obsession with the *vréel*—an obsession with the feminine psychic spaces repressed throughout 2,000 years of Western history. Their explosion today, into new languages—both liberating and destructive—is no accident according to Kristeva.

In her book, *Pouvoirs de l'horreur*, Kristeva explored what she sees as the fundamental condition of late-twentieth-century man— and by man, she means *men*: Abjection. Much stronger in French, this word designates the psychic state of the borderline subject who is no longer a subject and who no longer is sure of an object (or can't find one): the subject who is fascinated with the boundaries between subject and object, with the ambiguous, the mixed, *l'entre-deux*. As for exploring the intricacies of this new "male condition," I will leave you to the text. But I think it is important to point out briefly the place of this project within Kristeva's ethical trajectory. She ends the book in the following way, and we can see the same concerns that have haunted her work from the beginning surface once again:

Rivetted to meaning like Raymond Roussel's parrot to his chain, psychoanalysts, because they interpret, are no doubt among the rare contemporary witnesses to the fact that we are all dancing on a volcano. If there is where they are to find their perverse pleasure, so be it: on the condition that they help explode, by virtue of their qualifications as a man or woman *sans qualités*, the deepest logics of our anguishes and our hatreds. Can they x-ray that horror without capitalizing on the power it gives them? Exhibit the abject without confusing their own position with it?

Probably not. But at least they should know that, from this field of knowledge mined with forgetfulness and laughter, with the knowledge of the abject, he, she—they—are preparing themselves for the first really major demystification of Power (religious, moral, political, and verbal) that humanity has lived through, necessarily produced from within the demise of Judeo-Christian monotheism, the religion of sacred horror.

In the meantime, others will continue their long march toward idols and truths of all kinds, armed with the necessarily true faiths of wars to come, necessarily sacred wars.... (247–48; my translation)

The tone of this ending to Kristeva's book may appear apocalyptic— or even melodramatic to some—but that may be because those of us who rather stubbornly insist on continuing to function every day must put out of our minds the real or potential horrors of a contemporary world whose "deep logic" Kristeva seems to want to pursue on every page. (And as an aside and purely personal remark, I might just add that if feminists get upset because Kristeva does not center her work more around questions of female subjectivity, her male readers are getting even more upset, or perhaps hostile would be a better word, by her current rather relentless focus on the politics of male sexuality.)

Kristeva has most recently written on the most banal topic in the world: love, the inverse of abjection. But she has removed love from the television screen—as well as from the advertising pages of the NYRB—and put it back into our bedrooms and nurseries and, most importantly, back into history. She reminds us that there is a history of love, a history important to evoke in the context of radical shifts in the love stories being told today, stories in which what has been called love risks collapsing because of a lack of object in the language of the end of the twentieth century. Her unsentimental approach to this concept—in a contemporary world where, when not sentimentalized, love is thought of only in terms of desires that have lost, given up on, or banished their potential objects—promises some fairly interesting reading for the American pragmatic mind. So will, I'm sure, her current work on a third facet of our contemporary, dominant, male libidinal economy: the dark lining of love, the condition of melancholy.

Finally, I would like to pause for just a minute over one of Kristeva's last articles published in English. Entitled "Psychoanalysis and the Polis," it appeared in a special issue of *Critical Inquiry* on "The Politics of Interpretation" (77–92). I mention this article for two reasons: first, because it seems to me a perfect example of the Kristeva of the 1980s—a Kristeva whom, I hear, a lot of Americans don't like because they find her, well, *too psychoanalytic*. But that is the second reason I call attention to it. The article appears at the center of this volume of *Critical Inquiry* as the only *female voice*, and as the only voice from France, adopting the politics of *saying what is not being said*, adopting the micropolitics of psychoanalysis. She does this surrounded by eight Anglo-American males contemplating how awful everything is and pronouncing on what I can only describe as the Ethics, indeed Morality of our most popular modes of Interpretation—Marxist, Deconstructionist, Historical, and yes there is even a so-called male Feminist there. Into this Ultramoral—and rather transparent—context, Kristeva injected a very opaque text, preceded by a prefatory remark added after the conference at which these papers were read. In that preface, she reminds the reader of something that has been fundamental to French thinking for the last twenty years but which here, in the United States, seems just too difficult to confront: that "there are political implications inherent in the act of interpretation itself," whatever meaning that interpretation ultimately bestows. That to give an (empirically) political meaning to something is

perhaps only the ultimate consequence of the epistemological attitude which consists, simply, of the desire *to give meaning*. This attitude is not innocent but, rather, is rooted in the speaking subject's need to reassure himself of his image and his identity faced with an object. Political interpretation is thus the apogee of the obsessive quest for A Meaning." (78)

I would emphasize two things here: first of all, the words "reassure himself of *his* image and *his* identity" are no accident. That it should be uniquely a woman and feminist, Gayatri Spivak, who has taken the time to reply (if angrily) to Kristeva's article on the *male* politics of interpretation—including Kristeva's insistence on the contextual maleness of *this* inquiry—is fascinating to me (269–78). In any case—and secondly—Kristeva's lone voice and gesture at the center of this volume brings me back to my beginning. There I insisted on two kinds of reading and on my sense that the difference between these two kinds of reading is, above all, a political and ethical difference: a difference in attitude toward interpretation. *That*, also, is Kristeva's political difference. Kristeva knows and continues to remind us that the text—any text—can always be read *both* ways, transparently and opaquely, that what it signifies is always both possible and impossible, both can and cannot exist, both does and does not exist, and that, indeed, a text *must* be read both ways—its difference respected—with neither reading being excluded, overlooked, or denied because of convention, law, or privilege.

In my opinion, this is not to advocate some kind of warmed-over critical pluralism, but is, rather, to adopt purposefully a kind of . . . MORAL POSITION #3; an ethicity which, at least temporarily, might allow women to continue interpreting without being afraid of and without becoming *victims* of either modernity or feminism.

NOTES

1. I have not tried to cover the traces of my spoken text. Portions of this article have appeared in a differently written form in my book *Gynesis. Configurations of Woman and Modernity.*

2. The demand for clarity is not, of course, indigenously American, but comes from a long classical tradition more rigorously challenged in France than in the United States. That tradition in France had no more passionate advocate than Boileau: "Ce que l'on conçoit bien s'énonce clairement/ Et les mots pour le dire arrivent aisément." Nicolas Boileau, "L'art d'écrire" from L'Art Poétique (1674), Chant I, ll. 29–30.

3 This is true both literally and figuratively in that several of the writers in question—e.g., Cixous, Derrida, Kristeva—were not born in France, and in that all of them are at odds in some way with the dominant French tradition.

4. Most of this work has been pursued in the wake of Nietzsche. For the most concentrated introduction to what this has to do with modernity, see Jean-François Lyotard, *The Postmodern Condition: A Report on Knowledge.*

5. See my *Gynesis: Configurations of Woman and Modernity.*

6. Jacqueline Rose has suggested to me that, on the contrary, experience as an analyst may have made things more difficult and contradictory for Kristeva. I suspect that both of our observations are relevant. Kristeva's move in the 1970s from collective to individual labor (from *Tel Quel* to private practice) gave *her* a stronger, more independent voice (as someone primarily committed to the insights of Freudian analysis); yet that change in voice has no doubt rendered the interpretation of her *oeuvre* (committed to much more than Freud) more difficult and contradictory, perhaps, for us. See Jacqueline Rose's fine paper, "Julia Kristeva: Take Two," from the March 1985 Pembroke Center Conference, "Feminism/Theory/Politics."

WORKS CITED

Barth, John. "The Literature of Replenishment." *Atlantic Monthly* (January 1980), 245 (1): 65–71.

Boileau, Nicolas. "L'art d'écrire." *L'Art Poétique.* 1674.

Foucault, Michel. *The Order of Things.* New York: Random House, 1970.

Gilligan, Carol. *In a Different Voice.* Cambridge: Harvard University Press, 1982.

Jardine, Alice. *Gynesis: Configurations of Woman and Modernity.* Ithaca: Cornell University Press, 1985.

Johnson, Barbara. "The Frame of Reference: Poe, Lacan, Derrida." In *The Critical Difference.* Baltimore: Johns Hopkins University Press, 1980.

Kristeva, Julia. *Semeiotike/Recherches pour une sémanalyse.* Paris: Editions du Seuil, 1969.

—— *La Révolution du langage poétique.* Paris: Editions du Seuil, 1974. For the first half, see: *Revolution in Poetic Language.* Trans. Margaret Waller. New York: Columbia University Press, 1984.

—— *Polylogue.* Paris: Editions du Seuil, 1977. "Le vréel." In *Folle vérité.* Paris: Editions du Seuil, 1979.

—— *Pouvoirs de l'horreur.* Paris: Editions du Seuil, 1980. *Powers of Horror.* Trans. Leon S. Roudiez. New York: Columbia University Press, 1982.

—— "The Ethics of Linguistics." In *Desire in Language.* Ed. Leon S. Roudiez. Trans. Thomas Gora, Alice Jardine, and Leon S. Roudiez. New York: Columbia University Press, 1980.

—— "Psychoanalysis and the Polis." *Critical Inquiry* (September 1982), 9(1): 77–92.

Kristeva, Julia, ed. *La traversée des signes.* Paris: Editions du Seuil, 1975.

Lyotard, Jean-François. *The Postmodern Condition: A Report on Knowledge.* Minneapolis: University of Minnesota Press, 1984.

Rose, Jacqueline. "Julia Kristeva: Take Two." Pembroke Center Conference, March 1985, "Feminism/Theory/Politics."

Spivak, Gayatri Chakravorty. "The Politics of Interpretations." *Critical Inquiry* (September 1982), 9 (1): 259–78.

Pornography, Transgression, and the Avant-Garde: Bataille's *Story of the Eye*

SUSAN RUBIN SULEIMAN

You will have noticed that the title of this essay makes no mention of gender or the poetics of gender. But pornography (etymologically: writing about prostitutes) brings us close enough, and we will get to explicit considerations before long. These will arise from a reflection on different ways of reading Bataille's pornographic narratives—notably *Histoire de l'oeil* (*Story of the Eye*), which occupies the privileged position of liminary text in Bataille's *Oeuvres Complètes*. Like the equally famous *Madame Edwarda* (1941), *Histoire de l'oeil* never appeared under Bataille's own signature during his lifetime. This is one indication of the pornographic status of these texts, at least in a legal and sociological sense—a good place to start if one wants to define pornography. A pseudonymous author cannot be prosecuted, especially if his work appears in a very limited edition and bears a false place of publication.[1] Although in our permissive days such prudence may be deemed unnecessary, one does well to recall that only a few years before Bataille's death the Editions J.-J. Pauvert were brought to trial in Paris and heavily fined for publishing the works of Sade.[2]

The ways of reading I shall consider here I call textual, "ultrathematic," and thematic. The meaning of these terms will become clear soon enough. I wish to emphasize that my discussion is not meant to be purely academic. At stake is not merely an analytic desire to define and categorize, but the neccessity to understand the ideological aims and implications (by ideology, I mean of course also sexual ideology) of *any* way of reading.

Let us begin with an outstanding fact of recent cultural history: Georges Bataille, who at his death in 1962 (at age 65) was known only to a handful of Parisian intellectuals (and perhaps to a few provincial readers of the journal *Critique*, which he had founded after the war) became, in the space of a few years, one of the central references, a veritable culture hero, of the literary and philosophical movements that we associate with the renewal of French thought in the 1960s and 1970s—movements that would find a world-wide resonance.[3] In the decade following his death, Bataille's work elicited major essays by Roland Barthes, Julia Kristeva, Jacques Derrida, Philippe Sollers, Maurice Blanchot, and Michel Foucault, to mention only those who subsequently became culture heroes in their own right, in France and elsewhere. To this list one should add Susan Sontag, who with her usual intuition for significant intellectual trends on the Continent, devoted a long essay chiefly to Bataille as early as 1967.

The question obviously arises *why* Bataille's work should have been felt so deeply to correspond to a certain notion of textual and cultural modernity. It was not only, as some might think, a matter of promoting to a central place that which had been marginal—one of the characteristic gestures of any avant-garde. The French literary and philosophical avant-garde of the 1960s and 1970s found in Bataille's work an *exemplariness* that went far beyond a mere desire for paradox. But it will not be enough to suggest or even analyze the reasons for this correspondence; it will also be necessary to criticize them, in the radical, etymological sense: to make decisive, to separate, to choose. For we are not dealing with some safely distant question of cultural or literary history: the question of Bataille's relation to the problematics of modernity is contemporary, it concerns *us*. And this is nowhere more evident than in his practice of literary pornography.

In her 1967 essay, "The Pornographic Imagination," which remains one of the rare attempts to analyze the relations between pornography and modern writing, Susan Sontag stated that "books like those of Bataille [she was referring to *Histoire de l'oeil* and *Madame Edwarda*] could not have been written except for that agonized reappraisal of the nature of literature which has been preoccupying literary Europe for more than half a century" (44). Pornography, as practiced by a writer like Bataille, was one of the ways in which modern art fulfilled its task of "making forays into and taking up positions on the frontiers of consciousness," one of the manifestations of the modern artist's constantly renewed attempt to "advance further in the dialectic of outrage," to make his work "repulsive, obscure, inaccessible; in short, to give what is, or seems to be, *not* wanted" (45).

By situating Bataille's pornographic fictions in the French tradition—or more exactly, anti-tradition—of *transgressive* writing, a tradition whose founding father was Sade, Sontag manifested her own allegiance to the adversary values of the European avant-gardes of this century. For of course the avant-garde of the 1960s was not the first in our century to valorize an aesthetics of transgression. That had begun much earlier, with the Surrealists via their own reading of Sade and Lautréamont. It was the Surrealists, too, who placed eroticism at the center of their preoccupations with cultural subversion. But it was in the 1960s that the potential for a metaphoric equivalence between the violation of *sexual* taboos and the violation of *discursive* norms that we associate with the theory of textuality became fully elaborated. And it is here that both Bataille's practice as a writer and his thought as a philosopher became a central reference.

Philippe Sollers, in a long essay devoted to Bataille's book on eroticism (the essay appeared in *Tel Quel* in 1967), suggested that all of modern literature, from Sade's *Juliette* to Bataille's *Histoire de l'oeil*, was haunted by the idea of a "bodily writing" (*écriture corporelle*), to the point that the body had become the "fundamental referent of its [modern literature's] violations of discourse" (122).[4] Derrida, in an essay on Bataille published the same year, suggested that the transgression of rules of discourse implies the transgression of law in general, since discourse exists only by positing the norm and value of meaning, and meaning in turn is the founding element of legality (403–4). And already in 1963, in an essay devoted to *Histoire de l'oeil*, Barthes had explicitly stated: "the transgression of values, which is the declared principle of eroticism, has its counterpart—perhaps even its foundation—in a technical transgression of the forms of language" (244).[5]

The importance of this idea—which suggests that the transgressive content of a work of fiction, and of pornographic fiction in particular, must be read primarily as a metaphor for the transgressive use of language effected by modern writing—cannot be overestimated. What we see here is the transfer (or, to use a very Bataillean term, the "slipping over," *glissement*) of the notion of transgression from the realm of experience—whose equivalent, in fiction, is representation—to the realm of words, with a corresponding shift in the roles and importance accorded to the signifier and the signified. The signified becomes the vehicle of the metaphor, whose tenor—or as Barthes puts it, whose foundation—is the signifier: the sexually scandalous scenes of *Histoire de l'oeil* are there to "signify" Bataille's linguistically scandalous verbal combinations, not vice versa.

To fully appreciate the importance of this shift, we must consider briefly Bataille's own notion of transgression. For Bataille, transgression was an "interior experience" in which an individual—or, in the case of certain ritualized transgressions such as sacrifice or collective celebration (*la fête*), a community—exceeded the bounds of rational, everyday behavior, based on calculations of profit, productivity, and self-preservation. The experience of transgression so defined is indissociable from the consciousness of the limit or prohibition it violates; indeed, it is precisely by and through its transgression that the force of a prohibition becomes fully realized. The characteristic feeling accompanying transgression is one of intense pleasure (at the exceeding of boundaries) *and* of intense anguish (at the full realization of the force of those boundaries). And nowhere is this contradictory, heterogeneous combination of pleasure and anguish more acutely present than in the interior experience of eroticism, insofar as the latter involves the practice of sexual "perversions" opposed to "normal," reproductive sexual activity. In eroticism, as in any transgressive experience, the limits of the self become unstable, "slipping." Rationalized exchange and productivity—or, in this case, reproductivity—become subordinated to unlimited, nonproductive expenditure; purposeful action, or work, becomes subordinated to free play; the self-preserving husbandry of everyday life becomes subordinated to the excessive, quasimystical state we associate with religious ecstasy and generally with the realm of the sacred. These ideas were already present in Bataille's 1933 essay, "The Notion of Expenditure." They were developed and refined in his later works, in particular in L'*Erotisme* (1957), which presents a theory of eroticism in the historical and cultural perspective of transgressive practices in general.

What theorists of textuality like Barthes, Derrida, and Sollers accomplished was to transfer, or perhaps more exactly to extend, Bataille's notion of transgression to modern writing—that is, to *écriture*. For *écriture*, in the sense in which they used that term, is precisely that element of discursive practice which exceeds the traditional limits of meaning, of unity, of representation; and just as for Bataille the experience of transgression was indissociable from a consciousness of the limits it violated, so the practice of *écriture* was indissociable from a consciousness of the discursive and logical "rules," the system of prohibitions and exclusions that made meaning, unity, and representation possible but that the play of *écriture* constantly subverted.[6]

It now becomes clear why Bataille's writing, read in a particular way, could function as a central reference and as an exemplary enterprise for the French theorists of modernity of the 1960s and 1970s. His theoretical texts provided a set of concepts or "key words" whose applicability extended from the realm of cultural and individual experience to the realm of writing: expenditure, transgression, boundary, excess, heterogeneity, sovereignty — this last being a key term in Bataille's vocabulary, whose implications, as Derrida brilliantly demonstrated are the very opposite of Hegel's term, "mastery." Mastery is linked to work, and above all to the affirmation and preservation of meaning; sovereignty, on the other hand, is precisely that which enables an individual to expose himself to play, to risk, to the destruction or "waste" of meaning (373–84). Accompanying and complementing the theoretical texts, Bataille's pornographic fictions provided metaphoric equivalents for his key concepts, as well as a locus for their elaboration: the eroticized female body. Finally, Bataille's writing practice, tending toward the fragmentary and the incomplete, provided the example of a writing which (as Derrida put it) "will be called *écriture* because it exceeds the logos (of meaning, of mastery, of presence, etc.)"; the sovereignty of the Bataillean text, as of all *écriture*, resides in the text's "commentary on its absence of meaning" (392; 383–84).

As I say, what is involved here is a particular reading of Bataille—a very powerful reading which has (or had) at least two advantages: first, it is integrative, allowing the commentator to consider *all* of Bataille's varied writings as part of a single artistic and intellectual quest. In this integrative view, the pornographic narratives

Bataille did not sign with his own name or did not publish even under a pseudonym during his lifetime become as much a part of Bataille's signature as any of his other writings; thus, Julia Kristeva noted in her 1972 essay on Bataille that "Bataille's novels are inseparable from his theoretical positions and give them their real value" (286).[7] Maurice Blanchot, in a similar move, began one of his essays by stating that central to an understanding of Bataille's thought are not only his theoretical works but also "the books he published under a name other than his own," whose "power of truth is incomparable" (301).

The other advantage of this kind of reading—which I call the "textual" reading—is that it is generalizable: not only are Bataille's varied writings seen as parts of a single enterprise, but that enterprise becomes emblematic of modern transgressive writing in general.

If there is one thing, however, that the theorists of textuality have taught us, it is that no reading is innocent. Every reading is an interpretation, and every interpretation is an appropriation of a text for its own purposes. Every interpretation has its blind spot, which I like to think of not only as the spot or place from which the interpreter cannot "see" his or her own misreading of a text, but also as the spot or place *in* a text from which the interpreter averts his or her gaze.

What is the spot in Bataille's text from which the powerful textual reading averts its gaze? To answer that question, it is necessary to turn to an *other* reading, one that has its own significant blind spot but that nevertheless has the advantage of making us see Bataille— as well as the theory of textuality in whose service he was so powerfully enrolled—in a new, problematic light: I refer to the recent feminist reading of Bataille's pornographic fiction and of his theory of eroticism and transgression.

I know at least two versions of this reading, which complement rather than contradict each other. In the United States, Andrea Dworkin has discussed *Histoire de l'oeil* in the context of a political attack on pornography. In France, Anne-Marie Dardigna has discussed Bataille in a sophisticated analysis of the modern (male) erotic imagination.[8] What Dworkin and Dardigna both succeed in doing, albeit in different ways and with different degrees of persuasiveness (Dardigna being a great deal more persuasive to my mind than Dworkin), is to focus our attention on that from which the textual reading averts its gaze: the representational or fantasmatic content of Bataille's (and other modern writers') "pornographic imagination," and the political (in the sense of sexual politics) implications of that content. I stated earlier that the textual critics considered Bataille's pornographic narratives indissociable from his other writings. At the same time, it is striking to note how very few have devoted any kind of sustained analysis to these narratives. Blanchot and Kristeva insist on the importance of the pornographic novels, but then go on to more general and abstract considerations. Sollers writes about L'*Erotisme*, but not about any of Bataille's novels. Derrida at no point explicitly mentions them. As for Barthes, his essay on Histoire de l'oeil remains one of the most interesting—as well as one of the rare—commentaries on that text. The whole thrust of Barthes's analysis, however, is to bracket the representational content of the fiction and to insist on the play of metaphoric and metonymic transformations (egg-eye-testicle; milk-urine-sperm, etc.) which underlie and ultimately determine the "surface" progression of the narrative. It is only at the end, in a comment I have already quoted, that Barthes makes explicit mention of the transgressive content of the story of Histoire de l'oeil—but he does *that* only in order to affirm the primacy of Bataille's linguistic violations over the sexual and cultural violations that the narrative represents.[9]

No doubt this averting of the gaze by textual critics is due more to their general suspicion and critique of *representation* in art, and in narrative fiction in particular, than to sexual timidity, or what the French call *pudeur*. Nevertheless, it seems not indifferent that in their pursuit of the metaphoric equivalences between textual violation and the violation of bodies, what they passed over was precisely the *view* of the body and of the body's generally hidden organs, which were displayed and verbally designated on almost every page of Bataille's pornographic texts.[10]

"But let us leave the scene and the characters. The drama is first of all textual." This remark by Derrida (which I am quoting slightly out of context, for Derrida was not referring to Bataille's fiction, but to the "story" of Bataille's relationship to Hegel) sums up, I think, the strategy—and the symptomatic swerve away from representation—that characterizes the textual reading of Bataille (372). What characterizes Dworkin's reading is exactly the opposite. I am going to concentrate on hers rather than on Dardigna's, because it is more concise and also a lot simpler, allowing me to make my point by exaggeration, as it were. I am calling this reading not thematic but "ultrathematic," for reasons that will become evident. Here is how Dworkin begins her discussion of *Histoire de l'oeil*:

The story is told by a narrator in the first person. He grew up alone and was frightened of the sexual. When he was sixteen he met Simone, the same age. Three days after they met they were alone at her villa. Simone was wearing a black pinafore. She wore black silk stockings. He wanted to pick up her pinafore from behind to see her cunt, the word he considers the most beautiful one for vagina. There was a saucer of milk in a hallway for the cat. Simone put the saucer on a bench and sat down on it. He was transfixed. He was erect. He lay down at her feet. She stayed still. He saw her cunt in the milk. They were both overwhelmed. (167)

And so on for seven more pages of deadpan summary, detailing Simone's and the narrator's sexual exploits, which culminate in the rape and murder of a priest in a church in Seville, followed by their embarking on a schooner from Gibraltar to sail to further adventures. By means of this unwavering attention to "the scene and the characters," Dworkin flattens Bataille's narrative into a piece of pulp pornography. *Histoire de l'oeil* becomes, in the space of her summary, indistinguishable from novels with titles like I *Love a Laddie* or *Whip Chick* (which she summarizes in exactly the same way), or the photograph in *Hustler* magazine entitled "Beaver Hunters," showing a spread-eagled naked woman tied to a Jeep, the trophy of two gun-carrying male hunters (Dworkin describes and analyzes this photograph and the accompanying caption in detail, pp. 25–30). In effect, Dworkin recontextualizes Bataille's novel, or in more technical terms relocates it in what Gérard Genette would call a new "architexte," a new generic category.[11] This was precisely the kind of reading, or misreading, that Susan Sontag foresaw and tried to ward off, when she insisted that Bataille's novels had to be read in the context of European avant-garde writing: "lacking that context," she wrote, the novels "must prove almost unassimilable for English and American readers—except as mere pornography, inexplicably fancy trash" (44).

The interesting thing is that Dworkin has read Sontag— but she refuses to "buy" Sontag's argument. In the analysis that follows her summary of H*istoire de l'oeil*, she seems to be replying to Sontag, and indirectly to Barthes as well, whose essay Sontag had evidently read although she didn't refer to it explicitly. Where Sontag, following Barthes, admired Bataille's "spatial principle of organization," which consists in "the obscene playing with or defiling" of a limited number of objects (chief among them being the eye of the title), Dworkin merely notes, sarcastically, that "High-class symbols are . . . essential to high-class pornography: eggs, eyes, hard-boiled, soft-boiled" (75). Where Sontag saw the power of Bataille's writing in its dark view of sexuality ("as something beyond good and evil, beyond love, beyond sanity; as a resource for ordeal and for breaking through the limits of consciousness" [58]), and above all in the fact that "Bataille understood more clearly than any other writer I know of that what pornography is really about, ultimately, isn't sex but death" (60), Dworkin replies:

The intellectual claim made for the work is that Bataille has revealed a sexual secret: the authentic nexus between sex and death. . . . But in fact, Bataille has obscured more than he has uncovered. He has obscured the meaning of force in sex. He has obscured the fact that there is no male conception of sex without force as the essential dynamic. . . . The grand conceptions—death, angst—cover the grand truth: that force leading to death is what men most secretly, most deeply, and most truly value in sex. (176)

Obviously, the crucial words here are "male" and "men." What Sontag saw as the revelation of a troubling truth about human sexuality, Dworkin diagnoses as the particular truth of *male* desire, or the male imagination of sex, in our culture.

Now I am going to embark on a series of spiraling "Yes, but's."

Yes—politically, I find Dworkin's argument important, in the same way that Kate Millett's argument in *Sexual Politics* was important. There is something in our culture that endorses and reinforces violence against women (as any daily newspaper will confirm), and this violence seems to be indissociable from very old, deeply ingrained, essentially masculine attitudes toward sex.

But—rhetorically, as a reading of Bataille, or even as a reading of a single work by Bataille (for Dworkin claims no general knowledge of Bataille's *oeuvre*), Dworkin's pages on H*istoire de l'oeil* are by any standard less than satisfying. If the textual critics avert their gaze from representation, Dworkin cannot take her eyes off it. She is so intent on looking at "the scene and the characters" that she never sees the frame—I am using "frame" here as a shorthand for all those aspects of a fictional narrative that designate it, directly or indirectly, as constructed, invented, filtered through a specific medium: in short, as a *text* rather than as "life itself." Not unlike those consumers of pornography who skip the descriptions to get to the "good parts," Dworkin reads too quickly: she devours the text in order to get to its "core," or to change metaphors she traverses it without attention to its shape or the grain of its surface. Where the text says: "I stood for some time before her, without moving, the blood rushing to my head and trembling while she looked at my stiff prick make a bulge in my kneepants," Dworkin reads: "He was transfixed. He was erect." Where the text says: "Then I lay down at her feet without her having moved and, for the first time, I saw her 'pink and black' flesh cooling itself in the white milk" (12–13),[12] Dworkins reads: "He lay down at her feet. She stayed still. He saw her cunt in the milk."

As you notice, I have not chosen anodyne sentences as my examples. Bataille's text is without a doubt pornographic. But certainly one thing that contributes to its effect—even to its pornographic effect—is the contrast one feels between the long, sinuous, grammatically "exquisite" sentences (which in French appear even more so because of the use of the *passé simple* and the imperfect subjunctive, indices of traditional literary narration) and the explicitly sexual, obscene words ("stiff prick") that crash through the structure of the syntax, as Simone's transgressive behavior crashes through the stillness of a summer afternoon. In the second sentence, the text avoids naming Simone's sexual part explicitly, using instead a periphrasis set off by quotation marks, which suggest a literary or pictorial allusion: "her 'pink and black' flesh" ("sa chair 'rose et noire' "). The allusion is to Baudelaire's famous verses about Lola de Valence, who was also represented in a famous painting by Manet: "Mais on voit scintiller en Lola de Valence/Le charme inattendu d'un bijou rose et noir." In Baudelaire's poem, there is a "displacement upward" (to use Freud's phrase) from the woman's genitals to the jewel she wears, or possesses. This displacement is founded on both a metaphoric and a metonymic equation between genitals and jewel—a very nice coup, rhetorically speaking. Bataille does Baudelaire one better, however. He characteristically displaces things downward, for "sa chair rose et noire" (which here clearly refers to the lower part of Simone's body) could also refer to a woman's face, with the adjective "noire" having slipped over, in both cases, from hair to flesh by means of a transgressive metonymy: flesh cannot, literally or logically, be both pink and black, but one can have pink flesh framed by black hair—as in Proust's recurrent descriptions of Albertine's face, for example, or as in the narrator's view here of Simone's genitals framed by black pubic hair.[13]

Bataille's implicit equation of face with genitals—which, as in Baudelaire's poem, can be read both metaphorically and metonymically—is much more shocking and violent, especially if it is read as metaphor, than Baudelaire's equation of jewel with genitals. This rhetorical violence, whose other manifestation is the metonymic "slippage" of the adjective *noire* (pink *and* black flesh?), is consonant with the transgressive behavior represented in the scene. Without losing sight of the scene, we must remark (and our remark will be a great deal closer to Barthes than to Dworkin) how closely the language of the text "repeats" or "doubles" the content of its representation.[14]

Yes, but. Dworkin, responding to my reading, would no doubt accuse it, and me, of a culpable formalism. She is obviously aware of the language of the text, even in English translation, but the argument of her book—which is that pornography is harmful to women because of the scenes or images it represents—requires that she consider Bataille's language as mere ornament, and as a dangerous ornament, since it "stylizes the violence and denies its meaning to women" (176).

Yes, but. Dworkin's argument also obliges her to see, in every book she reads, simply more of the same thing. This prevents her from noticing differences that might lead to a more significant questioning—and a more persuasive critique—of Bataille's text. For example, Dworkin writes about the character of Simone that "she exists in the male framework: the sadistic whore whose sexuality is murderous and insatiable. . . . She is a prototypical figure in the male imagination, the woman who is sexual because her sexuality is male in its values, in its violence. She is the male idea of a woman let loose" (176). Now it may be true that Simone's sexuality is male; but if so, then it is precisely the nature of male sexuality that is figured in Bataille's text as problematic. Simone is presented throughout the novel as a sister soul of the narrator, who in true Bataillean fashion is never more tormentedly aware of the Law than when he is transgressing it. Neither she nor the narrator fit the description of "sadistic whore." The signif- icant thing about Simone is precisely that she is not a whore, but a "young girl from a good family," a virginal-looking adolescent who, like the narrator himself, experiences sex as profoundly scandalous (from Greek *skandalon*: trap, snare, stumbling block).[15] And just as she is not a whore, Simone is not sadistic in Sade's sense: the Sadean hero, or heroine, puts a premium on transgression, but transgression in Sade occurs when a sovereign subject defies an external Law. In Bataille, the Law is internalized; the drama of transgression occurs *within* the subject. (He did not have a Catholic childhood for nothing).

Now it is also the case that in Bataille's fiction the privi- leged locus of this drama is the female body. Bataille's internally divided subject is, emblematically, a woman: Simone, Madame Ed- warda, Marie in *Le Mort*, the narrator's mother in *Ma mère*, Eponine in *L'Abbé C*, Dorothea ("God's gift," whose nickname is Dirty) in *Le Bleu du ciel*. The question one should ask, it seems to me, is: why is it a woman who embodies most fully the paradoxical combination of pleasure and anguish that characterizes transgression—in whose body the contradictory impulses toward excess on the one hand and respect of the limit on the other are played out? Dworkin cannot ask this question, for she has not read Bataille's text carefully enough to notice its specificity.

And yet (this is my last "yes, but"), despite its obvious flaws—perhaps even because of them—Dworkin's willful misreading, or flattening, of *Histoire de l'oeil* provokes at least one important question for anyone interested in modern writing: to what extent are the "high- cultural" productions of the avant-gardes of our century in a relation of complicity rather than in a relation of rupture vis-à-vis dominant ideologies? From the Surrealists to the *Tel Quel* group and to some of the so-called "postmodernists" in American writing, twentieth-century avant-gardes have proclaimed, and in a sense lived on (or off) their adversary, subversive relation to the dominant culture. But insofar as the dominant culture has been not only bourgeois but also patriarchal, the productions of the avant-garde appear anything but subversive.

I have argued this point in some detail elsewhere, in connection with the novels of Robbe-Grillet.[16] This is also the chief argument of Anne-Marie Dardigna's book, *Les châteaux d'Eros*. Dardigna reads Bataille, Klossowski, and other French avant-garde writers not, like Dworkin, as "ordinary pornographers" but precisely as pseudosubversive ones. "The twentieth century," she writes in her conclusion,

is characterized in literature by the total freedom of the subjective instance; the subject can finally tell all about its fantasies, its perversions, its hidden desires. That is well and good. . . . But what voices are heard then? Always those of men. And what do they say? Nothing new: that women are dangerous, that they must be dominated, that their "flesh" must be conquered by assimilating them [to a male model] or by putting them to death . . . in any case, that they must be suppressed. (312–13)

In this conclusion, Dardigna rejoins, by a different route, the critique of masculine sexual economy—based on the suppression of what is "other" in female sexuality—that one finds, for example, in the work of the feminist philosopher and psychoanalyst, Luce Irigaray.

Where does all this leave us, as far as a poetics of gender is concerned? Should we, echoing Simone de Beauvoir's one-time question about Sade, ask whether to "burn Bataille"? That question, which Beauvoir asked only rhetorically, but which was also asked (equally rhetorically?) by a French Communist journal around the same time about Kafka, is perhaps—as Bataille suggested in his own essay on Kafka—the permanent temptation of any dogmatism when faced with texts it considers "harmful," or even merely "irresponsible."[17] But contemporary feminist criticism is, or has been at its best, precisely the opposite of a rigid dogmatism. If, as I believe, a genuine poetics of gender is indissociable from a feminist poetics, then a feminist reading of Bataille's and other modern male writers' pornographic fictions must seek to avoid both the blindness of the textual reading, which sees nothing but *écriture*, and the blindness of the ultrathematic reading, which sees nothing but the scene and the characters. Such a reading, necessarily thematic but not "ultra," is adumbrated in Dardigna's book. However, the design of her book is such that Dardigna at no point reads one of Bataille's novels in its entirety—and I would argue that a fully realized feminist/thematic reading needs to do just that. It needs to look at a text, or at a whole *oeuvre* if time and space allow, patiently and carefully, according it all due respect—but also critically, not letting respect inhibit it.[18]

Patiently and carefully, because like all modern writing with any claim to significance, Bataille's texts themselves go a long way toward providing the necessary commentary on them. In *Histoire de l'oeil*, for example—and this is something that neither Dworkin nor Dardigna finds important—the narrative of sexual excesses is only Part One of the work. The second part consists of a commentary that traces the fantasmatic elaboration of the obscene narrative from a number of events and people in the narrator's life. The representational content of the fiction is thus retrospectively designated as fantasy—and not only that, but as a fantasy whose source is Oedipal. The turning point in the narrator's life, we are told, came one day when he heard his mad, blind, syphilitic father cry out, while his mother was in the next room consulting with his doctor: "Say, doc, when will you finish fucking my wife!" "For me," writes the narrator,

this sentence, which destroyed in one instant the demoralizing effects of a strict upbringing, left behind it a kind of constant obligation, which until now has been involuntarily and unconsciously felt: the necessity to continually find its equivalent in every situation in which I find myself and that is what explains, in large part, *Story of the Eye*. (1:77)

"This sentence which destroyed in one instant the demoralizing effects of a strict upbringing..." What the father suddenly reveals (or recalls?) to the son is that the mother's body is sexual. The knowledge that a "strict upbringing" has always tried to repress, in a male child, is that his mother's body is *also* that of a woman. The recognition of the mother's body as female, and desirable—a recognition forced on the son by his blind but still powerful father—is thus designated as the source of the narrator's pornographic imagination.

This, I think, might explain why in Bataille's fiction it is always a woman (and in the posthumous *Ma mère*, is the mother herself) in whose body the drama of transgression is played out. For the female body, in its duplicity as asexual maternal and sexual feminine, is the very emblem of the contradictory coexistence of transgression and prohibition, purity and defilement, that characterizes both the "interior experience" of eroticism *and* the textual play of the pornographic narrative.

One could also, in a more classically Freudian perspective, suggest that the mother's sexual body traumatizes the son by exhibiting its (and his own potential) "castration." In Bataille's pornography, the male protagonist is often split between a passive and an active sexual role; this split is most clearly evident in L'*Abbé* C, where one of the identical twin brothers is the desired woman's lover, while the other brother, a priest dressed "in skirts," repeatedly witnesses their love-making and leaves behind him his own feces as a trace of his jouis-sance. This is strikingly similar to Freud's reconstitution of the primal scene in the case history of the Wolf Man, in which a crucial suppo-sition is that the child reacted to witnessing his parents' lovemaking by passing a stool (it's true that he was only eighteen months old!). Freud interprets this reaction as a sign (or a source?) of his patient's repressed homosexuality, his "anal" identification with the passive role of the mother.[19]

As far as Bataille's text is concerned, it is clear that which-ever interpretation one emphasizes, the focus is on the son's view of the mother's genitals, which invariably leads him to a recognition of sexual difference and to a split in his own experience: either through the combination of fascination and terror provoked by the mother's sexuality (in the first interpretation), or through the combination of fear and desire, manifested in active vs. passive sexual roles, as con-cerns his own castration (in the second interpretation). Paradoxical as it may seem, in both instances the real drama exists between the son and the father (who is at once "real" and "symbolic" in Lacan's sense), not between the son and the mother. The mother's body functions as mediation in the Oedipal narrative, whose only true (two) subjects are male.[20]

These observations are the result of a careful reading of

Bataille's own text, not against itself but insofar as it comments on itself. Kristeva, in one of her general remarks on Bataille's fiction, wrote: "Contrary to 'objective', historical or simply novelistic narratives which can be blind to their cause and merely repeat it without knowing it, [Bataille's] 'opération souveraine' consists in meditating on the Oedipal cause of the fiction and therefore of the narrating-desiring subject" (284). In its self-conscious meditation on its own Oedipal sources, Bataille's pornographic fiction (one finds this meditation, in one form or another, in all of Bataille's novels) is a far cry from the pulp novels or trashy magazine photos that serve up their fantasies straight. The difference between them is, one could argue, the difference between blindness and insight.

But the insight provided by Bataille's text about itself has its own limits. And that is why it must be read critically as well as carefully. Among the questions that Bataille's text cannot ask about itself—because in order to do so it would have to have both a historical and a theoretical distance from itself that it cannot have—are these: is there a model of sexuality possible in our culture that would not necessarily pass through the son's anguished and fascinated perception of the duplicity of the mother's body? Is there a model of *textuality* possible that would not necessarily play out, in discourse, the eternal Oedipal drama of transgression and the Law—a drama which always, ultimately, ends up maintaining the latter?[21]

Harold Bloom, in a moment of mock prophecy (and, one suspects, with some anxiety of his own) once predicted that "the first true break with literary continuity will be brought about in generations to come, if the burgeoning religion of Liberated Woman spreads from its clusters of enthusiasts to dominate the West. Homer will cease to be the inevitable precursor, and the rhetoric and forms of our literature may then break at last from tradition" (33). That time is still a while off, nor am I certain that it is what we should be waiting for. What does appear to me certain is that there will be no renewal, either in a poetics or in a politics of gender, as long as every drama, whether textual or sexual, continues to be envisaged—as in Bataille's pornography and in Harold Bloom's theory of poetry—in terms of a confrontation between an all-powerful father and a traumatized son, a confrontation staged across and over the body of the mother.

NOTES

1. *Histoire de l'oeil* was first published in a private edition (134 copies) in 1928, under the pseudonym, "Lord Auch." New, equally limited editions appeared in 1940 and 1941; although all three editions were published in Paris, the second and third gave Burgos and Seville as places of publication, respectively. The work appeared for the first time under Bataille's name in 1967, four years after his death (Editions J.-J. Pauvert). *Madame Edwarda* has a similar publishing history, and two other well-known works, *Ma mère* and *Le Mort*, were published only posthumously (in 1966 and 1967 respectively). The only two novels Bataille himself published under his own name are *Le Bleu du ciel* (1957, but written in 1935) and *L'Abbé C.* (1950).

2. For a transcription of the trial, see *L'Affaire Sade* (Paris: J.-J. Pauvert, 1957). Bataille was one of those testifying, unsuccessfully, on behalf of the publisher and in defense of Sade as a significant writer.

3. Paradoxically, Bataille himself remained virtually unknown to English-speaking readers until very recently, despite his enormous influence on French theorists who have a wide audience in England and in the United States. There are signs of change, however: the Winter 1984 issue of *Raritan* carried the translation of one of Bataille's important early essays, "The Notion of Expenditure" (trans. Allan Stoekl), as well as an essay by Allan Stoekl on *Le Bleu du ciel*. Even more recently, Stoekl has edited a volume of Bataille's selected writings in English, *Visions of Excess*. See also Michèle H. Richman, *Reading Georges Bataille: Beyond the Gift*, the first book on Bataille to be published in English. An excellent book on him in French is Denis Hollier's *La Prise de la Concorde: Essais sur Georges Bataille*.

4. All translations from the French are my own.

5. "La métaphore de l'Oeil" was first published in *Critique* (August–September 1963), in the commemorative issue devoted to Bataille after his death.

6. See Derrida, "De l'économie restreinte" (404–5): "The greatest force is that of a writing [*écriture*] which, in the most audacious transgression, continues to maintain and to recognize the necessity of the system of prohibitions (knowledge, science, philosophy, work, history, etc.). Writing is always traced between these two sides of the limit." I will return to the implications of this paradoxically conservative view at the end of my essay.

7. This essay, "Bataille," is reprinted as "L'expérience et la pratique" in *Polylogue*.

8. Andrea Dworkin, *Pornography: Men Possessing Women*; Anne-Marie Dardigna, *Les châteaux d'Eros ou l'infortune du sexe des femmes*.

9. The only sustained commentary on one of Bataille's pornographic works by a well-known "textual" critic is Lucette Finas's book on *Madame Edwarda*, *La Crue*. Finas's line-by-line reading, based on a principle of dictionary-inspired free associations to Bataille's text, is extremely interesting, and takes greater account of the representational content of the work than does Barthes's reading of *Histoire de l'oeil*. Finas's main emphasis, however, remains textual; what interests her chiefly is the way "*Madame Edwarda* [as] narrative is constituted by this effort, always disappointed, to envelop Her by him" (219).

In a somewhat different vein, one might also mention Brian Fitch's monograph, *Monde à l'envers, texte réversible: la fiction de Georges Bataille*, devoted exclusively to Bataille's novels. Fitch's elegant readings analyze the various forms of self-reflexive doubling in Bataille's fiction; but Fitch specifically excludes the question of eroticism and erotic representation, on the grounds that "Bataillean eroticism" is an experience to be understood only by reading the theoretical essays, not the novels (48). Here then is yet another reading of Bataille, a "strictly literary," formalist reading that manages to exclude even the metaphoric notion of transgression central to the textual reading. Bataille is shown to be a highly inventive, self-conscious writer—but one is tempted to say, "So what?"

10. This display was visual as well as verbal in the first (1928) edition of *Histoire de l'oeil*, which contained—printed on heavy paper in large format—eight original lithographs by André Masson, illustrating some of the more "scandalous" scenes. (I saw this edition at the Houghton rare book library at Harvard University) It is only a small step, after this, to associate the textual critics' "averting of the gaze" with the aversion traditionally inspired by the Medusa's head, which, the myth tells us, had the power to turn men to stone—and which, Freud has told us, is a symbolic representation of the female genitals. I shall argue later that the son's problematic "seeing" of the mother's genitals is centrally inscribed in *Story of the Eye*, which may then turn out to be a *mise en abyme* of the problematic "seeing" practiced by its critics. In a different perspective, Teresa de Lauretis has related Medusa to the question of female subjectivity and female seeing/spectatorship—see her *Alice Doesn't: Feminism, Semiotics, Cinema* (109–11, 136, and *passim*). My thanks to Nancy Miller for calling this book to my attention, and for reminding me about the beautiful Gorgon.

11. Gérard Genette, *Introduction à l'architexte*; also *Palimpsestes: la littérature au second degré*.

12. "Je restai quelque temps devant elle, immobile, le sang à la tête et tremblant pendant qu'elle regardait ma verge raide tendre ma culotte. Alors je me couchai à ses pieds sans qu'elle bougeât et, pour la première fois, je vis sa chair 'rose et noire' qui se rafraîchissait dans le lait blanc." This is the text of the 1928 edition, which Bataille revised extensively in 1940. The English translation, by Joachim Neugroschel (New York: Berkeley Books, 1982) follows the original version. The translations here are my own.

13. It is unfortunate that the English translation mitigates Bataille's stylistic transgression by rendering "rose et noire" as "pink and dark." There are some other problems with the translation as well (e.g., "cunt" for the less specific term "cul"), which I need not go into here. Dworkin's reading is based on the English version—but even based on that version, it is reductive. For another discussion of the "pink and the black" in Bataille, see Hollier's "Bataille's Tomb," p. 80ff.

14. During the discussion that followed the oral delivery of this paper at the Columbia Poetics Conference, Michael Riffaterre suggested that Simone's dipping her genitals in the plate of milk (which the text says was there for the cat, *le chat*) is already inscribed in the word *chat*, which, similar to the English "pussy," has an obscene slang meaning in French. This would be yet another example of Bataille's play with language—but whether the "shock value" or representational force of Simone's action is thereby diminished (since what she does, after all, is simply to put her *chat* in its "natural" place, in the milk) is highly debatable.

15. The fact that both of the main characters are adolescents is significant, since adolescence is that period when experimentation with sexual roles is indissociable from a more general search for the self. In both cases, the search is intimately bound up with an awareness of the (parental) Law and the possibilities of its infraction. This is repeatedly emphasized in *Histoire de l'oeil*. I consider the Oedipal implications of the fiction further on in this essay.

16. S. Suleiman, "Reading Robbe-Grillet." Somewhat similar conclusions regarding painting are drawn by Carol Duncan in her essay, "Virility and Domination in Early Twentieth-Century Vanguard Painting."

17. See his "Kafka" pp. 173–76; also Beauvoir, *Faut-il brûler Sade?*

18. Dardigna does devote several interesting chapters to reading Pierre Klossowski's trilogy, *Les Lois de l'hospitalité*. I find it all the more regrettable that in her latest book,

a full-length study of Klossowski's oeuvre, Dardigna has abandoned the feminist perspective altogether. Are respect for and "total immersion" in a writer's work somehow incompatible with critical distance and judgment? A question worth pondering, especially by feminist critics.

19. See Freud, "The Case of the Wolf-Man" (181–91, 214–30).

20. Nancy Vickers arrives at strikingly similar conclusions about the mediating role of the female body in her essay in this volume, which deals with a "text" altogether different from Bataille's. Denis Hollier, in a rich analysis of the father-son relation in Bataille and of its political and psychological implications, has suggested that the son's deepest desire may be a "glorious castration," at once violent and incestuous, at the hands of the father. In that case, the mother becomes superfluous, and indeed Hollier suggests as much ("La Tombe de Bataille"). Is the elimination of the mother, and a fortiori of female subjectivity, the "real" logic of Oedipus? For a far-ranging feminist critique of the Oedipal narrative, viewed as the single most powerful narrative model in patriarchal culture, see de Lauretis, *Alice Doesn't*, chap. 5. For an analysis of the Oedipal logic which leads to the male child's violent repudiation of the mother, see Benjamin, "The Bonds of Love."

21. See, for example, the passage I quoted from Derrida in note 6. The question of whether, and to what extent, the theory of *écriture* is "revolutionary," or even genuinely subversive, is an important one.

WORKS CITED

Barthes, Roland. "La métaphore de l'Oeil." In *Essais Critiques*. Paris: Seuil, 1964; pp. 238–45.

Bataille, Georges. *Histoire de l'oeil*. In *Oeuvres Complètes*, vol. 1, pp. 9–78. Paris: Gallimard, 1970.

——— "La notion de dépense" ("The Notion of Expenditure"). In *Oeuvres Complètes*, vol. 1, pp. 302–20. First English translation in *Raritan* (Winter 1984) 3(3):62–79. Trans. Alan Stoekl.

——— *L'Abbé C*. In *Oeuvres Complètes*, vol. 3, pp. 233–366.

——— *Le Bleu du ciel*. In *Oeuvres Complètes*, vol. 3, pp. 377–488.

——— *Le Mort*. In *Oeuvres Complètes*, vol. 4, pp. 37–52. Paris: Gallimard, 1971.

——— *Ma mère*. In *Oeuvres Complètes*, vol. 4, pp. 175–276.

——— *L'Erotisme*. Paris: Editions de Minuit, 1957.

——— "Kafka." In *La Littérature et le mal*. Paris: Gallimard, "Idées" edition, 1957; pp. 173–98.

——— *Visions of Excess: Selected Writings, 1927–1939*. Ed. Allan Stoekl; trans. A. Stoekl, C. Lovitt, and D. M. Leslie, Jr. Minneapolis: University of Minnesota Press, 1985.

Beauvoir, Simone de. *Faut-il brûler Sade?* Paris: Gallimard, 1955.

Benjamin, Jessica. "The Bonds of Love: Rational Violence and Erotic Domination." *Feminist Studies* (Spring 1980), 6(1):144–74.

Blanchot, Maurice. "L'expérience limite." In L'Entretien infini. Paris: Gallimard, 1969; pp. 300–42.

Bloom, Harold. A Map of Misreading. New York: Oxford University Press, 1975.

Dardigna, Anne-Marie. Les châteaux d'Eros ou l'infortune du sexe des femmes. Paris: Maspero, 1981.

Derrida, Jacques. "De l'économie restreinte à l'économie générale." In L'ecriture et la différence. Paris: Seuil, 1967; pp. 369–408.

Duncan, Carol. "Virility and Domination in Early Twentieth-Century Vanguard Painting." In Feminism and Art History. Ed. Norma Broude and Mary D. Garrard. New York: Harper & Row, 1982; pp. 293–313.

Dworkin, Andrea. Pornography: Men Possessing Women. New York: Perigee, 1981.

Finas, Lucette. La Crue. Paris: Gallimard, 1972.

Fitch, Brian. Monde à l'envers, texte réversible: la fiction de Georges Bataille. Paris: Lettres Modernes, 1982.

Freud, Sigmund. "The Case of the Wolf-Man." In The Wolf-Man by the Wolf-Man. Ed. Muriel Gardiner. New York: Basic Books, 1971; pp. 153–262.

Genette, Gérard. Introduction à l'architexte. Paris: Seuil, 1979.

—— Palimpsestes: la littérature au second degré. Paris: Seuil, 1982.

Hollier, Denis. La Prise de la Concorde: Essais sur Georges Bataille. Paris: Gallimard, 1974.

—— "La Tombe de Bataille." Unpublished ms.

—— "Bataille's Tomb: A Halloween Story." October (Summer 1985), 33:73–102.

Kristeva, Julia. "Bataille, l'expérience et la pratique." In Bataille. Ed. Roland Barthes et al. Paris: U.G.E., 1973.

Lauretis, Teresa de. Alice Doesn't: Feminism, Semiotics, Cinema. Bloomington: Indiana University Press, 1984.

Richman, Michele H. Reading Georges Bataille: Beyond the Gift. Baltimore: Johns Hopkins University Press, 1982.

Sollers, Philippe. "Le Toit." In L'Ecriture et l'expérience des limites. Paris: Seuil, 1968; pp. 105–38.

Sontag, Susan. "The Pornographic Imagination." In Styles of Radical Will. New York: Delta, 1981; pp. 35–73.

Suleiman, Susan. "Reading Robbe-Grillet: Sadism and Text in Projet pour une révolution à New York." Romanic Review (January 1977), 68(1):43–62.

Annie Leclerc Writing A Letter, With Vermeer

JANE GALLOP

In 1981, *Critical Inquiry*, one of the elite American journals of literary criticism and theory, published a feminist issue edited by Elizabeth Abel. That issue, whose title is "Writing and Sexual Difference," betokens a feminist criticism that is interested not only in feminist social, political, and psychological issues, but also in "writing," which is to say in literary issues. I first delivered the present paper at a colloquium entitled "The Poetics of Gender," which was the eighth in a series of poetics colloquia. That colloquium bespeaks the same moment in the history of feminist literary criticism. We might in fact line up "poetics" with "writing," and "gender" with "sexual difference," yet there is also a specific resonance in Abel's title. "Writing and Sexual Difference" is a revision of Jacques Derrida's *Writing and Difference*, likewise published by the University of Chicago Press. If "Writing and Sexual Difference" is a feminist revision of Derrida's title, then what is marked is not only feminism's entrance on the stage of high literary theory, but also that this entrance occurs through the play of something translated from the French.

Things from the French had already fully penetrated American literary theoretical discussion and had already insinuated themselves into American feminist criticism in a way that, I believe, made possible a feminist issue of *Critical Inquiry*, a certain coming together of literary theory and feminism, of poetics and gender. Conversely, the *Colloque* which had always been on *la poétique*, which until recently had been conducted in French, not only proceeded in English but had among its speakers a good number of critics from English departments. The new intercourse between literary theory and feminism seems to be concomitant with a permeation of the boundaries separating French and English departments.

"Writing and Sexual Difference" is thus in fact the scene of a double translation: from literary-philosophical terms—"Writing and Difference"—into sexual-feminist ones, as well as from French into English. L'écriture et la différence becomes Writing and Sexual Difference. And yet the two moves may be not simply coincidental but more deeply entwined one with the other. In English, perhaps the most immediate association to the locution la différence is the French expression Vive la différence!, by which we understand that THE Difference, for the French, is sexual difference, and by which we imagine that the French have a peculiarly affirmative and sexy relation to that difference.

In the Fall of 1982, the University of Chicago Press republished the feminist issue of Critical Inquiry as a book, including—along with the original essay—the "critical responses" that had appeared in a later Critical Inquiry as well as two other feminist articles that had been in the journal but outside the special issue. The book, likewise entitled Writing and Sexual Difference, is arguably the best anthology of feminist literary criticism to date, comprised of theoretically sophisticated and yet plainly forceful essays from some of our best feminist critics. Since all the essays in the book were already in the journal and remain unchanged, in some way the most exciting thing about the book when it appeared was the cover, which added a new "text" to the volume, one more striking and more "readable" than most covers.

The color is one of my personal favorites: a color which I, perhaps incorrectly, call mauve, one of those colors whose name in English is still in French. Almost pink: that color which is one of our markers of sexual difference and which, unlike its diacritical partner blue, remains—way past the nursery—marked as feminine. If blue, outside the infantile realm, is no longer a particularly masculine color, might not that relate to the phallocentrism which in our culture (as well as in most if not all others) raises the masculine to the universal human, beyond gender, so that the feminine alone must bear the burden of sexual difference? Pink then becomes THE color of sexual difference, carrying alone within it the diacritical distinction pink/blue. Sexual difference itself becomes feminine, so that L'écriture et la différence might glide into l'écriture féminine.

But, as I said, the cover of Abel's anthology is not quite pink but rather mauve. Not the blatant little-girl color, unseemly in its explicit, infantile femininity but a stylish, sophisticated version of that color, one that bespeaks not the messy, carnal world of the nursery but high culture, high feminine culture, the realms of interior decoration and *haute couture*, and also, of course, things from the French, as suggested by the word "mauve." The color suggests that this is a feminine book, but a highly cultured one, the feminine, bodily realm of the nursery sublimated through the mediation of Paris. (See figures 1a and 1b.)

We may indeed be able to judge this book by its color, but I actually want to draw your attention to the two black and white images on the cover. They are both pictures of people writing: on the front a woman, on the back a man. Together they compose a particularly well-articulated illustration of "writing and sexual difference." The woman is writing a letter; the man a book. Women write letters—personal, intimate, in relation; men write books—universal, public, in general circulation. The man in the picture is in fact Erasmus, father of our humanist tradition; the woman without a name. In the man's background: books. The woman sits against floral wallpaper, echoed in reverse by her patterned dress. Feminine Culture: interior decoration and clothes. Black and white, the writing of flowers. The woman's face is completely smooth; no sense of bones beneath that surface. The man's face is hewn and angular; the skeleton structures his flesh. Perhaps most significantly, the man holds pen to paper and his pen is echoed by the scissors hanging there (on the bookshelves), likewise aiming its sharp point at the smooth white paper. The scissors bring out the incisiveness, penetration, violence of the pen. I would hesitate to associate that threatening point with masculine sexuality—I would not want to jump to a phallic conclusion—were it not so tempting here in proximity to the image of the penless woman literally licking the paper.

Or maybe kissing it. In any case, her relation to the paper is not mediated through an instrument but is direct oral contact.

Sandra Gilbert and Susan Gubar have suggested that in the masculine tradition the text is a woman, the pen a penis, and writing understood as coitus. In the picture of the woman, her face is as white and smooth as the paper, so that when she brings it to her mouth, like embraces like. Is *écriture féminine* lesbian cunnilingus?

Ecriture féminine: something else from the French. Not only do we supposedly naive Americans think of the French as having a particular appreciation for sexual difference, but in the slang of our personal ads we refer to oral sex itself as French just as we give the French credit for our most seriously sexual sort of kiss. This picture of the woman licking paper is made by Mary Cassatt, an American woman who like many of us went to Paris in pursuit of her art.

Ecriture féminine, not only feminine but somehow French, a switch from the phallic to the oral sexual paradigm. Hélène Cixous, foremost spokeswoman for *écriture féminine* does not disappoint this expectation. In her 1977 essay, "La venue à l'écriture" (the second word is not "avenue" but "venue," feminine past participle of the verb *venir*, to come—I translate the title of this as yet untranslated essay as "Coming to Writing"), in "La venue à l'écriture" Cixous writes: "Texts I ate them, I sucked them, I kissed them." "I caressed [my books]. Page by page, oh beloved, licked." Not only as a reader, but as a writer does she affirm the model of writing as oral love: "To write: to love, inseparable. Writing is a gesture of love. . . . Read-me-lick-me, write-me love" (19, 30, 47–48).

"La venue à l'écriture" appears in a book by the same title along with essays by two other women: "Le corps dans l'écriture" ("The Body in Writing") by Madeleine Gagnon, and "La lettre d'amour" ("The Love Letter") by Annie Leclerc. Published in the 10/18 series "Feminine Future," a series directed by Cixous and Catherine Clément, this 1977 volume clearly functions as an important intervention in the politicized discussion of women's writing. And as you can tell from the titles ("The Body in Writing," "The Love Letter"), the three essays, although diverse in many ways, share a continual grounding of writing in the erotic body.

Leclerc's text, "La lettre d'amour," is, in fact, in its own way, a love letter. It contains a second-person addressee, a woman with whom she has just passed a night of lovemaking and to whom, after

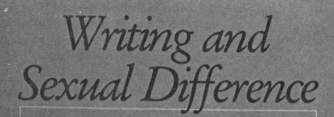

Figure 1a. Front cover of *Writing and Sexual Difference*.
Mary Cassatt, "The Letter." (Worcester Art Museum, Massachusetts)

Figure 1b. Back cover of *Writing and Sexual Difference*.
Quentin Metsys, "Portrait of Erasmus." (National Gallery of Ancient Art, Rome)

the morning's parting, Leclerc now wishes to express her love. A lesbian love letter. But of course this is also not a letter but an essay published in a book. Leclerc wishes precisely to heal the split portrayed on the cover of "Writing and Sexual Difference": women write letters, men books.

Love letters have always been written from the body, in connection with love. Leclerc wants all writing to have that connection; she wants love to enter into general circulation, inscribed knowledge, rather than remaining private and secret. A longish quote:

So many love letters [lettres d'amour, literally letters of, but also from love], but so few writings, real text, literature, science of/from love. . . . We who were so clever, greedy and generous in . . . billets . . . to the beloved . . . we nonetheless let them say, the true and the false. . . if our writings were of/from love, they risked their subversion only across intimacy and discretion. It was up to us, not them, to be philosophers. . . . we were the ones who remained in our body, we were in touch with love." (133–34)

We women must continue to write from our loving bodies, but we must break "discretion" and "intimacy" and "risk that subversion" in public, in print, in general circulation. And so Leclerc writes a letter to her lover which is also "real text, literature, science of/from love," philosophy from the body. This would seem to foretell Derrida's project in *La Carte Postale*, published in 1980, three years after "La lettre d'amour." Leclerc brings the love letter out of the closet and into the public domain.

Leclerc writes with excitement about the "extreme nudity" she experienced with her lover. She speaks of "dawn," of "birth," of "miracle," and one senses that this kind of love is a fresh discovery. In her book *Parole de femme*, published three years earlier, she seemed to write as a heterosexual; in that book the addressee is explicitly male. Only at one point in that earlier, heterosexual work, does she mention homosexuality. She has just been affirming the pleasure of difference and then suddenly: "But no I don't spit on homosexual pleasures. I simply refuse to see in them the expression of a lack of sexual differentiation. . . . And what I love in woman is everything that makes her different from you. In truth I only love in the perspective of difference" (80). "But no," she begins, denying something that threatens assertion.

For her, love is the celebration of difference, the encounter with difference, which risks sounding heterosexist, but she will not accept the notion that homosexuality is the pleasure of sameness. She wants to affirm difference in homosexuality, however much a contradiction in terms.

After the blatant heterosexuality of *Parole de femme*, we may be surprised that in "La lettre d'amour" Leclerc writes as a lesbian. But the quotation I just read prepares us for the particular quality of Leclerc's lesbianism, an acute sense of the otherness of the other woman. Leclerc's love letter is not an essentialistic affirmation of the universal, anatomically based identity of all women. In its assertion of difference within lesbianism, it in fact recalls for me a crucial point Gayatri Spivak makes in her article "French Feminism in an International Frame": "However unfeasible and inefficient it may sound, I see no way to avoid insisting that there has to be a simultaneous other focus: not merely who am I? But who is the other woman?" (179).

Leclerc's "Love Letter" offers us a different image of woman writing. Whereas on the cover of "Writing and Sexual Difference," the difference was between man writing and woman writing, in Leclerc's picture women's writing takes its place in a tableau of the difference between women. Leclerc's picture? There is no illustration in the text, but the text is accompanied by a painting to which it continually refers. As she writes her lover, as she writes her text, she comments: "*Alors, voilà*, she is always near me this Lady Writing a Letter and her Maidservant." The phrase "Lady Writing a Letter and her Maidservant" ("Dame Ecrivant une Lettre et sa Servante") is capitalized, and is in fact one of the titles of a painting by Vermeer. I found it under a similar English title—"Lady Writing a Letter, with her Maid"—but, in the volume I used, it was also listed under the simple title "The Letter" (see figure 2).

Leclerc's text is, in fact, a meditation on, an explication of, this painting. Like Cassatt, Vermeer has portrayed a woman writing a letter. She is, however, not simply a woman, but a "Lady" (actually, a *bourgeoise*) and with her is another woman, her servant. The difference between women is here, first of all, a difference of class. Yes, there is a tradition of women writing (writing letters at least), but the women are of a certain class: first the nobility, and then the bourgeoisie. There

Figure 2. Vermeer, "The Letter."
(Beit Collection, Blessington, Ireland)

is a class of women who write and a class who serve those who write. Leclerc writes: "Admit finally that there is in this woman writing, a spoiled woman (*femme gâtée*). . . a woman for whom the quill came into her fingers without her having to pluck it from the bird's wing" (138–39). Writing is not just a work of the spirit; there are material requisites. Labor must be done by another so that this woman can write. The labor has historical specificity, as does the scene: in 1667, the presumed date of the Vermeer, someone had to pluck a quill from a bird so a woman could write a letter. Obviously this is no longer the case, and yet if Leclerc, three centuries later, writes with a reproduction of this painting in the background it is because something about that relation still holds. Women no longer need servants to write letters; but what about the sort of open letters, public love writings Leclerc would write, that we would write? We must know the women of another class whose labor we rely on so that we can write: the women who clean our houses, care for our children, type our manuscripts; cleaning women and secretaries, for example.

Annie Leclerc identifies with the *bourgeoise* writing and she loves this picture. In fact she says that "the bad reproduction" of it which is in her possession is "the only object for which . . . (she) has . . . an undying attachment, the only object that is nourishment for (her)" (117–18). Rather than a source of paralyzing guilt, this picture is tremendously enabling for her. She contemplates the difference between these women and, rather than feeling guilt at the difference, rather than feeling pity, she feels desire. She writes: "I love the woman servant . . . oh no, not out of pity, not because I would take up the noble mantle of redressers of wrongs. . . but because I want to touch her, to take her hands, to bury my head in her chest, to smother her cheeks and neck with kisses" (143). Leclerc's position is not the liberal sense that she ought to do something for this poor unfortunate woman. She sees this woman as beautiful, as having something she wants. Leclerc in fact explicitly and frequently identifies the maid with the woman to whom she is writing her love letter.

Of course there is a long phallic tradition of desire for those with less power and privilege (women, for example) and I cannot but wonder about the relation of Leclerc's desire to this tradition. Just as I cannot but be reminded of the romantic and essentially conservative tradition of the happy and beautiful folk, the earthy, free working class. This is certainly a problem. Although Leclerc explicitly associates liberation and joy with socialist revolution, there is, after all, a revolutionary romantic tradition of idealizing the working class. Despite these problems I have with Leclerc's desire for the maid (an erotic attraction to women of another class which I share, I should add), I think it valuable as a powerful account of just that sort of desire, a desire that is frequently hidden under the "mantle of redressers of wrongs." Perhaps this desire gets us no closer than liberal superiority to knowing who the other woman is, but in its explicitness in Leclerc's text it allows us to see more clearly what is usually suppressed, repressed, or sublimated in our relation to the other woman.

Traditionally the maid carries letters between the lady and her beloved, a tradition Vermeer clearly draws on. There is, in fact, a painting entitled "The Love Letter," the same title as Leclerc's text, and she does briefly allude to it (see figure 3). The maid in another picture—entitled "Servant Handing a Letter to her Mistress"—resembles the one in Leclerc's Vermeer. You may recognize this picture from the cover of Terry Eagleton's *Literary Theory* (see figure 4). The maid serves as go-between, her labor makes possible the love connection, but she is not its recipient. In Leclerc's revision of Vermeer, however, the lady not only would hand the letter to the maid, the maid would be its addressee.

Not only do ladies give letters to maids but they receive letters from them as well. In Leclerc's revision, Vermeer's maid (and the female lover with whom she is identified) is not only the addressee of her writing but also in a certain way its source. Leclerc writes to her lover: "Come . . . my tongue will die if yours doesn't come and bring its warm saliva. Come, I would like so much to tell you the secret that I have from the lady writing, who has it from her maidservant" (119–20). She cannot speak if her tongue dies. She wants to tell her lover something, but first she must get her lover's saliva. The interlocutor is also an enabling source of speech. Leclerc is writing a chain letter, which carries a secret to her lover, a secret she gets from Vermeer's Lady who gets it from her Maid. If what women write is not just love but knowledge, the source of the knowledge in "La lettre d'amour" is not Leclerc the philosopher, not the educated, literate *bourgeoise*, but the maid.

And where does the maid get this knowledge? According

Figure 3. Vermeer, "The Love Letter."
(Rijksmuseum, Amsterdam)

Figure 4. Vermeer, "Servant Handing a Letter to Her Mistress."
(Frick Collection, New York)

to Leclerc, she "has it from the secret where women we are (*le secret où femmes nous sommes*)" (ibid.) The maid gets it from the source, from the secret itself, from some secret feminine space where we are women, where we can be women, where we have been women. The "we" may refer to all women, but it is also specifically the writer and her beloved addressee. It is, for example, the secret space of their loving, that space of discretion and intimacy. But that means it is a space where in the present of writing "we" are not, since she must summon her lover ("Come, my tongue will die"). Likewise it is a space to which her access is twice mediated, by a Lady writing a love letter and by her Maid.

For Leclerc, as for most proponents of *écriture féminine*, women's writing springs from a secret well of immanent femininity. "The secret where women we are" is not even the more grammatically common and predictable "where we are women (*où nous sommes femmes*): which might imply that here we are women, elsewhere we aren't. "The secret where women we are" ("*le secret où femmes nous sommes*") is a space of being, pure and simple (*où nous sommes*), being without attribute. Yet the woman writing has only a mediated relation to that space of feminine being. She is divided from that secret, a division figured by the space between the Lady Writing and her Maid. Leclerc's image of woman writing is an image of the rift between secret feminine knowledge—that is to say, pure feminine being—and writing. There is a space between *écriture* and *féminine*. (See figure 2.)

"From the woman servant to the woman writing," writes Leclerc, "an all-knowing plenitude is torn open" (136). The woman servant stands in all-knowing plenitude. She is full, present, solid, round, and she knows. Moving from her to the writer, that fullness of knowledge is ruptured. For Leclerc the fullness and the split are morphologically represented in the two women's figures. Here the curved and rounded arms, the warm and certain closure of the forearms, the hands tenderly linked. . . wedded. . . the splendid repose of a perfectly poised body" (ibid.) The plenitude is figured by the closure of the forearms and hands. She describes the forearms as "tenderly linked . . . wedded (*épousés*)." Her plenitude is an erotic self-sufficiency. I am reminded here of Luce Irigaray's description of female sexuality as two lips caressing each other ("Ce sexe qui n'en est pas un") as well as of Sarah Kofman's characterization of the narcissistic women (L'*énigme de la femme*). The maid is narcissistically, pleasurably whole unto herself, hence her desirability.

And then the contrast with her mistress: "Here. . . the closure of the forearms. . . and there, in the foreground, but no longer central, as if displaced. . . leaning. . . and above all those disjoined arms, those separated hands. . . divorced, the left one still woman-servant, curved and mute, and the right one woman-mistress, as if distant from the body" (136–37). The woman writing is displaced, decentered, removed from the locus of being, like her right arm, her writing arm is removed from her body, from the curve of an embrace. The disjunction between maid and woman writing is repeated as the difference between the mistress's left and right arms. Unlike the maid's erotic self-sufficiency, wedded arms, the mistress's arms are "divorced," erotically bereft, divorced by the very act of writing. The rift in feminine plenitude is at once the space between maid and mistress (the separation of the two female lovers) and repeated as the disjuncture within the woman writer, who partakes of the maid's feminine knowledge but in writing forsakes the maid's mute and perfect curvature, the closure of self-embrace.

Although in her left hand she still partakes of feminine plenitude, "the right one [is] woman-mistress as if distant from the body. . . dare I say it 'virile'?" (ibid.). The difference between the front and back covers of "Writing and Sexual Difference" is in Leclerc's version a difference within the woman writing, embodied in the contrast between her two arms. The right arm, the writing arm, is for Leclerc "virile." Speaking no longer about Vermeer's *bourgeoise*, but now directly about herself, she says: "If you only look at my. . . right hand, you'll see it at a distance from my body, you'll see it independent, abstract, male" (137). In writing, she becomes masculinized—as she puts it, "it's as if I wanted to play the man in wanting to write" (ibid.). Yet the difference between the maid and her is *not* the difference between feminine and masculine women. She is by no means fully masculine: it is only her right hand. Not masculine but split, both in touch with the maid's secret and abstracted from it.

She insists that, despite its masculinity, her right hand's "vocation is to formulate, to inscribe on the blank paper what in its shadow [her] wide and soft left hand whispers to it" (138). In the painting, the Lady's left hand is in the shadow (more discreet? more secretive?), her right is in the light. Leclerc describes her left hand as if it were a feminine object of desire: "my wide and soft left hand." Leclerc wants her right hand to copy down what the left hand knows. The mistress must write what the maidservant knows.

"She knows. She knows, the woman-servant who greets the babbling of sweet things in the light" (122). The curtain is pulled open to let light in for the mistress's writing, but it is the maid who contentedly gazes into the light. And what she greets, whence the source of her knowledge, is "babbling (*balbutiement*)." "*Balbutiement*" usually has negative connotations, except when used to describe the speech of infants, and then "balbutiement" can be used tenderly. The reception of the infant's tentative, wondrous efforts is precisely woman's work, domestic work. Leclerc explicitly and frequently identifies the maid with her mother. The women of another class who serve us recall the mother, recall her attentions to our material needs. The desire for the maid, along with the writer's resemblance to and difference from her must also be understood in terms of the mother. We need to understand how our relation to the mother colors our relation to women of the class who work for us.

Leclerc's ascription of knowledge to the maid can also be understood as an example of transference, in the psychoanalytic sense. It is not only that Leclerc transfers her relation to her mother (and her lover) onto the maid, but that the maid is for Leclerc "the subject presumed to know," which is Lacan's definition of transference. And as in the case of psychoanalysis proper the transference seems to depend upon the maid's silence, a silence which Leclerc often says hurts her. Leclerc writes: "She knows. . . . And me I want to tell you what she knows. But what she likewise does not say" ("*je veux te dire ce qu'elle sait. Mais ce qu'elle tait aussi*") (ibid.). The close resemblance between the verb for "knows" and the verb for "not to speak"—"elle sait" and "elle tait"—enforces a connection between the maid's feminine knowledge and her silence, a silence Leclerc sometimes reads as willful, a complacent unwillingness to speak which abashes Leclerc.

"Whence comes this difficult and delicious will which distinguishes me from her?" (ibid.). The will to write, to write what the maid, the mother, the lover knows but keeps to herself, keeps secret, distinguishes the writer from the other woman. "Are we not, she and I, of the same flesh, same woman servant, woman serving under the same constraint of father, master and husband?" (ibid.). Are not mother and daughter of the same flesh? Are not all women united in their common oppression? If the husband and master's constraint can be represented by the enclosure of the bourgeois household in which we find the two women, then it is the maidservant whose gaze goes outside, just as, presumably, she will physically carry the letter outside the house. Leclerc writes: "Admit that there is in [the woman writing] an abnegation, a consent to the limits, an adequation to the walls of the house" (139).

The two women are not the same. "How also to want this distance between us and which hurts me so?" Leclerc asks (122). The distance between them hurts Leclerc. But if she loves this picture, if it is the only object to which she is truly attached, it is certainly because it gives her an image of what, in her writing, she is striving for: an acceptance of the distance as well as the proximity between women.

We may well doubt whether the other woman here is anything but a projection of a woman who would be truly immanently feminine, who would not be split like the writer. The real woman, the pure being-in-itself, is always the other woman. And we traditionally project greater integrity of being to those with less power and privilege. And even beyond this big question we might well wonder why a painting by that seventeenth-century man Vermeer would tell us anything we need to know about woman's writing?

These problems with Leclerc's text are undeniable. Yet what I would like to hold onto from Leclerc's identification with Vermeer's Lady is the double image of the difference within *écriture féminine* in the hope of greater future understanding of the relation between these two rifts in an imaginary feminine and feminist plenitude. On the one hand the feminine psychological split: the internal division embodied in the figure of a right-handed writer who wishes to write precisely what only her left hand knows. On the other hand the feminist socioeconomic rift: the simultaneous proximity and separation, resemblance and difference between the bourgeoise woman writer and the other woman who may be our mother, lover, cleaning woman, or secretary. Future understanding not in order to close the divide and reach the space of pure and simple feminine being (*le secret où femmes nous sommes*) but in order precisely to "want this distance between us," in order better to ask the necessarily double and no less urgent questions of feminism: not merely "who am I?" But "who is the other woman?"

After I read the above paper at the Poetics of Gender colloquium, another woman (Nancy Miller to be exact) showed me the cover of *La venue à l'écriture* (see figure 5), a cover I had never seen since I had worked with a bound library copy of the book. They have deleted the maidservant and left only the single woman writing: this on the cover of the very book wherein Leclerc fairly sings her love for the maid. Thanks to this cover, I realize that the problem of *écriture féminine* is not, as some would have it, its insistence on sexual difference at the expense of some universal humanity, but rather, to my mind, its effacement of the differences between women in view of some feminine essence—in this case, the literal effacement of class difference—so as to represent woman alone at her writing table.

The difference between women, the question of the other woman, the rifts in feminist plentitude are extremely difficult to confront and even more difficult to hold on to. The temptation to essentialize is powerful, not so much in our texts, where difference is allowable, but on the cover, where we would like to encompass difference and get it all together. In our desire to make a book of it—a real book and not just letters—let us not forget the other woman.

WORKS CITED

Cixous, Hélène. "La venue à l'écriture." In H. Cixous, M. Gagnon, and A. Leclerc, *La venue à l'écriture*. Paris: Union Générale d'Editions, 1977.

Eagleton, Terry. *Literary Theory: An Introduction*. Minneapolis: University of Minnesota Press, 1983.

Irigaray, Luce. "Ce sexe qui n'en est pas un." In *Ce Sexe qui n'en est pas un*. Paris: Minuit,

Figure 5. Front Cover of *La venue à l'écriture*.

1977. *This Sex Which Is Not One*. Trans: Catherine Porter. Ithaca: Cornell University Press, 1985.

Kofman, Sarah. *L'énigme de la femme*. Paris: Galilée, 1980.

Leclerc, Annie. *Parole de femme*. Paris: Grasset, 1974.

—— "La lettre d'amour." In *La venue à l'écriture*. Paris: Union Générale d'Editions, 1977.

Spivak, Gayatri. "French Feminism in an International Frame." *Yale French Studies* (1981), 62:154–84.

Difference on Trial:
A Critique of the Maternal
Metaphor in Cixous,
Irigaray, and Kristeva

DOMNA C. STANTON

When the infinite bondage of woman will be broken, when she will live for herself and by herself, man—abominable until now—having discharged her, she too will be a poet! Woman will discover the unknown! Will her world of ideas differ from ours? She will discover strange things, unfathomable, repulsive, delicious; we will take them, we will understand them.

—Rimbaud

Woman becomes the possibility of a "different" idea.

—Irigaray

The future perfect that Rimbaud envisioned a century ago remains unrealized in our present imperfect: woman is still in(de)finitely in bondage, she exists in the real and the symbolic neither by nor for herself. And yet, during the past decade, most notably in France, female critics and theorists have used poetic modes of speech to explore *la différence féminine* and thus to subvert a phallocratic system predicated on the perpetuation of the same. For Hélène Cixous, Luce Irigaray, and Julia Kristeva—whom I consider emblematic of this tendency, notwithstanding undeniable dissimilarities in their work—the exploration of that sexual difference constitutes "the fecund horizon" of the future which will herald the birth of "a new era of thought... the creation of a new *poïetic*" (Irigaray, E*thique*, 13).[1] In their "maternal" pursuit of this poetic quest, the three exponents of difference, who are the subject of this study, have privileged metaphor, the trope upheld from classical to modernist times as the optimal tool for transporting meaning beyond the known (*meta-phorein*).[2] Metaphor, says Kristeva, creates "a surplus of meaning," which "manages to open the surface of signs toward the unrepresentable" (Histoires, 254, 344). Through this transporting metaphor, Cixous, Irigaray, and Kristeva strive to articulate the unrepresented, the female unknown repulsed by Rimbaud's abominable man.

According to Rimbaud's visionary scenario, "we" would expect man to take and understand the difference woman is discovering. However, something far more ambiguous has occurred. First, the emphasis on female difference is part and parcel of the philosophy of difference that pervades contemporary thought since Heidegger and dominates theories of modernity. Accordingly, the idea of female difference or the female as principal metaphor for difference has marked the work of Neumann and Marcuse, for instance, on this side of the Atlantic, Deleuze, Derrida, Lacan, and Lyotard on the other. As Alice Jardine has remarked, modernist masters in France have consistently coded as feminine that which exceeds the grasp of the Cartesian subject—be it called nonknowledge or nontruth, undecidability or supplementarity, even writing or the unconscious ("Gynesis," 54–63). It is possible, then, that the feminization of difference and its articulations involve a replaying of that age-old scene in which, and in contrast to Rimbaud's scenario, the male discloses, the female disposes. In effect, female-authored inscriptions of la *différence féminine* seem decisively, but often unavowedly, influenced by the texts of contemporary masters.[3] At the very least, these women's explorations represent a complex give and take with modernist discourse, a writing-between or re-writing, which comprises significant continuity and varying degrees of oppositional discontinuity. As Barthes reminds us in Writing Degree Zero, all writing, even the most intentionally subversive, is confined by the parameters of discourse at a particular moment, which is always an imperfect present.

Leaving aside the troubling relation between modernism and le *féminin*, which warrants its own extended analysis, the "quest for the Unknown Woman"— "la quête vers l'Inconnue" (Cixous, *Là*, 80)— pursued by these three female critics should be examined to determine how or whether it involves a transportation of meaning beyond the known. Despite or, in fact, because of its inspiring, empowering value for women, their challenging discourse should be probed for the traces of the same it contains—what Irigaray, with Heidegger, calls in-difference (*Ce Sexe*, 67ff.). It can be scrutinized, in other words, for the extent to which phallocentric scenes and semes are re-presented, despite the desire to subvert, eliminate, and replace them. In that process, metaphor itself must be interrogated to see whether it provides the best means for exploring the many aspects of the female unknown; or, then, whether other rhetorical strategies may be more propitious and productive. And finally, since this metaphorical discourse constitutes "a trial of difference"—"une épreuve de la différence" (Cixous, *Illa*, 65)—difference as teleology must be put on trial. Such an undertaking is critical to a dynamic feminist method(ide)ology, in my view. It seems crucial at a moment when American feminist critics are affirming *The Future of Difference* beyond earlier claims to equal value with men and to fundamental similarities among all women. It is particularly pertinent at a time when we are emphasizing the importance of *Writing and Sexual Difference* under the growing influence of French theories on the feminine. A partial investigation, of necessity both fragmentary and subjective, this study extracts and examines, in certain texts by Cixous, Irigaray, and Kristeva, the strands of an extended metaphor—woman as/is mother[4]—for its special relevance to the contemporary preoccupation with female difference, and beyond, the problematics of difference itself.

I

As mother of the virgin woman, in her comings and goings, in her search, she turns all the scenes of representation upside down, deconstructs the old cities and the new old cities, the whole imaginary and symbolic universe of the ancient men, with a merciless step renders obsolete the imperfect present.

—Cixous

In her radical re-writing of Rimbaud's scenario, Cixous delineates the metaphorically maternal role that she, like Irigaray and Kristeva, assumes to give birth to the unsaid feminine, "the virgin woman." In turn, the vehicle for this exploration of difference is essentially maternal, what Irigaray terms "the maternal-feminine" (*Ethique*, passim). Just as Cixous locates the "essence of femininity" in the womb, and hails the feminine as "the maternal sex" (*Illa*, 122, 204), so too does Irigaray affirm that "when we are women, we are always mothers" (*Ethique*, 27). And from *Revolution in Poetic Language* on, Kristeva depicts the feminine "function" as the maternal, and unrepresented feminine sexuality as maternal *jouissance* (*Rév*, 499–500). So saying, Cixous, Irigaray, and Kristeva take as their point of departure the primordial definition of woman in the phallocratic order, what could be viewed as the concrete agent of (its) re-production.

Now this valorization of the maternal marks a decisive break with the existentialism of *The Second Sex*, wherein de Beauvoir stressed the oppressiveness of motherhood as an institution and rejected maternity as a solution to the problem of female transcendence (*le pour-soi*). By contrast, Cixous considers feminist denunciations of the patriarchal trap of maternity a perpetuation of the taboo of the pregnant woman, and a new form of repression, the denial of the "passionate," "delicious" experiences of women's bodies (JN, 166). Likewise, Kristeva interprets the rejection of maternity as a feminist incapacity to transcend the phallocratic attitude of "idealized contempt" ("Héréthique," 30), and to see in the maternal the ultimate love for another ("Un nouveau," 6–7). Although the views of Kristeva and Cixous are not necessarily incompatible with those of de Beauvoir, their analyses are basically unconcerned with "the real" or the historical, despite occasional references to the "radical transformations in sociopolitical structures [which] would create a radically different inscription of difference" (Cixous, JN, 152–53).[5] Instead, their notion of the maternal difference centers exclusively on the symbolic and the imaginary. According to Kristeva, "only a full elaboration of maternity, and its relation to creation" can lead to "a true feminine innovation (in every single field)" ("Un nouveau," 6–7). More radically, Irigaray argues that such an elaboration predicates "another 'syntax,' another 'grammar' of culture" (*Ce Sexe*, 140). In *Le Corps-à-corps avec la mère* and *Amante marine*, and in direct opposition to Freud, she declares the murder of the mother to be the foundation of Western culture and society.[6] Thus to "think of the mother in every woman, of the woman in every mother" is a forbidden act, she claims, that will undermine the patriarchal edifice (*Corps*, 25, 27, 86), and bring about a revolutionary ethic of sexual difference (*Ethique*, 70, 71, 143).

In this symbolic context, it becomes clear that "the Mother" is, as Cixous states, "a metaphor" ("Laugh," 881). Accordingly, quotation marks often frame the "mother" in Cixousian texts: in *La Jeune Née*, "woman is never far from the 'mother' " (173); in *La venue à l'écriture*, "Woman is always in a certain way, 'mother' to herself and the other" (56). That Cixous upholds metaphor as desirable and efficacious ("Laugh," 882; JN, 271) presupposes faith in its capacity to transform existing meanings, ultimately, the system of significance. In effect, Irigaray maintains that similitude or analogy, in contrast to the rigor/ rigidity of male geometricity, "entails a reworking of meaning" (*Ce Sexe*, 108), especially when it involves "symbolism created among women" (*Ethique*, 103). And for Kristeva, the maternal, coupled with the paternal, represents a "theoretical bisexuality . . . a metaphor designating the possibility of exploring all aspects of signification."[7]

This venerated and idealistic conception of metaphor, however, ignores the problematic implications of metaphoricity. As the trope of similitude, metaphor affirms the verb to be—A is (like) B— or the notion of "being as," and thus has an ontological function, what Derrida describes as a hidden essence: "Metaphor is able to display properties, to relate to each other properties on the basis of their resemblance, without ever directly, fully or properly stating the essence, without itself making visible the truth of the thing itself" ("White Mythology," 50). Going further, Derrida concurs with Heidegger that the metaphorical exists within the metaphysical and represents a religious construct.[8] By that token, the maternal *sein* (breast) would partake of the ontotheological *Sein*, and already be caught up in the structures of phallogopresence. In fact, the trope of similitude itself could be regarded as a metonymy for the philosophy of sameness which, as Irigaray has convincingly shown in *Speculum de l'autre femme*, dominates Western thought from Plato to Freud. Not surprisingly, then, Kristeva subsumes metaphoricity under the paternal function (*Powers of Horror*, 53).

The hidden ontotheology of the maternal metaphor is ignored and implicitly denied by these exponents of *la différence féminine*, even though they oppose essentialist and religious thinking.[9] Kristeva's work, in particular, strives to undermine identity in favor of a subject always in process, on trial, or what she calls "a process without subject" (*Rév*, 489). She contrasts the Christian conception of the mother, which sustains the symbolic order and supports the dominant notion of the subject, with an-other, un-symbolic conception that can subvert phallogopresence, since "then every speaker would be led to conceive of its Being in relation to some void, a nothingness asymmetrically opposed to this Being, a permanent threat against first, its mastery, and ultimately its stability" (DL, 238). For Kristeva, the difference between the two conceptions of the maternal, which parallels the two conceptions of metaphor, is exemplified, on the one hand, by Leonardo's paintings of the madonna, a *père-version* ("Héréthique," 47) and, on the other, by certain Bellini madonnas, which suggest to her "the luminous serenity of the unrepresentable" (DL, 243). The same dichotomy appears in "Héréthique de l'amour": the right, the doxic side of the text exposes the ontotheological vision of maternity, while the left (the left out), inscribes in fragmented, elliptical images the female speaker's maternal experience. Concurrently, Kristeva cautions feminists against the "naively romantic" belief in identity, since "woman cannot *be*, is even that which does not go into *being*" (*Polylogue*, 519). The feminist assertion of being, she states, is theological: "women must stop making feminism a religion. . . or a sect" ("Un nouveau," 7).

Although Irigaray does not censure feminism as yet another man-ism, she too warns women against trying to "rival [man] by constructing a logic of the feminine which would still take for its model the ontotheologic" (*Ce Sexe*, 75). But that warning is addressed only to other women, while the speaking self urges women to substitute for god the Father "a goddess mother or woman, both mother and woman," and heralds in the future feminine a new *parousia* (*Ethique*, 71, 139). Like Kristeva, Irigaray does not put her own metaphorization of the maternal into question to probe and counteract its ontotheological traces. Even Irigaray's *Ce Sexe qui n'en est pas un*, which struggles self-consciously, haltingly to move beyond existing scenes of representation—"how can I say in another way?"; "how can I say it?," asks the speaker repeatedly (74, 77)—ends with the moment "when our lips speak together," finally free of the male-imposed fear of speaking properly, but also impervious to the implications of speaking metaphorically.

The tensions between a conscious repulsion of the ontotheologic and its enduring lures or traps are dramatized in Cixous's works. Although she states, like Irigaray, that there is no feminine essence, nature, or destiny (JN, 152; *Amante marine*, 91), her desire to create an empowering mythology or "magic without gods" (*With*, 185) leads to the affirmation of "a universal woman subject," "the New Woman" ("Laugh," 878), who would represent Adam in the feminine "if God had been a woman" (*With*, 89). To be sure, the Cixousian "I" occasionally recognizes and criticizes her "religious writing" (*Vivre*, 13). More important, the weight of the old phallosystem and the problematics of speaking in the new feminine are extensively inscribed. Typically, lyrically, the Cixousian text evokes the difficult rite of passage from the old order to the tentative, slippery moment of birth of that yonder feminine, which the Latin *illa* denotes, and which Aura (the future of the Latin, to have) symbolizes (*With*, 90). This strategy would seem to bypass the notion of presence/essence, but it transpires through the textual delineation of "the maternal sex" whose pervasive metaphoricity is never questioned. And it becomes particularly visible in the evocation of Clarice Lispector, the maternal Muse or Angela ("Ange-est-là"), who exemplifies feminine writing in a "present interior" in which "all women [speak] the same music" (*Illa*, 99, 129, 183). Self and other become a presence; so do things—"she has a way of pronouncing the essence of things, and things are there" (148)—so do "their presence-names . . . their names full of presence, their living, heavy, audible names" (*Vivre*, 72, 74). For the most Derridean of the exponents of feminine difference, as Gayatri Spivak has described Cixous (70–73), this emphatic presence marks a break with the symbolic father. But it remains a lyrical gesture that paradoxically reaffirms the phallophilosophy of presence which the maternal feminine is designed to efface.

As such examples suggest, *la différence féminine*, defined as absence, becomes present in the maternal text through the ontological maternal metaphor. To be sure, the very function of metaphor is to provide for a missing term, to say what lacks, is absent. As the metaphor is elaborated semantically, the unrepresented/unrepresentable feminine is recuperated into the scenes of representation that this maternal discourse aims to shatter.[10] Now it could be argued that far from constituting the critical difference, the unrepresentable has always been part of the discursive system. Indeed, in examining the principles of catachresis, "a foundation for our entire tropological system," the venerable Fontanier notes that this forced or abusive metaphor predicates the existence of "a new idea . . . having no sign at all or no other proper sign within the language" (*Figures du discours*, 213).[11] By extension, the unrepresented may be the very sign in our discursive system that sustains the illusion of its capacity to speak difference. Clearly, then, the problematic of the unrepresented is not peculiar to the maternal metaphor. It is endemic to any practice that tries to name the unnamed; it is embedded in the bind that all affirmation of difference creates. For either we name and become entrapped in the structures of the already named; or else we do not name and remain trapped in passivity, powerlessness, and a perpetuation of the same. Either way, to paraphrase Cixous, "we still flounder in the ancient order" (JN, 153).

II

> But is there an elsewhere? . . . If it's not yet "here," it's already there—in that other place . . . where desire makes fiction exist.
>
> —Cixous

Given the constraints of a global discursive bind, Cixous's question has particularly relevant, but more relative, implications for the maternal metaphor. To what extent does the metaphor, as a desirable fiction, bespeak an elsewhere, an-other place? Although philosophers of language, Derrida most recently, rightly insist that no thought is ever free of old metaphors, instances of extended metaphorization can represent varying degrees of "innovation," to use Kristeva's term, if not of difference in an absolute sense, which can effect a movement (*mouvance*) beyond sameness to some reworking of meaning (*Histoires*, 258). In the instance of the maternal, a more detailed analysis of the conceptual bases of the metaphor, and its constituent semes and scenes can help determine whether and in what specific ways inscriptions of the "new" feminine represent an elsewhere, a re-writing otherwise from the stereotypology of woman as mother.

At the outset, the elaboration of the maternal metaphor is grounded in the patriarchal Freudian text, for what it both says and silences. Refuting the oedipal version of maternity and girlhood, Cixous, Irigaray, and Kristeva focus instead on the pre-oedipal, that shadowy sphere "almost impossible to revivify," which Freud discovered through his female disciples, that "prehistory of women" which, he claimed, accounts "almost entirely" for the substance of their ulterior relations to father and husband (21:226; 22:119, 130). An absent presence, the pre-oedipal attracts maternal exponents of difference as a gynocentric space, even though, as the word implies, it remains bound up with the oedipal Weltanschauung. Still, the pre-oedipal can be rewritten to eliminate its pejorations in Freudian texts, suggests Irigaray (Ce Sexe, 46, 136). For Cixous, it can serve as an originary point for the future feminine: "As if there were, buried alive, between the breasts, under the clay curtains, in the chest, behind the fertile lungs, a woman in the cradle, hardly conceived, already perfectly formed, a living presence . . . daughter of woman, a female engendered without father . . . fruit of mother love, the kind that can be conceived *naturally* only in the regions of pre-oedipal culture" (*Illa*, 37; italics mine). This naturalization of a pre-historical, purely hypothetical construct points to the desire for an archaic past before the advent of the symbolic. Abducted and buried alive by man, like Persephone (203–9), that past can be recaptured as a "rebeginning" (205), insists Cixous, through the de-repression of unconscious or archaic memories: "the gods have lost their divinity, but memories, which replace them, keep their divine viscosity" (121). But the quest for the lost trace, for the origin that coincides with the telos, is, once again, religious in impulse. In fact, Irigaray unearths in "this ignorance . . . of woman's relation to her primordial desires, this nonelaboration of her relation to her origins" (Ce Sexe, 61) a primal plot based on man's and god's fear of the power of the archaic Mother (*Amante marine*). Its undoing would presumably be marked by a re-writing of John in the feminine. "In the beginning there was Woman," we read in Cixous's *With ou l'art de l'innocence*," and the beginning was woman" (201).[12]

In Kristeva's work, more than Irigaray's or Cixous's, the pre-oedipal is the cornerstone of her theory of subversive production. She names the "revival of archaic pre-oedipal modes of operation" the *semiotic*, a notion that is admittedly "only a theoretical supposition justified by the need for description" (*On Chinese Women*, 58; Rev-tr, 68). Logically and chronologically anterior to the imposition of the symbolic (or paternal) order, the semiotic is conceptualized as the pre-verbal moment when the child is bound up with, and dependent on, the mother's body, when instinctual drives are organized, and rhythmic models developed. This semiotic relation to the maternal body must undergo repression for the acquisition of language, a phenomenon that pervades the entire structure of the symbolic order (DL, 136). By that token, the semiotic is part of the dialectical process of *signifiance* through which all subjects constitute themselves. And yet, while re-maining "inherent in the symbolic," the semiotic "also [goes] beyond it and [threatens] its position" (Rev-tr, 81). In effect, only the reactiva-tion, the irruption of the semiotic/maternal can fracture and remodel the symbolic to produce the heterogeneous, which is the mark of the poetic (Rev-tr, 62ff.). Poetic language, art in general, is, then, "the semiotization of the symbolic" (79).

In more precise terms, however, the delineation of the subversive semiotic apparatus relies on a series of traditional images. Among these, the topos of the child at the breast. "The superego and its linear language," writes Kristeva, ". . . are combatted by a return of the oral glottic pleasure" of suction and expulsion, fusion, and, above all, rejection (*rejet*) (*Polylogue*, 74). Aside from the breast, the semiotic privileges the archetypal maternal voice and rhythms: "with a material support like the voice, this semiotic network gives 'music' to literature"; "melody, harmony, rhythm, 'gentle' and 'pleasing' sounds" (Rev-tr, 63; *Polylogue*, 73). By extension the semiotic produces alliterations, ana-phoric constructions, lexical repetitions or lapses which, for Kristeva, perturb the logic of the signifying chain. Such effects ultimately serve to "overturn the normativity of the language of communication: its semantics, its syntax, its contextual relations, its subjective instances" (Rev, 612). The radical quality of the poetic/semiotic text does not merely predicate a return of the repressed, but what Kristeva depicts as metaphorical incest: the artist/child commits the paternally forbid-den act of "appropriating the archaic, instinctual and maternal terri-tory" (DL, 136). By emphasizing the subject's desire to destroy the father and to (re)possess the mother, Kristeva's model for engendering the poetic does not then deviate fundamentally from the patriarchal oedipal script.

In a further echo of Freudian phallocentrism, Kristeva's

encoding of the artist/child privileges the male to the detriment of the female. "Son permanently at war with the father," he allies with the parent of the opposite sex, and commits the "son's incest. . . a meeting with . . . the first other, the mother" (*Polylogue*, 86; DL, 138, 191). The daughter, for whom the mother is not the other but the same (*Polylogue*, 475), forms a principal alliance with the father which makes her conform more rigidly to symbolic authority, and renders her implicitly less subversive/creative than semiotic man. Woman attains her creative limits "(and in our society *especially*) through the strange form of split symbolization (threshold of language and instinctual drive), of the 'symbolic' and the 'semiotic' [that] the act of giving birth" represents (DL, 240). Accordingly, she has the artistic function of articulating the repressed maternal experience. And yet, in Kristeva's work, the only articulate mother is the "I" in "Héréthique de l'amour," who recurs in the "Stabat Mater" of *Histoires d'amour*.[13] Although the maternal/semiotic is crucial to the Kristevan theory of art as the exemplary subversive practice, the mother remains, as the phallotext defines her, a passive instinctual force that does not speak, but is spoken by the male: "the artist speaks from a place where she is not, where she knows not. He delineates what in her is a body rejoicing (*un corps jouissant*)" (DL, 242).

By contrast, Cixous's work centers on the mother/daughter bond as the privileged metaphor for "femininity in writing" (JN, 170). She uses topoi of the maternal voice and breast far more extensively than Kristeva, although the voice represents, yet again, "[the] song before the law, before. . . the symbolic," which can "make the text gasp or fill it with suspense or silences, anaphorize it or tear it apart with cries" (170, 172). But Cixous opposes (masculine) "writing by the written" to (feminine) "writing by the voice" (*Illa*, 208), because of an essential connection to the voice that man lacks and maternal woman has. "The voice is the uterus," states the speaker in *Illa* (168), who internalizes the "woman-voice" of the maternal muse in her song for other women. Extending the metaphor for birthing and nourishing, the maternal poetic voice merges with the breast: "Voice. Inexhaustible milk. Is rediscovered. The lost mother. Eternity: voice mixed with milk" (JN, 173). More typical and exclusive, however, is the Cixousian assertion that "there is always in [woman] at least a little of the mother's good milk. She writes in white ink" (173). Transmuted into *le languelait* and the unique "knowledge of the breast" (With, 120, 202), maternal milk emerges as the predominant metaphorical vehicle for Cixousian writing in the feminine.

Voice and milk also serve to revisualize the traditional maternal trait of giving (as) love. "There are voices that . . . give birth to the gift," says the speaker in Illa (129–30), acknowledging the women who gave her life in/as writing: "there is a Gabrielle who gave me the bottle long after the end of the milk, beyond the law, in the absence of the first Mother" (104). Like "the Mother goddess" (196), woman gives/loves in ways that are radically different from proprietary man: "To love, to watch-think-seek the other in the other, to despecularize, to unhoard . . . a love that has no commerce with the apprehensive desire that provides against the lack and stultifies the strange, a love that rejoices in the exchange that multiplies" ("Laugh," 893). This essential capacity to give life/love to another in an-other way is concretized through the metaphor of the pregnant body. Indeed, the delights and mysteries of interiority unknown to man, the pleasures of an expansive waiting fertile with possibilities, and the uniquely maternal experience of arrival, issue (sortie), and separation number among the elements of a jouiscience (With, 219) metaphorically mined in Cixous's With to delineate the feminine elsewhere.

Aside from exploring the umbilical ties between mother and other, daughter or woman, the Cixousian vision of the elledorador (Illa, 32) invokes a maternal reconnection with the material things of nature. Just as Demeter's world is bereft of all vegetation when she grieves for her lost daughter, the return of flowers, "emitted maternally by the earth" (140), and of the lost fruits—Eve's apple, Clarice's orange—requires an obstetric act of deliverance, as the German obst (fruit) suggests (187, 194–95). With "delicate attentions . . . which wait patiently, patiently, and surrender to inspiration . . . the things which have always been present mute, make themselves heard," the speaker in Illa affirms: "There is no silence. The music of things always resounds, waiting for us to hear it faithfully" (155). Emulating the experiences of Proust's Marcel with hawthorne flowers, the female "I" rediscovers the "rose being" (la rose en soi) (159). Even more significant, she resurrects the bond between word and thing, guided by Clarice Lispector, whose voice "passes gently behind things and lifts them, gently bathes them, and [takes] the words in [her] hands" (133). The maternal muse bestows this transcendent gift to Illa, the third-person feminine beyond Demeter and Persephone, who reestablishes the Ariadnean thread of communication among women and things and brings on/back the *Primeverbe* (74, 141).

In her verbal rhapsody of traditional feminine symbols, Cixous does not merely valorize the *materrenelle*, woman as Mother Earth or earth mother (*With*, 201). Like Irigaray, she consistently exploits the age-old association of mother and water, capitalizing on the homophony between *mère/mer*: "it's my mother! The sea floats her, ripples her, flows together with her daughter, in all our ways. Then unseparated they sweep along their changing waters, without fear of their bodies, without bony stiffness, without a shell. . . . And sea for mother (*mer pour mère*) gives herself up to pleasure in her bath of writing" (*Là*, 143). While Cixous may favor topoi of the continuity and variety of the rhythms and songs of "our women's waters" (*Venue*, 62), both she and Irigaray uphold the unceasing movement (*mouvance*) of the sea as the very symbol of the feminine elsewhere (*Amante marine*, 19). Notwithstanding Irigaray's extended critique of Plato's identification of women and water in *Speculum, de l'autre femme*, the terrifying storminess of the sea which eludes mastery, even destroys identity, and its enchanting mysteries, which connote unfathomable alterity, are enlisted in her apotheosis of the liquid mother as the ultimate source of difference.[14]

Going beyond the global implications of the sea, Irigaray highlights an essential fluidity in/among women. Rejecting the notion of self and other as part of binary phalloeconomy, she depicts the feminine body/bodies in "When Our Lips Speak Together" as "always one and the other at the same time," open and shared, wall-less and boundless in multiplicity (72–73). Women's capacity for an (over)flowing diffusiveness that is "alien to unity" (*Amante marine*, 92)[15] is opposed to the phallocentric mentality fixated on "the privilege, domination, and sollipsism of the One" (*Ce Sexe*, 270). And the rigid hardness or "the solid that the penis represents" (112) is contrasted to an intrauterine, amniotically fluid sexuality, which Irigaray identifies as specifically feminine: "the sea (*marin*) element, as an attempt to mark a difference, is both the amniotic waters . . . and also . . . the movement of the sea, the coming and going, the continual flux. [It] seems to me quite close to my jouissance as a woman, completely foreign to an economy of erection and tumescence" (*Corps*, 49). Not surprisingly, then, "When Our Lips Speak Together" constitutes a paean to the female as *amante marine*:

How can I speak you, who remain in a flux that never congeals or solidifies? How can this current pass into words? It is multiple . . . ; yet it is not decomposable.. . . These streams don't flow into one, definitive sea; these rivers have no permanent banks; this body no fixed borders. This unceasing mobility, this life. Which they might describe as our restlessness, whims, pretenses or lies. For all this seems so strange to those who claim "solidity" as their foundation. Speak, nevertheless. Between us, "hardness" is not the rule.. . . Our density can do without the sharp edges of rigidity. We are not attracted to dead bodies. (76–77)

In this evocation of fluidity, softness, movement, life, antithetical to masculine solidity, hardness, rigidity, and death, the feminine, the devalued term in phallologic, becomes the superior value, but the system of binary oppositions remains the same. Indeed, in their maternal metaphorizations, Irigaray, Cixous, and Kristeva countervalorize the traditional antithesis that identifies man with culture and confines woman to instinctual nature, "always childlike, always savage" (Cixous, JN, 57). And they reproduce the dichotomy between male rationality and female materiality, corporeality, and sexuality, which Irigaray has traced to Plato and Plotinus (*Speculum*, 210–25, 375). The noncultural, nonintellectual, feminine elsewhere also suggests a return to Plato's cave redefined as a uterine symbol (347). Rejected by classical thinkers in favor of external reality, that shadowy, nocturnal, oneiric domain (386) is extolled by Romantics and exponents of difference as the interior locus of mystery and creativity. "I want to remain nocturnal and find again . . . my softly luminous night," intones Irigaray's "Lips" (78).[16] Ultimately, the maternal-feminine is the mysterious black continent, which Freud, symbol of protophallic man, feared, colonized and debased as *la contrée du con* (Cixous, "Laugh," 879). By contrast, the Cixousian "I" instructs the future feminine explorers:

To enter the domain where you can reclaim your nursling you will . . . have split the eardrums of resignation's preachers, punctured the crust of death's throes, threading your way into its entrails, into the black continent where women don't kill their dead. They relodge them in their flesh by bits scrupulously tasted . . . woman proceeds black in the black/feminine. . . . We who know that love illuminates and who have heard the psalms of the black continent and made them reverberate . . . we can affirm that black radiates, that the country of femininity reserves for us the most dazzling revelations. (*Souffles*, 147–48)

In this critical passage, the maternal-feminine voice moves from the future perfect to a present that proclaims "dazzling revelations." Judging from the present texts that explore *la différence féminine*, however, the maternal metaphor does not produce revelations so much as revalorizations or relodgings of topoi, images, and myths embedded in binary phallologic. Do these make an elsewhere reverberate? Do they signal movement (*mouvance*) to another place when inscribed by maternal women, and just because they are inscribed by women? Or is this a utopian vision that denies the bind of the present imperfect?

In more circumspect terms, Cixous has suggested that while we strive to "puncture the system of couples and oppositions" (JN, 179), *l'écriture féminine* must first steal (*voler*) male discourse in order to explode and fly (*voler*) beyond it:

If woman has always functioned "within" the discourse of man . . . it is time for her to dislocate this "within," to explode it, turn it around, and seize it; to make it hers, containing it, taking it into her own mouth, biting that tongue with her very own teeth to invent for herself a language to get inside of. And you'll see with what ease she will spring from that "within" —the "within" where once she so drowsily crouched. ("Laugh," 887)

Undeniably, the maternal metaphor exemplifies women "getting within," seizing, powerfully manipulating male discourse on women. Through extended play with signifiers and signifieds, the traditional conception of the maternal is expanded, swollen with meanings that move to the limits of the same. That feat alone should not be minimized in a system that equates femininity with passivity and silence; at the very least, then, these exponents of the feminine give voice to woman as a potently poetical/theoretical speaking subject. But the maternal metaphor, in my view, does not herald the invention of a different poetic or conceptual idiom. Indeed, it underscores not "the ease" but the unease of "springing from within" to a radical elsewhere.

Like Cixous, Irigaray has emphasized the necessity, even the desirability of reappropriating the feminine "within" binary phalloeconomy:

In the first stage, there is, perhaps, only a single "way," that which has historically been assigned the feminine: *mimeticism*. It's a matter of assuming this role deliberately, which is already to transform subordination into affirmation, and thereby to start spoiling the game. . . . To play at mimesis is, then, for a woman, to try to rediscover the locus of her exploitation by discourse, without being simply reduced to it. It is to resubmit herself . . . to "ideas" about her, elaborated in/by a masculine logic, but in order to "manifest" by ludic repetition what was to remain hidden: the recovery of a possible operation of the feminine in language. It is also to "unveil" the fact that if women mime so well it's because they cannot simply be reabsorbed in that function. *They also remain elsewhere.* (*Ce Sexe*, 73–74)

Despite the seductiveness of Irigaray's logic, the repetition of masculinist notions and images of the feminine does not necessarily have a ludic or subversive impact that points to an elsewhere. The adoption of the mimetic function, traditionally assigned to woman, may freeze and fixate the feminine at the mirror stage, rather than lead to a difference beyond the same old binary plays. As Irigaray herself recognizes, a revalorization that is "a simple reversal," a displacement of positive/negative value from one term to another in binary structures, "finally comes back to the same. To phallocratism" (32, 78). While *l'écriture au maternel* is anything but "simple," Irigaray's awareness does not preclude internalization, what Cixous terms "the risk of identification" ("Laugh," 887), and thus an enduring confinement within the parameters of the dominant discourse. In fact, since it depicts the maternal-feminine as voice, breast, giving, loving, plurality, fluidity, sea, nature, and body—this metaphorical body of work may be viewed, somewhat perversely perhaps, not as an elaboration of the unrepresented/unrepresentable, but rather—to use a metaphor—as an offspring delivered by/from the father; an appealing, empowering reproduction, not a different production. The assertion that the maternal constitutes the crucial difference even evokes the stance of the phallic mother, who lays down the Law of the father, rather than lays waste to it; who keeps, in so many words, both the symbolic baby and the bathwater.

III

... "that's not it" ... "that's still not it" ...

—Kristeva

That the maternal-feminine remains within sameness is, of course, no reason to bathe in despair or banish poetic women to silence. More usefully, this corpus underscores the need to confront the inescapable fact that any inscription of difference is (over)determined by the in-different dominant discourse. As Derrida suggests in "The Law of Genre," the symbolic order needs transgressions to sustain it; transgressions need the order to define their specificity; and thus, order and dis-order are inextricably bound one with the other (205). In this respect, Irigaray's "And the One Doesn't Stir Without the Other," a text that describes the daughter's attempts and failures to free herself from the mother, may be read as a metaphor for the inability to achieve freedom from the body of law, and that includes the maternal and the metaphorical.

Metaphoricity and binarism may be our (present) destiny. But the awareness that sameness permeates all efforts to speak dif-ference, and further, that every alternative practice tends to erect itself as ultimate authority can instill the imperative of unceasing vigilance and self-interrogation. This "permanent analytical attitude," which Kris-teva defines as dissidence itself ("Un nouveau," 7), is elaborated in her essay, "Semiology: A Critical Science and/or a Critique of Science":

semiology is, each time, a reevaluation of its object and/or its models, a critique of its models (and thus the sciences from which they are taken) and of itself (as system of constant truths). An intersection of sciences and of a theoretical process always in progress, semiology cannot consti-tute itself as one science, even less as *the* science: it is an open path of research, a constant critique that turns back on itself, in other words, an autocritique. (30)

Although it represents a demanding ideal, which semiology itself has failed to realize, autocriticsm needs to be interwoven in the fabric of *l'écriture au maternel*. It is not enough to proclaim a future feminine born "in the light of questions," the possessor of "a Gay ignorance" (Cixous, *Illa*, 208, 211), which is textually undermined by essentialist proposi-tions on woman-as-mother. Instead, there should be a critical negation

of the negation, not toward some imperial, Hegelian pinnacle, but as
an ongoing process with (a) telos. Thus the symbolic function that
Kristeva ascribes to woman—"negative, in opposition to what exists,
in order to say, 'that's not it,' and 'that's still not it' " (*Polylogue*, 519)—
should be inherent in explorations of *la différence féminine* and directed
at the maternal metaphor.

This is not to deny the importance of an initial counter-
valorization of the maternal-feminine as a negation/subversion of
paternal hierarchies, a heuristic tool for reworking images and meanings, above all, an enabling mythology.[17] But the moment the maternal
emerges as a new dominance, it must be put into question before it
congeals as feminine essence, as unchanging in-difference. In my view,
inscriptions of the maternal metaphor should have reached the symbolic point outlined in Monique Wittig's epic *Les Guérillères*, when the
women recognize that their feminaries, which are filled with images
and symbols, "have fulfilled their function" (49): "They say that at the
point they have reached they must examine the principle that has
guided them. They say it is not for them to exhaust their strength in
symbols" (72).[18] Closer to home, that critical voice has been assumed
by trans-Atlantic feminists weighing *The Future of Difference*. "Do we want
to continue reorganizing the relationship of difference to sameness
through the dialectics of valorization," asks Alice Jardine, "or is there a
way to break down the overdetermined metaphors which continue to
organize our perceptions of reality?" (xxvi). More specifically, Christiane
Makward warns that "the [French] theory of femininity is dangerously
close to recreating in 'deconstructive' language the traditional assumptions on femininity and female creativity" (96), while Josette Féral
cautions against neofeminine values becoming "newly imposed
norms, thereby reinstituting an antisystem that would be just as
repressive... a new dictatorship" (92).

Assuming the role of vigilant/dissident same/other, the
transatlantic feminist could also propose that the maternal as metaphor for *la différence féminine* undergo a symbolic renomination. In this
tentative scheme, "feminine," a signifier that seems to serve, in retrospect, to activate patriarchal scenes and topoi, would be replaced by
"female," and, more important, the status of the "maternal" would be
displaced from metaphor to metonymy.[19] For the maternal, which is

metaphorized as total being to substantiate a notion that can combat the paternal, represents only one aspect of potential female difference. To be sure, this displacement onto the metonymic is not innocent. It promotes a shift from the principal, indeed obsessive, preoccupation with the "difference from" man, which underlies the maternal-feminine, to "differences within" (a) woman, and "among" women; for if all women are maternal, where's the difference(s)? At the same time, this proposed displacement does not imply the (re)discovery of a virgin space free of phallocratic modes of thinking, much less of outworn metaphors. The conventional opposition between metaphor and metonymy, like Irigaray's distinction between metaphoric solidity and metonymic fluidity (*Ce Sexe*, 108ff.), still partakes of binary thinking.

Because of that discursive bind, I put "metonymy" into question, under erasure, even as I argue, after Lacan, that this figure evokes the more numerous elements that are missing and thus, in contrast to metaphor, suggests lack of being (515, 528). Because it does not cross the bar to truth, according to the French Freud, metonymy underscores the desire for the other, for something/somewhere else, a desire extended along an indefinite chain of signifiers by substitution, by a displacement that wanders off the subject (518, 528). By that token, a reconception of the maternal as a metonymy can help generate indefinite explorations of other desirable known and unknown female functions. In traditional rhetorical terms that should appeal to modernist exponents of difference, metonymy represents the trope that cannot be defined; as Hugh Bredin observes, it is composed of a "raggle-taggle collection of those tropes for which we can find no other name" (47). The left-over (50), the supplement that is multiple, metonymization can create propitious conditions within the present imperfect for speaking women in the plural, over and beyond the trinitarian mother, child, and the holy ghost of *illa*.

No less critical for my purpose is the possibility that the metonymic process would favor more concrete, contextual inscriptions of differences within/among women. Because of its association with contiguity, metonymy is context-bound, says Bredin, thus it exposes specific cultural values, prejudices, and limitations (57–58). By analogy and extension, metonymization would promote the recognition that the mother cannot symbolize an untainted origin, isolated in a virgin

black continent, and as such, an unbounded source or force of subversion; but rather, that this idea(l) is always/already inhabited by, and
accomplice to, the workings of contextual phallogocentric structures.
After all, even Demeter's daughter lives half the year in the masculine,
Hadean realm. So saying, I endorse for the moment Jakobson's decid-
edly arbitrary claim that the metonymic pole characterizes realistic
narratives ("Two Aspects," 76–82).[20] I do so not simply to reemphasize
a needed awareness of the essentialist traps of Romantic fictions and
poetic symbols. I do so primarily to promote female practices
grounded in contextual, sociohistorical discourses. A metonymic practice should/would displace focus from the utopian arche or future to
the imperfect past/present in which all processes of exploration are
located and all discoveries must begin.

It would also be utopian, however, to uphold the more
metonymic studies of American feminist scholars as models for undoing the fixation on the metaphorical process among French exponents of *la différence maternelle*. Although the American work on the
maternal, which has proliferated since 1975, has concentrated on sociohistorical critiques of institutions,[21] it still contains distinctly metaphorical tendencies and traits, which are nonetheless denied in the
name of a political criticism rooted in the real.[22] Even more, this
discourse on the maternal has undeniable traces of essentialism,
which can be detected in the influential texts of Adrienne Rich and
Nancy Chodorow, but are most dramatically revealed in Sara Ruddick's
"Maternal Thinking." These multidisciplinary studies repeatedly extol
pre-oedipal unboundedness, relatedness, plurality, fluidity, tenderness,
and nurturance in the name of the difference of female identity. In
what appears to be a repetition compulsion or contagion, today those
"different" traits are being reproduced far more extensively and inten-
sively in America than in France.

That women in two cultures with distinct philosophical
and methodological traditions have hypostasized the maternal in the
same decade leads the transatlantic feminist to ask what exigencies
their discourses fulfill. In what can only be a partial and ambiguous
answer, this body of work surely marks, on one level, the explosive
return of the repression of maternity in postwar feminist thought until

the late 1960s. Moreover, by exposing the suppressed mother/daughter bond, the work has served to validate and cultivate gynocentric connections and lineages. In fact, the metaphorization of the mother/daughter relation has provided an important vehicle for speaking the Lesbian relation in an enduringly homophobic hegemony. At the same time, the maternal may also satisfy conservative and fundamentalist imperatives allied with the (re)assertion of "traditional values," (more) conservative politics, even the irruption of militant religiosity. And from yet another perspective, the life-engendering, future-oriented vision of the maternal may be a compensatory response to a world imperiled by nuclear extinction. Whatever other global or partial factors may obtain,[23] the overdetermination of the maternal militates against our overcoming the conceptual impasse it represents. To displace/replace the maternal as the metaphor for female difference, and to conceive more compelling metonymic visions, may not be feasible at present, but must become the possibility of the future.[24]

There is no final analysis, no solution, nor should there be. Inevitably, however, predictably perhaps, the problematics of the maternal metaphor makes it imperative to question difference itself as the privileged construct of modernist masters. As Nancy Chodorow argues in The Future of Difference, "men have a psychological investment in difference that women do not have"; and, going further, Jessica Benjamin insists that "in theory and practice, our culture," even "Western rationality. . . knows only one form of individuality: the male stance of overdifferentiation" (14, 45–46). While those ideas are still binary-bound—but then, what idea is not?—they reinforce the possibility that difference as teleology is part of the phallocentric design. Thus they underscore the importance of deferring any affirmation of essential difference between male and female subjects bound within the same discursive order. But even that idea is not different, as Derrideans will confirm; nor is it phallogo-free. For metonymic deferral, postponement or putting off ironically represents the traditional feminine posture whenever a question of inter(dis)course arises. Nevertheless, in the present imperfect, that putting off, however offputting it may seem, is the more desirable course for diverse female explorations than excessive, tumescent metaforeplay.

NOTES

1. This study is, in some ways, a continuation of my "Language and Revolution: The Franco-American Dis-Connection," wherein I focused on the same three writers and interpreted their theories on the revolutionary force of the feminine as poetic discourse (75, 80–82). However, whereas I then urged American feminist critics to be receptive to the challenge of this body of work, the present essay, written five years after the first, expresses in much stronger terms a concern about a mystification of the feminine and, more generally, about the difficulties of getting "outside" phallogocentrism. In retrospect, I regard the two essays as complementary; they assume a different oppositional stance in response to what I perceive(d) as emerging or dominant tendencies or blindspots within American feminist criticism. An earlier version of this essay was read at the universities of Michigan and Montreal in 1982. Unless otherwise indicated, the translations are mine.

2. According to Ricoeur, for instance, "metaphorical utterance brings an unknown referential field toward language, and within the ambit of this field, the semantic aim functions and unfolds" (299). And for Lacan, metaphor represents a "crossing of the bar" of repression that allows meaning to emerge "as a poetic or creative effect" (515).

3. Discrete references to this influence appear in Féral, Makward, and Spivak, and more extensively in relation to Lacan, in Gallop's *The Daughter's Seduction*.

4. It must be emphasized that this is not a global analysis of the maternal metaphor in contemporary French women's writing, which would have to include, for example, texts by Chantal Chawaf, Marguerite Duras, Sarah Kofman, Eugénie Lemoine-Luccioni, Marcelle Marini, and Michèle Montrelay. Nor is this a global study of the work of Cixous, Irigaray, and Kristeva, but rather a symptomatic reading of some texts published in the last decade. It goes without saying that their dense and demanding texts cannot be reduced to an inscription of the maternal metaphor.

5. See also Irigaray, *Ce Sexe*, 123–25. However, as I argued in "Language and Revolution," these exponents of difference regard their work as profoundly political, or at least, as Cixous puts it, "poetically political, politically poetic" (Conley, 139ff.).

6. In *L'Oubli de l'air*, which could be entitled *L'Oubli de la mère*, the repression or forgetting of the mother is considered the foundation of the Western conception of Being.

7. Quoted in Burke, "Rethinking the Maternal," 112.

8. Opposition to the Derridean/Heideggerian view of metaphor has been voiced by Ricoeur (257–311) among others.

9. In *Histoires d'amour*, Kristeva confronts the metaphysical implications of metaphor and attempts to circumvent the problem posed by Derrida by relocating the production of metaphor to the transference between analysand and analyst and, by analogy, the transference of affect between two lovers.

10. Jacobus argues that *l'écriture au féminin* is not essentialistic, but that it is constrained by the conditions of representability (139); Berg, however, shares my concern for the essentialism of the maternal and the metaphysics of presence it sustains.

11. On catachresis, see also Derrida, "White Mythology," 57, and Ricoeur, 62ff.

12. In *With*, which implies "to be with child," the origin and telos of the feminine is conceived as a "pre-legal childhood" (67) of freedom, joy, and especially of "innocence beyond ignorance" (139), which is personified by Aura. The same pre-oedipal qualities are ascribed to the unbound, "delivered" female lover in *Le Livre de Promethea*.

13. The only female writer discussed in Kristeva's work is the seventeenth-century mystic, Jeanne Guyon (*Histoires*, 277–96). With one or two exceptions, notably in *Histoires*, Kristeva's texts deal solely with avant-garde male writers from Mallarmé to Sollers.

14. Even air, the irreducible, but forgotten, element explored in *L'Oubli de l'air* is

consistently liquefied and maternalized as "the first fluid along with blood given freely and unconditionally in the mother" (*Ethique*, 122). See also *L'Oubli*, 16, 31, 34–38, 77–78.

15. The capacity to overflow has led Irigaray and Cixous to idealize feminine hysteria, even madness (*Corps*, 82; JN, 161–68) and Kristeva to probe the abject that lacks ego boundaries (*Powers of Horror*). Moreover, an element like the mucous, which eludes both numerical order and fixity, and which "always |becomes| the fluid, merges boundaries" (*Passions*, 18) is, in Irigaray's view, imperative for "thought of or in the feminine" (*Ethique*, 107–8).

16. See the opposition between mother/night and male/day in *L'Oubli de l'air*, 50, 90, 99; see also *Passions élémentaires*, 46ff.; *Ethique*, 144–45.

17. See Abel, preface, 6.

18. It is possible that some such examination of their *modus operandi* informs the most recent texts of Cixous and Kristeva. As Conley observes, Cixous's "desire to write *with* presence"—indeed, as *Le Livre de Promethea* indicates, to depict the "real," "true" female other accurately and faithfully—may represent, notwithstanding the impossible nature of this goal, "a writing-out of a certain guilt for . . . taking the metaphoric vehicle" (124). Although Kristeva's *Histoires* upholds the idealistic conception of metaphor, her analyses of literary texts and psychoanalytic cases are not markedly metaphoric. Irigaray's *modus scribandi* has not changed, although her focus of concern in *Ethique* is the ethics of relations between the sexes founded on acceptance of sexual (maternal) difference.

19. In keeping with recent practice (e.g., Jakobson and Lacan), I take metonymy to include synecdoche, although the two were considered different tropes in traditional rhetoric (e.g., Quintilian, Ramus, Fontanier); see Bredin, 45–47. However, Schor has privileged synecdoche in elaborating what she calls a "clitoral theory" of writing (219).

20. Jakobson's often-cited polarization and characterization of the metaphoric and the metonymic have been criticized by Ricoeur (178ff.) and Ruegg among others.

21. Because of the dimensions of this body of work, I refer the reader to Hirsch's very useful review essay.

22. See Gallop's critique in "The Difference Within."

23. For instance, the timing of the maternal fixation could be related to the ticking of the biological clock for a generation of female/feminist critics who "came of age" during the last decade and, more paradoxically perhaps, to the legalization of abortion in France (1974) and America (1973).

24. I note that Cixous's *Le Livre de Promethea*, Irigaray's *Ethique*, and Kristeva's *Histoires* all privilege woman as lover in her relation to man or, in Cixous's case, to woman. Although its inscriptions do not seem nearly as rich or compelling as the maternal, this notion may signal a new departure; but only time and texts will tell.

WORKS CITED

Abel, Elizabeth, ed. *Writing and Sexual Difference*. Chicago: University of Chicago Press, 1982.

Barthes, Roland. *Writing Degree Zero*. Trans. Annette Lavers and Colin Smith. New York: Hill and Wang, 1968.

Beauvoir, Simone de. *The Second Sex*. Trans. H. M. Parshley. New York: Vintage Books, 1974.

Benjamin, Jessica. "The Bonds of Love: Rational Violence and Erotic Domination." In *The Future of Difference*. Ed. Hester Eisenstein and Alice Jardine. Boston: G. K. Hall, 1980; pp. 41–70.

Berg, Elizabeth L. "The Third Woman." *Diacritics* (Summer 1982). Special Issue: "Cherchez la femme," pp. 11–20.

Bredin, Hugh. "Metonymy." *Poetics Today* (1984), 5(1):45–58. Issue on "Metaphor and Metonymy Revisited."

Burke, Carolyn. "Rethinking the Maternal." In *The Future of Difference*. Ed. Hester Eisenstein and Alice Jardine. Boston: G. K. Hall, 1980; pp. 107–13.

Chodorow, Nancy. "Gender, Relation, and Difference in Psychoanalytic Practice." In *The Future of Difference*. Ed. Hester Eisenstein and Alice Jardine. Boston: G. K. Hall, 1980; pp. 3–19.

—— *The Reproduction of Mothering*. Berkeley: University of California Press, 1978.

Cixous, Hélène. *Illa*. Paris: Editions des Femmes, 1980.

—— *Là*. Paris: Gallimard, 1976.

—— *La Jeune Née*. Paris: Union Générale d'Editions (10/18), 1975. (JN)

—— "La Venue à l'écriture." In Cixous, Madeleine Gagnon, and Annie Leclerc. *La Venue à l'écriture*. Paris: Union Générale d'Editions (10/18), 1977; pp. 6–62. (*Venue*)

—— *Le Livre de Promethea*. Paris: Gallimard, 1983.

—— *Souffles*. Paris: Editions des femmes, 1975.

—— "The Laugh of the Medusa." Trans. Keith Cohen and Paula Cohen. *Signs: Journal of Women in Culture and Society* (Summer 1976), 1(4):875–93. (*Laugh*)

—— *Vivre l'orange*. Paris: Editions des femmes, 1979. (*Vivre*)

—— *With ou l'art de l'innocence*. Paris: Editions des femmes, 1981. (*With*)

Conley, Verena Andermatt. *Hélène Cixous: Writing in the Feminine*. Lincoln, Nebraska: University of Nebraska Press, 1984.

Derrida Jacques. "The Law of Genre." Trans. Avital Ronell. *Glyph* (1980), 7:202–32.

—— "White Mythology: Metaphor in the Text of Philosophy." Trans. F. C. T. Moore *New Literary History* (Autumn 1974), 6(1):5–74.

Féral, Josette. "The Powers of Difference." In *The Future of Difference*. Ed. Hester Eisenstein and Alice Jardine. Boston: G. K. Hall, 1980; pp. 88–94.

Fontanier, Pierre. *Les Figures du discours*. Ed. Gérard Genette. Paris: Flammarion, 1968.

Freud, Sigmund. *The Standard Edition of the Complete Psychological Works*. 25 vols. London: The Hogarth Press, 1975.

Gallop, Jane. *The Daughter's Seduction: Feminism and Psychoanalysis*. Ithaca: Cornell University Press, 1982.

—— "The Difference Within." In *Writing and Sexual Difference*. Ed. Elizabeth Abel. Chicago: University of Chicago Press, 1982; pp. 283–90.

Hirsch, Marianne. "Mothers and Daughters." *Signs: Journal of Women in Culture and Society* (Autumn 1981), 7(1):200–22.

Irigaray, Luce. *Amante marine: de Friedrich Nietzsche*. Paris: Editions de Minuit, 1980.

—— "And the One Doesn't Stir Without the Other." Trans. Hélène Vivienne Wenzel. *Signs: Journal of Women in Culture and Society* (Autumn 1981), 7(1):60–67.

—— *Ce Sexe qui n'en est pas un*. Paris: Editions de Minuit, 1977. (*Ce Sexe*; the last chapter has been translated by Carolyn Burke and will be cited as "When Our Lips Speak Together.")

—— *Ethique de la différence sexuelle*. Paris: Editions de Minuit, 1984. (*Ethique*)

—— *Le Corps-à-corps avec la mère*. Ottawa: Editions de la pleine lune, 1981. (*Corps*)

—— *L'Oubli de l'air*. Paris: Editions de Minuit, 1983.

—— *Passsions élémentaires*. Paris: Editions de Minuit, 1982.

—— *Speculum, de l'autre femme*. Paris: Editions de Minuit, 1974.

—— "When Our Lips Speak Together." Trans. Carolyn Burke. *Signs: Journal of Women in Culture and Society* (Autumn 1980), 6(1):69–79.

Jacobus, Mary. "Is There a Woman in This Text?" *New Literary History* (1982):117–41.

Jakobson, Roman. "Two Aspects of Language and Two Types of Aphasic Disturbances." In *Fundamentals of Language*. The Hague: Mouton, 1956; pp. 55–82.

Jardine, Alice. "Gynesis." *Diacritics* (Summer 1982). Special Issue: "Cherchez la femme," pp. 54–63.

—— "Prelude: The Future of Difference." In *The Future of Difference*. Ed. Hester Eisenstein and Alice Jardine. Boston: G. K. Hall, 1980; pp. xxv–xvii.

Kristeva, Julia. *Desire in Language: A Semiotic Approach to Literature and Art*. Ed. Leon Roudiez. Trans. Tom Gora, Alice Jardine, and Leon Roudiez. New York: Columbia University Press, 1980. (DL; I cite the translations from *Polylogue* included in this volume wherever possible.)

—— "Héréthique de l'amour." *Tel Quel* (Winter 1977), 74:30–49. Special Issue: "Recherches féminines." ("*Héréthique*")

—— *Histoires d'amour*. Paris: Denoël, 1983. (*Histoires*.)

—— "La Sémiotique, science critique et/ou critique de la science." In *Semeiotike: Recherches pour une sémanalyse*. Paris: Editions du Seuil, 1969; pp. 27–42.

—— *La Révolution du langage poétique*. Paris: Editions du Seuil, 1974. (*La Rév*) Pages 11–204 of this text have been translated by Margaret Waller as *Revolution in Poetic Language*. Ed. Leon Roudiez. New York: Columbia University Press, 1984. (Waller's translation will be used wherever possible and will be noted as Rev-tr.)

—— *On Chinese Women*. Trans. Anita Barros. New York: Urizen Press, 1976.

—— *Polylogue*. Paris: Editions du Seuil, 1977.

—— *Powers of Horror*. Trans. Leon Roudiez. New York: Columbia University Press, 1982.

—— "Un Nouveau Type d'intellectuel." *Tel Quel* (Winter, 1977), 74:3–8. Special Issue: "Recherches féminines." ("*Un Nouveau*")

Lacan, Jacques. *Ecrits*. Paris: Editions du Seuil, 1966.

Makward, Christiane. "To Be or Not to Be . . . A Feminist Speaker." In *The Future of Difference*. Ed. Hester Eisenstein and Alice Jardine. Boston: G. K. Hall, 1980; pp. 95–105.

Rich, Adrienne. *Of Woman Born*. New York: Norton, 1976.

Ricoeur, Paul. *The Rule of Metaphor*. Trans. Robert Czerny. Toronto: Toronto University Press, 1977.

Ruddick, Sara. "Maternal Thinking." *Feminist Studies* (Summer 1980), 6(2):342–67.

Ruegg, Maria. "Metaphor and Metonymy: The Logic of Structuralist Rhetoric." *Glyph* (1977), 6:141–57.

Schor, Naomi. "Female Paranoia: The Case for Psychoanalytic Feminist Criticism." *Yale French Studies* (1981), 62:204–19. Issue on "Feminist Readings: French Texts/American Contexts." Repr. in *Breaking the Chain: Women/Theory, and French Realist Fiction*. New York: Columbia University Press, 1985.

Spivak, Gayatri Chakravorty. "French Feminism in an International Frame." *Yale French Studies* (1981), 62:154–84. Issue on "Feminist Readings: French Texts/American Contexts."

Stanton, Domna C. "Language and Revolution: The Franco-American Dis-Connection." In *The Future of Difference*. Ed. Hester Eisenstein and Alice Jardine. Boston: G. K. Hall, 1980; pp. 73–87.

Wittig, Monique. *Les Guérillères*. Trans. David Le Vay. New York: Avon, 1973.

Tradition and the Female Talent

SANDRA M. GILBERT and SUSAN GUBAR

> Towards the end of the eighteenth century a change came about which, if I were re-writing history, I should describe more fully and think of greater importance than the Crusades or the Wars of the Roses. The middle-class woman began to write.
> —Virginia Woolf, A Room of One's Own

> In the nineteenth century men were confident, the women were not but in the twentieth century the men have no confidence.
> —Dashiell Hammett to Gertrude Stein, in Everybody's Autobiography

> The existing monuments form an ideal order among themselves, which is modified by the introduction of the new (the really new) work of art among them.
> —T.S. Eliot, "Tradition and the Individual Talent"

On December 30, 1927, Max Beerbohm wrote Virginia Woolf a strangely ambiguous fan letter. Praising her criticism for its likeness to her father's work—"if he had been a 'Georgian' and a woman, just so would he have written"—he went on quite unexpectedly to attack her fiction: "Your novels beat me—black and blue. I retire howling, aching, sore; full, moreover, of an acute sense of disgrace. I return later, I re-submit myself to the discipline. No use: I am carried out half-dead."[1] What was bothering the incomparable Max? Certainly, in the context of his admiration for The Common Reader, his somewhat paranoid association of Woolf's novels with bondage and discipline seems inexplicable, almost bizarre.

To be sure, Beerbohm goes on in the same letter to provide

an explanation of his pain which would appear to suggest that his quarrel with Leslie Stephen's daughter is part of a larger generational conflict in the world of letters. "I don't really, insidious though you are, believe in your Cambridge argument that a new spirit exacts a new method of narration," he explains, identifying himself with "Homer's and Thackeray's method, and Tolstoy's and Tom's, Dick's, and Chaucer's, Maupassant's and Harry's," all presumably methods grounded in the modes and manners of traditional realism. Thus he sets himself, as a late-Victorian man of letters, against Woolf, as a representative of Cambridge/Bloomsbury modernism. Despite this explanation, however, Beerbohm's description of the effect Woolf's novels have on him, together with his list of the Toms, Dicks, and Harrys who constitute his literary patrilineage, implies that more than a conflict of cohorts is being enacted here. Curiously enough, moreover, the rhetoric of his letter echoes a story he had published seven years earlier, a story about a literary battle not between the generations but between the sexes. Indeed, Beerbohm's image of a generational struggle masks a more profound sexual-literary struggle dramatized not only in his fiction but also in the fiction of many of his contemporaries.

"The Crime," which was included in Beerbohm's *And Even Now*, describes the acute "sense of disgrace" experienced by a nameless narrator who impetuously flings a woman writer's novel into a fireplace but cannot seem to burn the book up. Vacationing in a rented cottage in a remote county, this lonely man of letters compares himself at the outset of the story to "Lear in the hovel on the heath" (246). Idly looking for something to read, he picks up the latest novel by a well-known woman writer whom he has met and been daunted by on several occasions: "She had . . . a sisterly, brotherly way. . . . But I was conscious that my best, under her eye, was not good . . . she said for me just what I had tried to say, and proceeded to show me just why it was wrong" (247). In fact, he reminisces, his few conversations with her led him to speculate on the "'sex war'" that, "we are often told, is to be one of the features of the world's future—women demanding the right to do men's work and men refusing, resisting, counter-attacking" (248). While he claims that he himself has never had his "sense of fitness jarred; nor a spark of animosity roused" by most feminist demands, he confesses that he is disturbed by the idea of a woman practicing the art of writing. More specifically, he admits that he is bothered if a woman is "an habitual, professional author, with a passion for her art, and a fountain-pen and an agent, and sums down in advance of royalties on sales in Canada and Australia" (248–49).

But the novelist whose book Beerbohm's man of letters picks up in his country cottage is emphatically all these things and, worse still, her work, as its jacket copy suggests, is characterized by "immense and intense vitality"; her newest novel, say the critics, is "a book that will live" (247). Furthermore, when he begins reading this book, he soon discovers that the novel is itself a *Künstlerroman* about a successful woman of letters, a mother who sits "writing in a summerhouse at the end of a small garden," her pen traveling "rapidly across the foolscap" (249). It is no wonder, then, that he feels "exquisite satisfaction" when he discovers that, following "an impulse. . . almost before I was conscious of it" (250), he has committed the heinous crime of flinging his landlord's copy of this woman's book into the fire, where it stands for a moment gloriously glowing. But although at first "little tongues of bright colour" (251) leaping from the binding let him exult that "I had scored. . . perfectly" against this "Poor woman!," he soon discovers to his dismay that the text itself refuses to be burnt. Enacting a cross between a ritual rape and a sacrificial burning at the stake, this increasingly obsessed narrator "rakes" the book "fore and aft" with a poker, "carve[s]" it into sections, "subdivide[s] it, spread[s] it, redistribute[s] it" (251–52). Yet still its intense and immense vitality proclaims that "it [is] a book that will live—do what one might" (252). Finally, therefore, Beerbohm's disgraced man of letters has to concede that his female antagonist has "scored again." Not only has he been unable to destroy her book in "the yawning crimson jaws" of his hearth, her book has itself damped his flames. As his fire goes out (252), he is left alone in a small and chilly room, as dispossessed as a parodic Lear confined to the prison of his consciousness.

Beerbohm's story is, of course, a masterfully comical satire on the futile rage with which men of letters greeted female literary achievement. At the same time, however, it is also, as the author's own letter to Virginia Woolf suggests, an enactment of that futile rage. What the juxtaposition of the letter and story suggests, therefore, is that the existence of a tradition of "habitual, professional" women authors led to a battle of the sexes over the province and provenance of literature, a battle which men, rightly or wrongly, felt they were losing in the years when Beerbohm wrote.

Not surprisingly, the author of *Zuleika Dobson* (1906), that ultimate comedy of the femme fatale, was no noncombatant in the war between men and women that had been gathering force since the late nineteenth century. Always masking his masculinist anxieties with elegant irony, Beerbohm nevertheless understood the deeply dialectical relationship in which men and women found themselves by the fin de siècle, a relationship that, as Virginia Woolf herself pointed out, was historically unprecedented.

Eight years after Beerbohm wrote "The Crime," after all, Woolf observes in a passage from A *Room of One's Own* that we have used as an epigraph here that "toward the end of the eighteenth century a change came about which, if I were rewriting history, I should describe more fully and think of greater importance than the Crusades or the War of the Roses. The middle-class woman began to write" (68). Earlier, moreover, in just the year when Beerbohm wrote "The Crime," Woolf had analyzed the empowering implications of the entrance of women into literary history, noting in a letter to *The New Statesman* that "the seventeenth century produced more remarkable women than the sixteenth. The eighteenth than the seventeenth, and the nineteenth than all three put together. . . . When I compare the Duchess of New-castle with Jane Austen, the matchless Orinda with Emily Brontë, Mrs. Haywood with George Eliot, Aphra Behn with Charlotte Brontë, the advance in intellectual power seems to me not only sensible but immense" ("Response to 'Affable Hawk' "). Describing the evolution of a tradition of immense and intense vitality, Woolf's statement almost seems to gloss the dilemma Beerbohm dramatizes in "The Crime." Moreover, the implicit dialogue between Beerbohm and Woolf that we have traced here seems itself to gloss the asymmetrical response of literary men and literary women to the strong new presence of women in the literary marketplace. For, as we shall argue throughout this essay, when the middle-class woman began not only to enter the professions but specifically to enter the profession of letters, both sexes reacted with powerful but powerfully different changes in their views of the world and themselves. To begin with and most dramatically, male writers like James in America and Wilde in England could not help noticing that theirs was among the earliest generations to have female precursors. But what did it mean for such men to have to confront not only the commercial success of, say, Harriet Beecher Stowe in America and Mary Elizabeth Braddon in England, but also the cultural achievement of, say, George Eliot, Elizabeth Barrett Browning, and Charlotte Brontë in England?

As we shall show, the historical change was disquieting for them because it had several ramifications: first, because women's new autonomy smashed the Oedipal paradigm in which the mother represents a figure who is to be possessed rather than self-possessed, the change suggested, as Ann Douglas has demonstrated, a frightening feminization of culture, an emasculating engulfment by the mother; second, and perhaps even more important, because for late nineteenth- and early twentieth-century literary sons the Oedipal struggle to take the place and the possession of the father was now in some sense doomed from the start, this historical change reinforced the sense of belatedness—the anxiety about the originary power of the father—upon which, as Harold Bloom has shown, literary men had already been brooding for several centuries. What Matthew Arnold defined as "this strange disease of modern life" became a dis-ease with what James's Basil Ransom called in *The Bostonians* "a feminine, chattering, canting age" (318). At the same time, however, the very disease fostered by this unprecedented cultural crisis worked paradoxically to the advantage of many literary men. For as the richness of the (male) modernist tradition attests and as we shall argue later, for many male writers Beerbohm's futile rage became fertile rage, fueling the innovations of the avant-garde in order to ward off the onslaughts of women.

Recently, casually, and almost comically, Harold Bloom declared that "the first true breach with literary continuity will be brought about in generations to come if the burgeoning religion of Liberated Woman spreads from its clusters of enthusiasts to dominate the West. Homer will cease to be the inevitable precursor and the rhetoric and forms of our literature then may break at last from tradition" (33). Bloom seems to be speculating provisionally about some future catastrophe, yet it is possible to argue that what he describes in such ironically apocalyptic terms is an event that has already occurred. Certainly, his remarks appear to gloss a novella that the young Aldous Huxley published in the same year that Max Beerbohm published "The Crime." "The Farcical History of Richard Greenow" was the lead work in a volume with the resonantly and resolutely nihilistic title Limbo, and in keeping with such nihilism Huxley's tale traced the misadventures and growing misogyny of a literary man who lives out in his own person the living end of masculine history that Bloom describes.

Dick Greenow, the antihero of Huxley's farcical Künstlerroman, starts as a sensitive boy with a domineering younger sister named Millicent, whose dollhouse fascinates him, although, as if she had already read Ibsen, "it simply didn't interest her" (Limbo, 2) Enduring the standard late Victorian male education, first at a public school called Aesop and then at Cantaloup College, Oxford, he falls hopelessly in love at the age of sixteen with one Francis Quarles, a handsome incarnation of classical literary history who inspires him to fits of sentimental verse-writing from which he is luckily awakened by a sudden sense that he had been "suffering from anemia of the brain" (23). Later, at college, he dedicates himself to "all that [is] most intellectually distinguished" (29), but soon unnervingly discovers that he has been possessed by the spirit of a female novelist named "Pearl Bellairs," who takes over his body to write long, saccharine romances while he is asleep. "Her" first work is entitled Heartsease Fitzroy: The Story of a Young Girl and, ironically enough, its instant success helps finance his "unproductive male labours" (38). After going down from college "in a blaze of glory," therefore, Dick pragmatically continues his dual career. While he works on his New Synthetic Philosophy, Pearl indefatigably completes La Belle Dame Sans Morality and Daisy's Voyage to Cytherea, along with a series of articles "for the girls of Britain" (49). But, as Dick gradually loses his intellectual potency and becomes little Dick, Pearl (with her fanciful belle airs) increasingly manifests herself as the belle heir, a twentieth-century inheritor of the women's tradition founded by such precursors as Jane Eyre. Worse still, as his writing becomes increasingly elitist and occult, her work, inspired by his readings of George Sand, Elizabeth Barrett Browning, and Mrs. Humphrey Ward, becomes ever more powerful and popular.

The crisis of Dick's life, which seems to parody an intensified historical crisis for literary men, comes with the advent of World
War I. As he travels toward London, planning to become a conscien-
tious objector, even the wheels of the train "refus[e] to recite Milton,"
as if prophetically warning him about the demise of the cultural history
he had hoped to inherit. Finally, moreover, his experiences during the
war document that demise, for while his sister Millicent supervises
three hundred clerks at the Ministry of Munitions with "unsurpassed
efficiency" (95), Pearl writes jingoistic propaganda for the "Women of
England." Distraught about the "horrible Bluebeard's chamber of his
own brain" (67), Dick visits a psychiatrist whose word association test
elicits a response which seems to offer some solution to the mystery
of his schizophrenic seizures, for the word "woman" seems to lead
inexorably to the word "novelist" (67). Though Dick continues to stage
dramatic antiwar protests as an intellectual socialist/pacifist, therefore,
he slowly sinks into madness, with Pearl demonically possessing his
brain and pen. By the end of the war, when she is strong enough to
emerge and register to vote, he is confined as a lunatic and force-fed
the way the suffragists had been. Filled with revulsion at Pearl's pro-
liferating vulgarity, he desperately tries to will his body to science, but
even here she intervenes, wresting the pen from him and begging to
be buried "in a little country church-yard with little marble angels." In
the end, his last desperate scribblings, the fragments he has tried to
shore against his ruin, are "thrown away as being merely the written
ravings of a madman" (115).

To be sure, despite the desolation of Dick's fate, Huxley's
story is as farcical as its title indicates; like Beerbohm's it seems to
have been intended as a deliciously sardonic diversion. As Huxley
himself indicates in the text, moreover, he is creating a comedy of
doubles like Jekyll and Hyde in fiction or William Sharp and Fiona
McLeod in real life. Nevertheless, it seems significant that Richard
Greenow emerges as a prototypically modern alienated intellectual
specifically within the context of a tale depicting degrading femininity
let loose in a culture where the apocalypse Bloom described was
already taking place. For little Dick Greenow does seem to be the
apotheosis of a *poète maudit* and he seems to have become such a
figure precisely because of the excursions of his sister, Millicent, and
the incursions of her double, Pearl. At the same time, their assaults

upon his integrity seem to have been made possible by the intellectual and moral impoverishment, the historical weariness, of great male centers of learning like Aesop and Cantaloup.

That Huxley and Beerbohm were not alone in their sense of a literary apocalypse set in motion by the changing relations of the sexes to modes of literary production is further suggested by the work of Henry James. His famous "The Death of the Lion," for instance, counterpoints the ignominious demise of a truly great man of letters and the horrifying rise of two vulgarly popular literary transsexuals, while his "The Next Time" traces another male literary fall associated with a female literary rise, specifically the fall of a novelist who fails to descend to the level of what would be commercially successful in an age of "trash triumphant" (245) and the rise of a woman writer who produces voluminous bestsellers with the greatest of ease. Similarly, James's "Greville Fane" portrays the "imperturbable industry" of a woman novelist "who could invent stories by the yard but couldn't write a page of English" (155). Although James's narrator is in many ways sympathetic to this "dull kind woman" who has been, as he shows, ruthlessly exploited by her children, he condescendingly explains that he "liked her" because "she rested me so from literature," which was to him "an irritation, a torment" (154). His sense of his own "admirably absolute" failure, in other words, is set against his vision of the Ouida-like Greville Fane as "an old sausage-mill" grinding out "any poor verbal scrap that had been dropped into her" (156) and receiving lucrative rewards for such vigorous banality. In all three of these James tales, then, the male writer is rarified, marginalized, and impoverished, while the female writer, like Beerbohm's woman novelist and Huxley's Pearl Bellairs, achieves an "immense vitality" and a sinister centrality.

Historically speaking, which figure comes first, the neurasthenic man of letters or the imaginative female romancer? Does Pearl Bellairs gain her strength from Dick's weakness or is Dick weakened by her strength? Huxley's story, like James's tales, emphasizes the second of these alternatives while not discounting the first. To begin with, after all, Dick Greenow is certainly not a powerful heir of his patrilineage, but his physical fragility and mental effeminacy are matched by, say, the bovine stupidity of the supposedly powerful

Francis Quarles. Because neither of these men can be an inheritor, culture inevitably falls into the hands of Pearl and Millicent. But increasingly, as the story progresses, these two female demons of efficiency become themselves the causes of Dick's diminution. Like Beerbohm's woman writer, who says for the narrator "just what [he] had tried to say" and then proceeds "to show [him] why it [is] wrong" (247), Pearl usurps even Dick's language, as she invades "the sanctities of his private life" and tramples "on his dearest convictions, denying his faith" (62). As the novella goes on, indeed, Huxley uses the rhetoric of parasitism and vampirism to describe Pearl's insistent and untiring appropriation of Dick's body: she is "greedy for life" (71); "watching perpetually like a hungry tigress for her opportunity," she takes "possession of his conscious faculties" so that he is "lost, blotted off the register of living souls while she [performs] with intense and hideous industry, her self-appointed task" (73–74). Like Zuleika Dobson, she is a femme fatale whose voracity requires the suicide of the literary man; like those of Beerbohm's woman of letters—or, indeed, those of his Virginia Woolf—her "insidious" ways utterly destroy the male and the culture he represents; like those of James's imaginative women, her fantasies cripple man's fancy, and her "hideous industry" and "immense vitality" leave him with "an acute sense of disgrace."

Given the vampiric and parasitic qualitites of this paradigmatic literary woman, one cannot help thinking that she seems uncannily like a female prototype Thomas Hardy once created: his famous 1898 "Ivy Wife." Looking for a host to feed on, Hardy's vegetable femme fatale tries first "to love a full-boughed beech/ And be as high as he," then to give "the grasp of partnership" to a plane tree, but finally in her "affection" she strives "to coll an ash," who "in trust" receives her love. But that the ash accepts her embrace, as the other trees do not, implies, in terms of the question we have been raising here, that some secret death-wish, some ashen neurasthenia, is in fact a precondition for female triumph. And certainly the victory of the Ivy Wife is in some ways significantly analogous to the triumphs of Pearl Bellairs and her fictive sisters, for, as she tells us, "with my soft green claw/ I cramped and bound him as I wove . . . / Such was my love: ha-ha!" After all, like Pearl and the others, she is a tenaciously successful parasite, cramping her host's style with what appears to be

her virtue but is really her "hideous industry." Worse still, her exhila-
rated assertion—"Such was my love: ha-ha!"—expresses the alien
urgency of female desire, with its threat to male potency.

Perhaps more than his modernist successors, however,
Hardy feels free to imagine a punitive plot in which his Ivy Wife is
destroyed by her own aspirations.

> But in my triumph I lost sight of afterhaps. Soon he
>   Being bark-bound, flagged, snapped, fell outright,
> And in his fall felled me!

While this may in some sense by the story of Pearl Bellairs, it is
emphatically not that of Beerbohm's or James's women (and even Pearl
Bellairs will, after all, live on through her amazingly successful writing).
No doubt because Hardy still feels himself hardily embedded in the
sexual conventions of Victorian culture, he is able to annihilate his
overreaching female Faust. Yet he does also have to kill the male host
along with the female guest, and the anxious ambiguities his poem
enacts therefore point to a story he published in 1893, a story about
an "Ivy Wife" which provides a significant background to the struggles
over literary primacy that we have been tracing here.

Hardy's "An Imaginative Woman," which was included in
Life's Little Ironies, dramatizes the increasing infatuation of a would-be
poet named Ella Marchmill, who seems in her female submissiveness
like a paradigmatic *elle*, with a true poet who has the appropriate name
of Robert Trewe. The only daughter of a struggling man of letters and
the wife of a "commonplace" small-arms manufacturer, Ella publishes
what Hardy makes quite clear is second-rate verse under the pseudonym of John Ivy, and an Ivy Wife is what, metaphorically speaking,
she becomes in her relationship both to her husband and to the
fantasy lover/double into which she transforms Robert Trewe. For
though the most striking irony in this tale of one of life's little ironies
is that Ella never actually meets Trewe, she becomes obsessed with
him when she and her family rent his rooms in a seaside resort for a
month one summer. A poem of his, Ella recalls, had appeared in large
type at the top of a page in a magazine on which her own poem about
the same subject was published in small type at the bottom. He had
then assembled his poems in a volume that sold successfully, but

when she tried to follow his example her own collection had fallen "dead in a fortnight—if it had ever been alive" (9).[2] For some time, indeed, "with sad and hopeless envy Ella Marchmill had often and often scanned the rival poet's work, so much stronger as it always was than her own feeble lines. She had imitated him, and her inability to touch his level would send her into fits of despondency" (9).

No wonder, then, that when she finds herself actually inhabiting Trewe's room she feverishly studies the relics of identity he has left behind. Possessed by the Ivy Wife's passion to "be as high as he," she dons his macintosh and hat, imagining his coat as "the mantle of Elijah" and praying "would it might inspire me to rival him, glorious genius that he is!" (12). But although "His heart had beat inside that coat and *his* brain had worked under that hat," her "weakness beside him [makes] her feel quite sick" (13). Similarly, when she finds his picture secreted behind a photograph of the royal family, she studies his "striking countenance" adoringly (16) but soon confesses that "It's *you* who've so cruelly eclipsed me these many times!" (17). Finally, and most dramatically, she scans "the half-obliterated pencillings on the wall-paper" next to his bed (17), perceiving "the least of them" as "so palpitating, that is seemed as if his very breath . . . fanned her cheeks from those walls" (17). Enclosed by the ghostly traces of Trewe's script, she voraciously invokes his presence, imagining that "she was sleeping on a poet's lips, immersed in the very essence of him, permeated by his spirit as by an ether" (18). In a number of ways, then, she seems as vulnerable, passive, and secondary as the Ivy Wife. Disciple to master, student to teacher, even Danäe to Zeus, Mary to Holy Spirit, "permeated" by male authority, she appears more threatened than threat.

Yet, oddly enough, while Ella continues humbly to hope for a meeting with this deific man of letters, the distant Trewe responds with cursory civility to the letters she writes him as "John Ivy" and misses a meeting she has arranged. Trewe, it appears, has gone into a bizarre decline which we soon learn is not unrelated to his new volume of verse, *Lyrics to a Woman Unknown*, a book whose impetus is a mysterious passion for a kind of *Ferne Geliebte*, an "imaginary woman alone," for—he himself insists—"in spite of what has been said in some quarters" there is "no real woman behind the title" (26). Soon, we learn that he has actually committed suicide and that he has done so because of this "imaginary woman." On the one hand, therefore, Trewe appears to have been sapped of strength because there was no mother, sister, or female friend "tenderly devoted" to him (26); on the other hand, although he says "there is no real woman" behind the title of his newest volume, the "imaginary woman" whose absence triggers his death seems suspiciously related to the "imaginative woman" named Ella Marchmill. To make matters worse, moreover, although Ella is genuinely distraught at Trewe's demise, she soon, in what Hardy insinuates is another one of life's little ironies, gives birth to the poet's successor, a son who "by an inexplicable trick of Nature" (32) looks uncannily like this man she has never seen.

To be sure, she herself dies in labor, confessing to her husband that she has been mysteriously "possessed" (31), but in fact her production of this apparently illegitimate child suggests that she has radically subverted the very patrilineage which refused to acknowledge her poetry, for, by creating an alien heir to literary tradition, she has triumphed over both Trewe and her husband, supplanting the one and undermining the other. Like the Ivy Wife, in other words, she "nurtures a love" which "cramps[s] and bind[s]" her male hosts, even though their "fall felled" her; and like Pearl Bellairs, she leaves a legacy of chaos which dramatically expresses her sense of herself as a second-rate poet and a second-rate person. For, at least subtextually, Hardy's language implies that Ella's ambition somehow causes the sexual frustration that kills Trewe, since the reality of the fiercely "imaginative" woman annihilates the dream of the nurturing "imaginary woman." Finally, then, and most ironically, Ella does not merely destroy Trewe; more terribly, she recreates him in diminished form as an effeminately vulnerable and potentially disenfranchised child. As early as 1893, then, Hardy was brooding on the very issues that Beerbohm, Huxley, and James were more ferociously and comically to dramatize.

The prominent turn-of-the-century authors whose stories we have reviewed here were not merely paranoid, for their fictions document the astonishing rise of commerically successful women of letters throughout the middle and late nineteenth century in England and America. The prototypes of such stereotypes as Huxley's Pearl

Bellairs and James's Greville Fane were not only, after all, stellar figures like Harriet Beecher Stowe and Mary Elizabeth Braddon; they were part of what Hawthorne once called "a damned mob of scribbling women" (in Ticknor, 142), a "mob" that had begun to invade the literary marketplace with alarming success and striking visibility as early as 1855, when Hawthorne made his defensive remark, and for several reasons the first impact of this invasion was felt in America by men like Hawthorne. Cut off not only from the long history of the English fatherland but also from the literary patrilineage that, drawing on a tradition from Chaucer and Shakespeare to Milton and the Romantics, endowed the man of letters with the powers of a priest or prophet, American artists felt emasculated and thus reacted to the achievement of women more quickly and with more virulent misogyny than their British contemporaries did. Indeed, it could be said that they began to create a myth of America as a country of aggressive women; expressing such a male sense of assault and invasion, one anonymous commentator complained in 1856 that "France, England, Germany, Sweden, but most of all our own country has furnished forth an army of women in the walks of literature. . . quite to the shame of manhood" (in Habegger, 239). His feelings, moreover, are confirmed by the fact that out of 558 poems published in the 1870s by the prestigious *Atlantic Monthly*, 201 were by women. By 1896 the poet Louise Guiney felt confident enough about the poetic achievements of her sex to write that "The women over here are regular Atalantas in the poetic race" (in Walker, 201).

As for what Nina Baym has called "Woman's Fiction," and what Henry Nash Smith has defined as the scribbling woman's "cosmic success story," it is arguable that by the mid-nineteenth century in America such a genre defined and dominated the literary marketplace ("The Scribbling Woman," 47–70). Henry James, for instance, believed that "women, with their free use of leisure, were the chief consumers of novels and therefore were increasingly becoming producers of them. The feminine attitude, now disengaging itself from that of men, was in point of fact coming to be all that the novel was" (in Ziff, 275). Commenting on the same phenomenon, the critic Thomas Beer observed that "if you were a proper editor. . . you did not trifle with the Titaness and for her sake you issued tales of women, by women, for women" (*The Mauve Decade*, 31–32). No wonder, then, that Edmund Clarence Stedman characterized this period in his American literature anthology as "the woman's age" (in Walker, 117) and no wonder, either, that just a few years ago Leslie Fiedler in the *New York Times Book Review* described the nineteenth-century American "struggle of High Art and Low" as "a battle of the sexes" in which the serious male author was "condemned to neglect and poverty by a culture simultaneously commercialized and feminized." Despite the special historical and social problems with which American literary men were confronted, however, their response to this "Woman's age" provided a crucial paradigm of what was to become an equally passionate anxiety on the other side of the Atlantic. For though it can be argued that at least in England a tradition of male feminism extends from Godwin and Shelley to Mill, Meredith, Gissing, and Shaw, the very existence of such a tradition suggests the unnerving centrality of the "woman question" in nineteenth-century Britain. By the fin de siècle, moreover, even the most seemingly supportive Englishmen were as nervous about female literary power as their American precursors.

Oscar Wilde, for instance, the son of a woman poet, the editor of *Woman's World*, and the author of an apparently celebratory essay on "English Poetesses," defended himself against the threat of female autonomy by annihilating the desirous daughter of Herodias in *Salome*. Furthermore, even while praising "the really remarkable awakening of woman's song that characterizes the latter half of our century in England" (*The Artist as Critic*, 105) Wilde undercut his affirmation of English poetesses by singling out figures like "Eliza Haywood, who is immortalized by the badness of her work, and has a niche in *The Dunciad*" (107), "Mrs. Ratcliffe [sic], who introduced the romantic novel, and has consequently much to answer for" (108), and "poor L.E.L., whom Disraeli described in one of his . . . letters . . . as 'the personification of Brompton' " (108). In fact, Wilde's principal thesis is that the only great English poetess is Elizabeth Barrett Browning, with all the others being characterized essentially as versions of Ella Marchmill.

In thus defining and degrading "scribbling women" in an 1888 issue of England's *Queen*, Wilde would seem to have been doing exactly what such satirists as Bret Harte and Mark Twain had done earlier in America. Harte's "Miss Mix by Ch–l–tte Br–ntë" (1867) is a hilarious parody of *Jane Eyre* that the American humorist reinterprets as a melodramatic farce in which the smugly virtuous heroine leaves her childhood home at "Minerva Cottage" to enter the service (and the arms) of "Mr. Rawjester," the polygamous master of "Blunderbore Hall," who bears a "remarkable likeness to a gorilla." As for Twain, one of the most comical characters in his *Huckleberry Finn* (1885) is the lugubrious lyricist Emmeline Grangerford, whose 'Ode to Stephen Dowling Bots, Dec'd" is merely one of the inadvertently humorous mortuary verses that she grinds out with fatal fluency: "she could rattle off poetry like nothing," explains Huck. "She didn't ever have to stop to think" (120–21). Like Wilde's Eliza Haywood and Harte's "Ch–l–tte Br–ntë," Emmeline is "immortalized by the badness of her work" and, as we quickly discover, she was killed by her own eager vulgarity just as surely as she is buried by Twain's hilarious recounting of it, for "she pined away and did not live long" after the traumatic occasion when she "hung fire on a rhyme for [a] dead person's name, which was Whistler" (121).

To be sure, what Harte and Twain offer are apparently light-hearted caricatures, and yet the motivating force behind their comedy—as behind the comedy of Huxley and Beerbohm—is precisely the sexual anxiety experienced by writers like Poe, Hawthorne, and Melville. It is not impossible either, however, that such sexual anxiety is what drew the modernist English novelist D. H. Lawrence to write about an unlikely subject for him—namely, the masters of the so-called American Renaissance. His *Studies in Classic American Literature* was, interestingly enough, the first major critical assessment of these artists, and though he does not emphasize the point, he may well have been attracted to them by a secret sense of the parallels between their situation and his. Lamenting a world occupied by "Cock-Sure Women" and "Hen-Sure Men," Lawrence complained in "Figs" that "the year of our women has fallen over-ripe," for, demanding an equal place in the sun, "our women" have horrifyingly "bursten into self-assertion" (284). In articulating such anxieties, however, Lawrence was really speaking for his generation of literary men both in England and America. Male novelists from James to Joyce were dismayed, as Robert Adams observes, by the world's "ready acceptance of frank unashamed trash" and specifically by the way in which "lowbrows avidly devoured rhetorical romances by such as Elinor Glyn, Marie Corelli, Mrs. Henry Wood, Miss Rhoda Broughton, Mary Elizabeth Braddon, Maria Susanna Cummins and other weird sisters" (*After Joyce,* 5).

Perhaps the best example of the highbrow male modernists' disgust with the lowbrow female scribbler is Joyce's parody of Maria Cummins's *The Lamplighter* in the "Nausicaa" chapter of *Ulysses.* Writing in what he calls a "namby pamby marmalady drawersy style," he satirizes Gerty MacDowell's girls' school language, which both revolts and titillates him, for even as he attacks this vulgarly genteel virgin's sentimentality, he gets to transcribe not only her voice but the vices of one of the foremost of Hawthorne's "damned mob of scribbling women."[3] More recently, as if to summarize and clarify the feelings that fuel such satire, Nathaniel West in *Miss Lonelyhearts* helps his newspaper reporters revenge themselves against their own nihilism by letting them savor stories about lady writers with three names: "Mary Roberts Wilcox, Ella Wheeler Catheter, Ford Mary Rinehard"—"what they all needed was a good rape"—and West records the men's special pleasure in the beating of a "hard-boiled woman writer" in a bar frequented by mugs: "They got her into the back room to teach her a new word and put the boots to her. They didn't let her out for three days. On the last day they sold tickets to niggers" (13–14).

Besides being driven to such ferocious misogyny and racism by feelings of anxiety and competitiveness, however, a number of modernist male writers became as enraged by their economic dependence on women as they were troubled by women's usurpation of the marketplace. A striking characteristic of the twentieth-century avant-garde, after all, was its determinedly anticommercial cast. Perhaps there has been no circle of writers since the sixteenth century who were more dependent on private patronage; and like such sixteenth-century figures as Sidney and Spenser, Yeats, Lawrence, Joyce, and Eliot, among others, were subsidized by a series of wealthy women or publicized by a set of powerful women. Yeats, of course, was financially dependent on Lady Gregory; Lawrence was sponsored by Ottoline Morrell and Mabel Dodge Luhan; Joyce was generously helped not only by Lady Gregory but also by Harriet Weaver and Sylvia Beach;

Eliot was aided by May Sinclair and Virginia Woolf. In addition, all these men were in some sense at the mercy of entrepreneurial female editors like Harriet Monroe, Jane Heap, Margaret Anderson, Dora Marsden, and Marianne Moore. Finally, the careers of such writers were significantly furthered by female facilitators like Amy Lowell, Gertrude Stein, Natalie Barney, Peggy Guggenheim, and Bryher.

But perhaps the most daunting aspect of women's entrance into literary history was the fact that some female authors were neither scribblers nor facilitators; some, quite terrifyingly, were great artists. Like Bret Harte, who may well have been as disturbed by Charlotte Brontë's power as he was dismayed by her popularity, such men as Poe, Hawthorne, Emerson, and Higginson brooded on the charismatic creativity of Margaret Fuller while others, like Henry James and Leslie Stephen, were awed by the mysterious mastery of George Eliot, an artist who, confided James, "has a larger circumference than any woman I have ever seen" (in Haight, 417). From novels like *The Blithedale Romance*, in which Hawthorne both celebrates and castigates the potency of Margaret Fuller as Zenobia, to stories like Kipling's "The Janeites," in which a World War I regiment becomes dependent on a lifesaving code evolved from characters in Jane Austen's novels, moreover, these writers demonstrate their sense of diminishment by a surprisingly strong female literary tradition. So large does this tradition loom in male imaginations that by the end of the nineteenth century a significant number of poets and scholars actually began to redefine their ideas about a classical history that had heretofore excluded the accomplishments of women: in *The Authoress of the Odyssey*, Samuel Butler proposes that Homer may at least in one of his epics have been a pseudonym for a woman, while such diverse figures as T. W. Higginson, Swinburne, Aldington, Robert Graves, and William Carlos Williams meditate on and translate the works of Sappho, about whom Graves, in *The White Goddess*, reports one scholar remarking that "that's the trouble; she was very very good" (372).

But if these writers felt about so ghostly a precursor as Sappho that she might have been "very [threateningly] good," they were even more troubled by the competition of female contemporaries who might also be "too good." A kind of scribbling sibling rivalry is almost established between pairs like James and Wharton, Yeats and

Lady Gregory, Hemingway and Stein, Lawrence and Mansfield (or H.D.), Wells and Richardson (or West), Eliot and Woolf, Graves and Riding, Miller and Nin, and in almost every case the male half of the pair devises a variety of strategies for defusing his anxiety about the threat represented by his female counterpart. Such strategies included mythologizing women in poems to align them with dread prototypes, fictionalizing them in novels to dramatize their destructive influence, slandering them in essays and memoirs, prescribing alternative ways of being for them in many genres, and ignoring or evading their achievements in critical texts.

James, for instance, mythologizes Wharton as "the whirling one . . . the Angel of Destruction" (Wolff, 144–45), while Yeats—though he does not speak directly on the subject of Lady Gregory—displaces anxiety about female contemporaries into more general mythic statements about the woman artist. It is the dancer Loie Fuller's "dragon of air," for instance, that he remembers when he predicts the second coming of Herodias's daughters, and we are reminded that even the actress Maud Gonne's beauty "like a tightened bow" is potentially ruinous when the poet asks, "Was there a second Troy for her to burn?" (*Collected Poems*, 89). As for fictionalized portraits, Lawrence's versions of the artist as a young woman frequently emphasize her sterility as they recount the "frictional white seething" of her aesthetic as well as her sexual desire (e.g., *Women in Love*: 454–55). In *Women in Love*, Lawrence (at least in part) fictionalizes Katherine Mansfield as Gudrun, whose "nerve-brain" irony, together with her miniaturized art, suggest that her murderous rejection of Gerald is an expression of the implacable female will that manifests itself when women burst "into self-assertion," while in *Kangaroo* he even more frankly transforms H.D. into one of those "poetesses" his hero "feared and wondered over" (253).

But if Lawrence derogates Mansfield and H.D. in anxious or angry fiction, writers like Williams and Hemingway record distinctly unpleasant memories of such literary women in autobiographies and memoirs. Williams, for instance, consistently portrays H.D.—a woman toward whom he had once, admittedly, had romantic feelings—as foolish and pretentious. Similarly, but even more fiercely, Hemingway castigates his onetime mentor, Gertrude Stein, throughout A *Moveable Feast*. More generally, he vilifies the voracious mouths and wombs of literary ladies in a poem called "The Lady Poets With Footnotes":

One lady poet was a nymphomaniac and wrote for Vanity Fair.[1]
One lady poet's husband was killed in the war.[2]
One lady poet wanted her lover, but was afraid of having a baby
When she finally got married, she found she couldn't have a baby.[3]
One lady poet slept with Bill Reedy got fatter and fatter and made
half a million dollars writing bum plays.[4]
One lady poet never had enough to eat.[5]
One lady poet was big and fat and no fool.[6]

We might note that behind the misogyny of this catalog lurk Edna St. Vincent Millay, Alice Kilmer, Sara Teasdale, Zoe Atkins, Lola Ridge, and Amy Lowell (88 Poems, 77).

In poems and essays, Yeats, Lawrence, and Graves surface the imperatives that underlie such misogyny when they admonish female contemporaries and descendants to relinquish "self-assertion" and, as Yeats tells his daughter, "become a flourishing hidden tree," since for women in particular "an intellectual hatred is the worst/ So let her think opinions are accursed" (Collected Poems, 187). "The great flow of female consciousness is downward," insists Lawrence, so that "the moment woman has got man's ideals and tricks drilled into her, the moment she is competent in the manly world—there's an end of it" (Psychoanalysis and the Unconscious, 215–16). Similarly, in The White Goddess Graves claims "it is the imitation of male poetry that causes the false ring in the work of almost all women poets," declaring that "a woman who concerns herself with poetry" should either be "a Silent Muse" or should "be the Muse in a complete sense . . . and should write . . . with antique authority" (372), an authority which, by its very antiquity, seems to preclude the threat of contemporary competition.

Yet another way of precluding such a threat, however, involves the construction of a literary history that denies the reality of women writers, a gesture that returns us to the act of Blutbrüderschaft with American male precursors that Lawrence performed in Studies. But it also reminds us that the existence of a self-valorizing female tradition may have had to be more generally countered with critical ceremonies of male self-certification so that the emergence of modern male literary theoretical discourse, exemplified by canon-forming works like "Tradition and the Individual Talent," The ABC of Reading, Seven Types of Ambiguity, and The Well-Wrought Urn, could be seen as an attempt to construct "his" story of a literary history in which women play no part. It is possible, indeed, that even a seminal study like *The Great Tradition*, which seems to acknowledge the existence of a female literary past, places the texts of major figures like Austen and Eliot in a context that desexualizes and therefore defuses their power. Perhaps to men from Hawthorne to Wilde and Beerbohm to Joyce, Lawrence, and Eliot a literary landscape populated by women, whether they were scribblers, facilitators, or great artists, would have seemed like a No Man's Land, a wasted and wasting country that left them with "an acute sense of disgrace."

Perhaps, too, the acute sense of disgrace we associate with the alienation and anomie of such a waste land arises from the fact that, as much as the industrial revolution and the fall of God, the rise of the female imagination was a central problem of the twentieth-century male imagination. Because texts like *Women in Love* and *The Waste Land*, *Ulysses* and "The Second Coming" have been universalized and privileged as documents in a history of cultural crisis, the sexual anxieties they articulate have been seen mainly as metaphors of metaphysical angst. But though they do, of course, express such angst—God did, after all, disappear in the nineteenth century and the smoke of dark Satanic mills did shadow Europe—it is significant that modernist formulations of societal breakdown consistently employed imagery that was specifically sexual and, even more specifically, imagery of male impotence and female potency.

Can it be that the literary sterility described by writers like Beerbohm, Huxley, and Hardy translated itself, paradoxically enough, into fertile imagery of biological sterility, castration, and impotence in modernist delineations of such famous figures as Eliot's Fisher King, Hemingway's Jake Barnes, Faulkner's Benjy, Joyce's Leopold Bloom, and Lawrence's Clifford Chatterley? Can it be that the voracity of Yeats's "daughters of Herodias," the haunting ferocity of Stephen Daedelus's mother, the triumphant endurance of Faulkner's Dilsey or the necrophiliac potency of his Emily Grierson, the sinister wisdom of Eliot's lady of situations or his Madame Sosostris, and the virulent victories of Hemingway's Lady Brett reflect a corollary anxiety about a world in which women have "bursten into self-assertion"? As Theodore Roszak has shown, our assessment of early twentieth-century intellectual history has been skewed because critics and scholars, whether consciously or not, have massively repressed the centrality of "the woman question" in this period ("The Hard and the Soft," 88). But Virginia Woolf herself, after all, observed in 1928 that "no age can ever have been as stridently sex-conscious as our own; those innumerable books by men about women . . . are a proof of it," and she went on to speculate that "the Suffrage campaign was no doubt to blame. It must have roused in men an extraordinary desire for self assertion" (A Room of One's Own, 103). Thus, as Roszak and Woolf together imply, when we foreground women's increasingly successful struggle for autonomy in the years from, say, 1880 to 1920, we find ourselves confronting an entirely different modernism, a modernism constructed not just against the grain of Victorian male precursors, not just in the shadow of a shattered God, but as an integral part of a complex response to female precursors and contemporaries. Indeed, if Roszak and Woolf are right, we might hypothesize that a misogynistic reaction-formation against the rise of literary women became not just a theme in modernist writing but a motive for modernism.

Even the establishment of a supposedly antiestablishment avant-garde can be seen as part of this phenomenon, for the twin strategies of excavation and innovation deployed in experimental works like The Cantos, The Waste Land, and Ulysses reconstitute the patriarchal hierarchies implicit in what T. S. Eliot called in "Tradition and the Individual Talent" "the mind of Europe." More specifically, the excavation of that mind's fragments functions to recover and reinscribe the noble fatherhood of precursors from Homer to Shakespeare, while the linguistic innovation associated with the avant-garde—the use of puns, allusions, phrases in foreign languages, arcane and fractured forms—functions to occult language and limit access to meaning so that only an initiated, even priestly elite can participate in the community of high culture. To be sure, a few women like Gertrude Stein and Djuna Barnes did intermittently join in such a community, but by and large it remained (and may have been unconsciously designed as) a men's club, and therefore it is not surprising that on his first reading of The Waste Land Joyce noted that T. S. Eliot's masterpiece "ends [the] idea of poetry for ladies" (in Ellman, 510).

But how did the ladies react to such reactions? Did Woolf and her literary sisters form a women's club comparable to the male society created by Eliot and his brothers? Even more important, what did it mean for late nineteenth- and early twentieth-century women writers that they no longer needed to "look everywhere," as Elizabeth Barrett Browning did, "for grandmothers, and find none" (*The Letters*, 1:231–32). These are issues which we have begun to explore in another paper.[4] Briefly, however, our research so far suggests that women experienced the dynamics of maternal literary inheritance differently from what we might expect if we only listened to the male side of the modernist sexual dialogue. Given the anxiety expressed by figures like Beerbohm, Huxley, and (to a lesser extent) Hardy, we might suppose that they were hearing fiercely exultant female voices, voices of "immense vitality" and victory. Strangely, though, when we turn to works by female contemporaries of, say, Beerbohm, we often find that such women feel imperiled rather than empowered by what has been defined for them as "the crime" of female literary ambition. Often, too, these women experience and express an "acute sense of disgrace" at least as intense as, though very different from, Beerbohm's, and they no doubt feel such shame precisely because texts like Beerbohm's tell them to. For, as is so frequently the case in the history of sex relations, men perceive the smallest female steps toward autonomy as threatening strides that will strip them of all authority, while women respond to such anxious reaction-formations with a nervous sense of guilt and a paradoxical sense of marginalization. At the same time, however, some women do feel empowered by every advance toward cultural centrality so we suspect we shall see, as we continue to study the particular issue of male-female literary relations in the modern period, that the female half of the dialogue is considerably more complicated than the male.

Interestingly, a poem Emily Dickinson wrote some years before the issue was so dramatically confronted by artists like Woolf and Eliot seems almost to predict the modernists' dilemma. Beginning in what appears to be the voice of the Ivy Wife, Dickinson articulates exactly the female exultation that men from Hardy to Huxley dread:

> I rose—because He sank—
> I thought it would be opposite—
> But when his power dropped—
> My Soul grew straight.

Yet as she recounts the decline of her "fainting Prince," Dickinson's speaker becomes oddly anxious, even guilty, and in a desperate attempt to revive male power, she struggles to reconstruct her lover's history, telling him of "worlds I knew—/ Where Emperors grew—." Finally, the fallen man becomes a burden that she has to strain to resurrect:

> And so with Thews of Hymns—
> And sinew from within—
> And ways I knew not that I knew—till then—
> I lifted Him—
>
> *(Collected Poems, #616)*

Taken as a narrative, Dickinson's poem implies that the deconstruction of male primacy is not necessarily matched by a construction of female potency. Rather, male dis-ease is often balanced by female unease; for both sexes, the shock of the new—and specifically the new world of women's words—required shocking sociocultural redefinitions. T. S. Eliot himself may not have understood the radical implications of the relationship between tradition and the individual talent that he described in a 1919 issue of *The Egoist* (a journal, incidentally, which began its career as a suffrage periodical called *The Freewoman* and then *The New Freewoman*). But Eliot's theory that new works of art alter not only our sense of the past but also our sense of what art might *be* actually seems to articulate the sexual crisis that underlies modernism. For inevitably, the "ideal order" of patriarchal literary history was radically "modified by the introduction of the new (the really new) work of art"—and, as Woolf remarked, that "really new work" was women's work.

NOTES

This essay was researched and written with the support of the Rockefeller and Guggenheim Foundations, both of whom we wish to thank. In addition, we would like to thank Ruth Stone, Elliot Gilbert, Cara Chell, and Stephen Wolfe for helpful advice and suggestions. Finally, we are grateful to colleagues and audiences at a number of institutions where we have tested out these ideas, including Georgetown University, Northeastern University, the California Institute of Technology, Southwest Texas State University, the University of Texas at Austin, the University of Delaware, and the School for Criticism and Theory at Northwestern University.

1. Unpublished letter. We are grateful to the University of Sussex for allowing us to reprint this passage.

2. In a prefatory note, Hardy explains that "An Imaginative Woman" originally appeared in *Wessex Tales* (1888) "but was brought into this volume as being more nearly its place, turning as it does upon a trick of Nature, so to speak."

3. On Joyce's use of Maria Cummins' *The Lamplighter* (1854), see Burgess, *Joysprick* (103).

4. See our " 'Forward Into the Past': The Complex Female Affiliation Complex."

WORKS CITED

Adams, Robert Martin. *After Joyce: Studies in Fiction After Ulysses.* New York: Oxford University Press, 1977.

Arnold, Matthew. "The Scholar Gypsy." 1853.

Baym, Nina. *Woman's Fiction: A Guide to Novels by and about Women in America, 1820–1870.* Ithaca: Cornell University Press, 1978.

Beer, Thomas. *The Mauve Decade.* New York: Vintage, 1960.

Beerbohm, Max. "The Crime." In *And Even Now.* London: Heinemann, 1920.

—— Unpublished letter. University of Sussex Library.

Bloom, Harold. *A Map of Misreading.* New York: Oxford, 1975.

Browning, Elizabeth Barrett. *The Letters of Elizabeth Barrett Browning.* Ed. Frederick G. Kenyon. 2 vols. in one. New York: Macmillan, 1897.

Burgess, Anthony. *Joysprick: An Introduction to the Language of James Joyce.* New York: Harcourt, 1973.

Clemens, Samuel L. (Mark Twain). *Adventures of Huckleberry Finn.* Ed. James K. Bowen and Richard Vanderbeets. 1885; repr. Glenview, Ill: Scott, Foresman, 1970.

Dickinson, Emily. *The Collected Poems of Emily Dickinson.* Ed. Thomas Johnson. Boston: Little Brown, 1955.

Douglas, Ann. *The Femininization of American Culture.* New York: Knopf, 1977.

Ellman, Richard. *James Joyce.* New York: Oxford, 1959.

Ellman, Richard, ed. *The Artist as Critic: Critical Writings of Oscar Wilde.* Chicago: University of Chicago Press, 1982.

Eliot, T. S. "Tradition and the Individual Talent." In *Selected Essays of T. S. Eliot.* 1919; repr. New York: Harcourt, 1950.

Gilbert, Sandra M., and Gubar, Susan. " 'Forward Into the Past': The Complex Female Affiliation Complex." In *Historical Studies in Literary Criticism.* Ed. Jerome McGann. Madison: University of Wisconsin Press, 1985.

Graves, Robert. *The White Goddess: A Historical Grammar of Poetic Myth*. New York: Creative Age, 1948.

Habegger, Alfred. *Gender, Fantasy and Realism in American Literature*. New York: Columbia University Press, 1982.

Haight, Gordon S. *George Eliot: A Biography*. London: Oxford University Press, 1968.

Hardy, Thomas. "The Ivy Wife." In *The Complete Poems of Thomas Hardy*. Ed. James Gibson. New York, Macmillan, 1976.

—— *Life's Little Ironies*. 1894; repr. London: Macmillan, 1953.

Harte, Bret. "Miss Mix by Ch–l–tte Br–ntë." In *American Literature, Tradition and Innovation. vol. 2, Romantic and Realistic Writing*. Ed. Harrison T. Meserole, Walter Sutton, and Brom Weber. Lexington, Mass: D.C. Heath, 1969. Text taken from Harte, *Condensed Novels and Other Papers*. New York, 1867.

Hemingway, Ernest. "The Lady Poets With Foot Notes." In *88 Poems*, Ed. Nicholas Georgiannis. New York: Harcourt, 1979.

Huxley, Aldous. *Limbo*. New York: Doran, 1920.

James, Henry. *Stories of Writers and Artists*. Ed. F. O. Matthiessen. New York: New Directions, n.d.

Lawrence, D.H. *Psychoanalysis and the Unconscious and Fantasia of the Unconscious*. 1921–22; repr. New York: Viking, 1960.

—— *Women in Love*. 1920; repr. New York: Viking, 1960.

—— *Kangaroo*. 1923; repr. New York: Viking, 1960.

—— *The Complete Poems of D.H. Lawrence*. Ed. Vivian de Sola Pinto and Warren Roberts. New York: Viking, 1964.

Roszak, Theodore. "The Hard and the Soft." In *Masculine/Feminine: Readings in Sexual Mythology and the Liberation of Women*. Ed. Betty Roszak and Theodore Roszak. New York: Harper, 1969.

Smith, Henry Nash. "The Scribbling Woman and the Cosmic Success Story." *Critical Inquiry* (September 1974), 1:47–70.

Stein, Gertrude. *Everybody's Autobiography*. 1937; repr. New York: Vintage, 1973.

Ticknor, Caroline. *Hawthorne and His Publishers*. Boston: Houghton Mifflin, 1913.

Walker, Cheryl. *The Nightingale's Burden: Women Poets and American Culture Before 1900*. Bloomington: Indiana University Press, 1982.

West, Nathaniel. *Miss Lonelyhearts and the Day of the Locust*. New York: New Directions, 1962.

Wolff, Cynthia Griffin. *A Feast of Words: The Triumph of Edith Wharton*. New York: Oxford, 1977.

Woolf, Virginia. *A Room of One's Own*. New York: Harcourt, 1928.

—— "Response to 'Affable Hawk' (Desmond MacCarthy)." In *The New Statesman* (2 October 1920). Repr. in Virginia Woolf, *Women and Writing*. Ed. Michèle Barrett. New York: Harcourt, 1979.

Yeats, William Butler. *Collected Poems*. New York: Macmillan, 1955.

Ziff, Larzer. *The American 1890's: Life and Times of a Lost Generation*. New York: Viking, 1966.

Iconoclastic Moments: Reading the *Sonnets for Helene,* Writing the *Portuguese Letters*

ELIZABETH L. BERG

This paper is about reading and writing as iconoclastic activities, as activities that undo images of identity, of truth, of authority. The image of reading in Ronsard's *Sonnets for Helene,* and of writing in Guilleragues's *Portuguese Letters,* provide positions from which to question assumptions about the value of the literary work, in particular its value to women readers and writers.

Ronsard's love poetry is not only *about* the woman; it is also primarily addressed *to the woman.* The *Sonnets for Helene* are intended to be read by Helene and, in particular, are intended to produce a reaction in her. They are, to be precise, instruments of seduction. Ronsard insists repeatedly in the poems on the necessary inscription of poetry in reality, that is to say, on his standard that the poetic narrative must accurately represent a preexisting reality, and that it must in turn produce a modification in that reality. The truth of the poetry is thus authenticated by its certification as an accurate portrayal of reality, as well as by its efficacity in influencing the course of the events represented. Thus the poetry is judged by a double standard of representational truth (the standard of history) and of performative force (the standard of authority).[1]

In this system the woman acquires a privileged status, and a particular power as reader, since justification of the poetic narrative depends (for both standards) on her response. Only Helene's estimation of the poetry establishes the poetry as worthy of its subject matter:

If Homer chose you as fertile subject,
I can, following in his path which goes without companion,
In singing of you, honor myself, and not you, unless
It please you to admire my rough poetry.

Si pour sujet fertil Homere t'a choisie,
Je puis, suivant son train qui va sans compagnon,
Te chantant, m'honorer, & non pas toy, sinon
Qu'il te plaise estimer ma rude Poësie. (Book II, Sonnet 37)

To the extent that the world has not yet recognized Helene's worth, only Helene herself is qualified to judge whether the poetry is an accurate reflection of its subject. In I, 26, Helene appears explicitly as reader of the *Sonnets*. She is here given the chance to "speak," filling the first two stanzas with her commentary on the poetry. There in the midst of the *Sonnets*, the voice of this privileged reader/subject is called upon to express her judgment of the poems. Her response is a curiously ambiguous one, at once approving of the poetry and yet in such a way as to provoke an accusation from Ronsard that she is trying to destroy him by her treachery. Helene expresses her admiration for the poems. Yet, in expressing her approval, she at the same time undermines Ronsard's affirmation of their value by her substitution of a whole different criterion:

Walking along all alone, you said to me, Mistress,
That a song displeased you if it was sweet:
That you liked the complaints of unfortunate lovers,
Any voice that is lamentable and full of sadness.
    And for that reason, you said, when I am far from the crowd,
I choose your Sonnets which are sadder:
Since on a song which is proper to a languorous subject
My nature and love wish me to feed.
    Your words are treacherous. If you cared
About those whose heart is tearful and dying,
You would have pity on me by sympathy:
    But your prudent eye, too trickily subtle,
Cries in reciting my verses, like the crocodile,
In order to better by feigning take my life.

Nous promenant tous seuls, vous me dites, Maistresse,
Qu'un chant vous desplaisoit, s'il estoit doucereux:

Que vous aimiez les plaints des chetifs amoureux,
Toute voix lamentable, & pleine de tristesse.
   Et pource (disiez vous) quand je suis loin de presse,
Je choisis voz Sonets qui sont plus douloureux:
Puis d'un chant qui est propre au sujet langoureux,
Ma nature & Amour veulent que je me paisse.
   Voz propos sont trompeurs. Si vous aviez soucy
De ceux qui ont un coeur larmoyant & transy,
Je vous ferois pitié par une sympathie:
   Mais vostre oeil cauteleux, trop finement subtil,
Pleure en chantant mes vers, comme le Crocodil,
Pour mieux me desrober par feintise la vie. (I, 26)

Helene substitutes for the criteria of truth and power her own, much more partial, criterion of personal taste. She prefers Ronsard's sonnets not because they accurately portray a reality outside the poetry; she gives no sign of recognizing herself in the poems. Neither does she make any move to respond to the poetic pleas, which would imply her reading of them as a statement on the part of her interlocutor taking place in reality and demanding a response in reality. Ronsard's reproach is based on her indifference to (and thus her refusal to acknowledge) his real-life suffering. Instead Helene responds to the poetry as a work of fiction, requiring neither an assessment of accuracy nor a real response, but rather a judgment of pleasure. In fact, the poetry is so far removed from inscription in reality that she is able to find pleasure in the plaintive laments she has ostensibly provoked. Helene simply refuses to take the poetry personally (as well she should according to the general consensus of the critics: any woman would have done just as well, at least any woman with as evocative a name).[2]

Ronsard accuses Helene of trying to kill him by her feigning of a reaction to the poetry, thus insisting on the continuity between poetry and life and taking her response as if it were a direct response to a statement of love rather than the aesthetic judgment of a work of art. But Helene has introduced the possibility of illusion into the poetry. With no acknowledgment of the referent's existence outside the scope of the poetry, much less an assurance of the poetry's adequacy to that referent, there is no longer any certainty that the poetry has any truth at all, or any connection to an outside world existing other than in Ronsard's head. The poetry increasingly turns back on itself to question what it is describing and the grounding of its authority to do so.

Ronsard had opposed to the belief in reason as the criterion of truth, a superior truth to be found in the irrational insights of inspiration (Cave, 197). As a poet inspired by the muses as well as by love, Ronsard had claimed for himself privileged access to this transcendent truth which guaranteed the value of the poetry as a revelation of hidden truth. In the *Sonnets for Helene*, however, doubt begins to undermine Ronsard's faith in the value of these irrational insights. Critics have repeatedly pointed out the marked presence of illusion in the *Sonnets*;[3] Ronsard seems unable to convince himself that he has attained a superior truth through his love. An internal debate continues throughout the sonnet cycle over whether Ronsard's submission to love means he is being guided toward truth by a god, or deceived by a blind prankster. Images of feverish delusion, accusations of dissimulation or lies, and suggestions of folly or madness abound, ending at times in desperate justifications like, "Fooling oneself in love is not a bad thing" ("S'abuser en amour n'est pas mauvaise chose") (II, 23).

Each of the images produced to ground the authority of the poetry is seen also to undermine that authority. The conventional signs of authority are no longer trustworthy. Is the placement of Helene's room on the top floor—thus nearer the gods—a guarantee that Ronsard's mounting of the stairs is a movement toward greater perfection? Does his age guarantee wisdom or is it possible that he is only an old fool blinded by delusion? The faltering of these images reflects a crisis in the belief in inspiration as truth; Ronsard's emblems of inspiration continually betray him, revealing the possibility of illusion in what was intended to represent a transcendent truth. Terence Cave suggests that this crisis of faith in inspiration then leaves poetry with no guarantee except its intrinsic power to create, to maintain a dialogue between reality and imagination (207). Ronsard is thus thrown back all the more hopelessly on the need to create a bridge between the poetry and life through Helene's response.

Helene's refusal to respond to the poetry as a real speech act inscribed in reality, segregating it into a realm of fiction where it no longer requires a response, then sabotages the authority of the text, reducing it to a pretty game without further significance. Basically, she pops Ronsard's bubble; in treating the poems as "just literature," she eliminates the source of Ronsard's power—his promises of eternal life through the poetry lose their power of seduction. She denies the wider significance of the poetry, its transcendental value, thereby robbing the author of his power base, transforming him from the wise old poet to an old lecher trying to con young women with promises of immortality. Ronsard appears as the emperor clothed only in imagination, only in fiction. He is left standing, winded, at the top of the stairs, seeing himself as an old fool unable to keep up with this young woman and asking himself if love has made him see more clearly or if it has rather blinded him. He questions the very foundation of his identity as poet: has he all this time been writing nonsense? Is there no transcendence in literature, but only falsehood and deception—blindness, delusion, dream, madness, lies?

My students began a discussion of Baudelaire's *Le Mauvais Vitrier* the other day by asserting that were the poem a description of something that really happened they would be revolted, but if it were only a story then they were amused by it. They further elaborated that the episode was particularly valuable as a story precisely because they would not approve of it in reality, thus establishing some kind of relationship of mutual exclusion between literature and life, fiction and history. I of course rushed to the defense of my profession, protesting that literature is only of value insofar as it is read *as if* it were fact, thus lending it the seriousness of real life. I am now questioning that response.

What my students were doing was undermining Baudelaire's authority as author by removing his writing into a realm of fantasy well insulated from the real world. A writer's power resides only in the referential aspect of his or her work: only in its claim to represent and affect reality. In refusing that referential aspect, the reader disarms the text, since the text's only power over reality—its only opening onto an outside—is through a reader. By treating the *Mauvais Vitrier* as an amusing story, one neutralizes its power: Baudelaire's flowerpot can never reach my panes of glass because we don't exist in the same space. The flowerpot can only enter my world if I allow it to affect me by taking it seriously. The authority of literature is grounded in a pact between writer and reader to read the text *as if* it were real;[4] in reading the text as fiction the reader reclaims his or her power to determine the meaning and significance of the work.

One could, of course, counter with one's own version of the facts—throw one's own flowerpot, so to speak. That is not disarming the text, however; that is simply fighting back. In the end it amounts to playing Baudelaire's game, in that it is simply a mirror image of his tactic. I am looking for an exit from the endless attack and counter-attack scenario in which descriptions of reality are set against each other, each claiming to represent the truth. The appeal to an outside referent inevitably engages one once again in this battle of truths.

In ignoring Ronsard's poetic pleas—in not taking them seriously—Helene makes herself unreachable. She is not seduced over to his side, but neither is she aligned against him. It is precisely her refusal to react in any way to him, to say either yes or no, that makes her such an infuriating reader, and which introduces the specter of illusion in the poetry. She provides Ronsard with neither approval nor a position to fight against (and hopefully win over); she erects no barrier between them, but rather vanishes into the "no-man's-land" of individual preference. She undermines the confrontation by placing herself on his side, but in a different relationship.

This different relationship is that of partiality: Helene expresses a partiality for a certain type of poetry, that is to say, a personal preference with no claim to exclusivity, truth, or universality. Through this partiality, she reveals Ronsard's poetic statement as equally partial, equally rooted in personal preferences having no claim to universality. In the absence of a universal, transcendent standard, their relationship is also transformed: they are no longer in opposition, seeking to impose the universal for themselves. To the extent that their differences are not solidified into opposition, then, the partiality of their positions opens the way for exchanges, intersections, possible congruences.

One may find in the *Sonnets* an image of reading that one might call the "frivolous" model, and which I am proposing as a strategy for undermining the domination of masculine writing. "Serious" reading takes as its rules the conception of writing, and thus of reading, set down by the text. It takes literature seriously. Frivolous reading neither accepts nor rejects the image put forth by the text; instead it ignores the rules set down by the text in order to extract from it what it wants. It eliminates confrontations as well as seductions by displacing the relationship, stepping out of the reader's appointed place in order to defy fixed battlelines.

In thinking about resistance to masculine power in terms of strategies of reading, one is immediately drawn to the reverse question: what is the effect of our own writing? What is the part or value of performative force in women's fiction? We have come to take for granted the importance of women's writing as a means of introducing real change into society; are we also taking ourselves too seriously?

The *Portuguese Letters*, although probably only ostensibly written by a woman, may serve as a means of addressing questions of women's writing and identity to the extent that the feminine narrator of the texts herself reflects on these questions. I would like to use this text to address questions of the value and use of women's writing, particularly in relation to the construction of identity. In the *Portuguese Letters* one may trace the vague outline of a trajectory toward the loss, or better yet, the deconstruction of identity through the act of writing the letters. Through her interaction with the narratee, Mariane finally arrives at a dismantling of the self that frees her from the relationship the letters serve to describe.

Mariane moves back and forth in the letters between, on the one hand, an image of herself as entirely defined by her love, and, on the other hand, a total lack of identity. She continually sharpens this opposition, using the alternative of identity/nonidentity as a means of persuading her wandering lover of her unalterable dependency on him. Her accusations, and her dilemma, are centered around the word "abandonment": she has abandoned herself to him and thus finds her identity only in him, but he has abandoned her and thus leaves her without an identity. As Peggy Kamuf has shown, Mariane desires to maintain the illusion of the closed circle formed by the two lovers' silent exchange of gazes, but finds that complete reciprocity is now dispersed in writing (57). The self-image mirrored back to Mariane by her lover's eyes is lost, leaving a void. She had previously seen herself only through him: "It seemed to me that I owed you the charms and the beauty that you found in me and which you made me perceive" ("Il me semblait que je vous devais les charmes et la beauté que vous me trouviez, et dont vous me faisiez apercevoir") (176). In his absence (her abandonment), she is left with nothing in which to mirror herself.

Her attempts to deal with her solitude fluctuate between two affirmations: of her fidelity to her lover (and thus consistency in the identity he provided for her) and of the emptiness he inflicted on her in leaving. Her attempt to maintain the identity he revealed to her (gave her or imposed on her, depending on one's perspective) takes the form of hyperbolic statements of fidelity tending toward masochism. She insists on devoting her entire life to him: "I make it my honor and my religion only to love you hopelessly all my life, since I have begun to love you" ("Je ne mets plus mon honneur et ma religion qu'à vous aimer éperdument toute ma vie, puisque j'ai commencé à vous aimer") (153). This fidelity, however, can only be put in action in the act of writing the letters to him; at the moment when she finishes the letter, that identity is lost and she is plunged into uncertainty. Thus her reluctance to end letters: "Goodbye, it is harder for me to finish my letter than it was for you to leave me perhaps for forever" ("Adieu, j'ai plus de peine à finir ma lettre, que vous n'en avez eu à me quitter, peut-être, pour toujours") (167–68).

One might remark on the similarity of this remark to Mlle de Scudéry's refusal to end letters: "I never finish the letters I write by that common insistence on being all my life what I am" ("Je ne finis jamais les lettres que j'écris par cette protestation commune d'estre toute ma vie ce que je suis") (84). But whereas Scudéry flatly refuses to find out what lies beyond the end of the letters, in that other world of silence and the death of "what one is," Mariane continually wrestles with the possibility of exploring that other region. She suggests at times that she would be happy to "lose herself"—to finally be rid of what holds her in her identity: "Some remaining hope sustains me still, and I will be very content (if it must have no sequel) to lose it completely and to lose myself"—"Quelque reste d'espérance me soutient encore, et je serai bien aise (si elle ne doit avoir aucune suite) de la perdre tout à fait, et de me perdre moi-même") (166).

She questions the possibility of "surviving" her present

identity, of whether something might lie beyond the death of her present self: "What would I do, alas! without so much hate and so much love which fill my heart? Could I survive what occupies me constantly in order to lead a tranquil and languishing life? That emptiness and that insensibility cannot suit me." ("Que ferais-je, hélas! sans tant de haine et sans tant d'amour qui remplissent mon coeur? Pourrais-je survivre à ce qui m'occupe incessamment, pour mener une vie tranquille et languissante? Ce vide et cette insensibilité ne peuvent me convenir") (163). What she perceives as lying beyond her present self is loss of identity, "emptiness," "insensibility," "tranquillity," elsewhere she will call it "uncertainty." At stake in her attachment to her lover is a question of self-preservation—"that common insistence on remaining all one's life what one is." The question she asks—whether she could "survive," having lost the object, or the passion, that occupies her entire self and which is the unique source of her self-definition— is a question of what lies beyond identity, what one is in the absence of a self-image, whether one can live without a self-image.

The fifth (and last) letter indicates this emptiness as what lies beyond the closing of the correspondence. Her lover's "indifference" has become apparent from his coldly polite response to her letters. The indifference displayed in his letter destroys the mirroring function he had served; the letter no longer gives back any image to Mariane. It shows no "movement in his heart" but only the unreadable indifference of friendliness and politeness. His indifference is a function of her indifference—her lack of delineation—in his mind. One might go a step further and suggest that what the letter shows her is precisely a vision of herself *as* uncertainty, as a confused image, as undifferentiated in the mind or heart of the only person whose perception matters, the only source of images.

Mariane embraces this vision of herself as uncertainty, insisting that her lover make no further attempt to communicate with her in order that there be no risk of this hazy image being disturbed by some hint of a reaction to her final letter. She asks to be allowed to remain in her uncertainty: "Do not take me from my uncertainty: I hope that I will make something tranquil of it with time" ("Ne m'ôtez point de mon incertitude: j'espère que j'en ferai, avec le temps, quelque chose de tranquille") (171). It is not another identity that Mariane projects in her last letter; it is rather an exploration of herself in her complexity, beyond the simple certainty of her identity as lover. She will adopt uncertainty as her "image" (or nonimage) of herself, as a representation of the complex play of oppositions and partial definitions that constitute the self. Thus she sends back to him all of his letters except the last two (the polite ones), which she promises to reread often in order not to "fall back into [her] weaknesses" ("retomber dans [ses] faiblesses"). She retains only the blank mirror, a denial of the deluding self-image she had previously clung to in her weakness.

Mariane ends the correspondence with a question about writing: "Am I obliged to give you an exact account of all my various movements?" ("Suis-je obligée de vous rendre un compte exact de tous mes divers mouvements?") (177). If we decide to read this as a real question, it may become useful in elaborating the question of women's writing. How can we attempt to answer this question of the obligation to render an account of oneself? Earlier in the letter Mariane had contrasted her situation with that of a married mistress in order to show the preferability of nuns as mistresses. Speaking of the difficulty for the lover of knowing for sure that a married mistress truly takes no pleasure from her husband, she comments. "Oh! they must be wary of a lover who does not make them render an exact account on that subject" ("Ah! qu'elles doivent se défier d'un amant qui ne leur fait pas rendre un compte bien exact là-dessus") (173). Here rendering an account of oneself is necessary as a means of reassuring the lover of his exclusive claim on his mistress's affections, if not her body. In this context, Mariane might be understood at the end simply as stating (or perhaps asking) once again that the relationship is ended and there is no longer any need for giving accounts of her feelings to her lover.

On the other hand, one might read her final sentence as asking a much more disturbing question: what is the status of writing in the state of "tranquillity" which Mariane promises herself? The problem the married mistresses address in their writing is one of identity. They need to put their identity into writing because their identity is double: they are both wife and mistress and must define the claims of each, resolving ambivalent emotions into a fixed division. The exact account here serves to determine a division, to resolve ambiguity into a manageable opposition. Mariane questions whether this exact account is either feasible or desirable in her "uncertainty." Given that she has no self-image except that of uncertainty, is it possible to put this uncertainty into writing? Unlike the married mistresses, Mariane has no simple identity (or even a double identity) to give an account of. Her diversity cannot be resumed by any image, nor divided into its constituent parts.

To the extent that giving an account of oneself implies some necessity of reducing uncertainty to an image or a representation such that it may be fitted into an "exact account," it is legitimate and even necessary to question in general this obligation of self-representation. Where does the obligation to produce this image come from? Does it reflect a desire to reveal women in their own terms, thus rectifying an imbalance in the great bulk of literature, or does it rather reflect a desire to enclose women's "uncertainty" in an image or account of woman as only the specular reflection of man, thus serving to perpetuate the system in which all that is visible is masculine? (Irigaray, 203–17). One might ask: in whose service are institutions such as women's studies programs, or conferences on the poetics of gender? Does the representation of woman eventually benefit women, or does it inevitably serve only to limit their possibilites by circumscribing their identity within rigid limits, in particular, by reducing identity to one facet of the self, one's sexual identity? To some extent the feminist emphasis on sexual identity as being of primary importance in the determination of the individual only perpetuates—and perhaps even deepens—the phallogocentric repression of women by once again defining women only in relation to men (that is, by their sexual identity). This emphasis on sexual identity only reduces the multiplicity of their identifications, the complexity of their insertion in the signifying system, and thus the fundamental *uncertainty* of their position, which is never one simply of sexual oppression, but rather a much more complicated and more uncertain configuration of relations. It has been part of the repression of women to be reduced to being always women first, exclusive of whatever else they may be. Here I refer you to Laurie Anderson's "Let $X = X/IT$ Tango," where the man's way of not hearing anything the woman says is through his refrain,

"Isn't it just like a woman?" The question that remains at the end of the *Portuguese Letters* is whether it would be possible to envisage a kind of writing that does not reduce uncertainty to a univocal image, that does not determine a simple identity, that does not define women in relation to men.

We have looked at two texts: one by a man addressed to a woman and one by a woman addressed to a man. These two texts may be seen as mirror images of each other, each depicting an indifferent reader confronted with an attempted written seduction. The lover's reading of Mariane's letters is essentially the same as Helene's reading of Ronsard's poems. Each undermines the power of the text simply by reading it as fiction, by not taking it seriously, by displaying their indifference to what is being said. Each provokes a crisis in the writer's construction of identity and eventually the termination of the writing project. What role does the difference in gender then play in these two readings or writings?

The only difference I can see concerns what one might call the "aftertext"—the perspective envisaged beyond the termination of the writing. While Ronsard ends with a reference to the death of the King, an image of loss that seems to sum up the whole experience recounted in the *Sonnets*, Mariane (at least partially) looks forward to a new "tranquillity" which she will construct out of her newfound nonidentity. What for Ronsard was pure loss is the basis of a different existence for Mariane.

Should I conclude by claiming that women have a superior adaptive capacity? Or that multiplicity, fluidity, lack of identity define the feminine? That women are more accustomed to indifferent readers and therefore cope better? It is tempting, but let me resist, for this one iconoclastic moment, defining an opposition based on gender that would reinstate a sexual hierarchy—even a reversed hierarchy. I will say only that these two writers have somewhat different (and also somewhat similar) reactions to the loss of identity provoked by indifferent readers. The more important consequence of what I have been doing here concerns the possibilities arising from this dissolution of identity (including sexual identity).

A writing project based on identity sets up one of two

possible relationships to the reader: one of seduction or one of confrontation. That is, the reader may accept what is set down by the writer and be seduced (or persuaded) over to the writer's side, or else the reader may refuse the writer's determination and set himself up in opposition to the text. In either case, the relationship is one of specularity, where the reader can only mirror the writer, either in direct or inversed image. In eliminating identity from this relationship, in refusing the unitary, coherent determination of positions, instead allowing contradictions, partial meanings, inconsistencies, qualified agreements, etc., to remain, one may make possible a relationship between writer and reader (or between text and reader) based on congruences, intersections, encounters. Sexual identity, like any other identity, then becomes a temporary configuration, structuring a particular relationship. It is a partial identity constructed of heterogeneous elements and having meaning only within a particular context, which determines that identity and is in turn determined by it. Only in exploring sexual identity as a configuration of elements, as a construction within a particular context and taking place in response to a defined situation, can one hope to escape the binary opposition that maintains the oppression of women. It is the double move of reifying a diversity of traits into a determination as masculine or feminine, and then essentializing that determination, that holds one in the hierarchy of the sexes.

Finally, in the context of this encounter as feminists, it is important to insist on the partial nature of sexual identity, to remind oneself that gender is not the only difference among people, nor even the essential difference, that the move to privilege gender as the primary defining characteristic of people participates in the same logic of oppression as the masculine philosophy one criticizes, for by that gesture one subsumes what is different from oneself (a different color, a different class, a different sexual orientation, a different belief) into a universal that denies that other even as it pretends to represent it. Feminism, if it is to escape the phallocentric, or egocentric, appropriation of all representation, must be partial; more than that, it must be a continual reminder that there is nothing impartial.

NOTES

1. One might discern here a hesitation around the proper grounding of a concept of fiction that Graham Castor has described in terms of the historical transition from grounding in a concept of truth to grounding in a concept of fiction and the *vraisemblable*. *Plêïade Poetics*, 114–25.

2. See, for example, Desonay (3:241–50).

3. See, for instance, Graham Castor, "The Theme of Illusion in Ronsard's *Sonets pour Hélène* and in the Variants of the 1552 *Amours*."

4. One might extend this idea to the analysis of power outside literature. It is not only fiction that requires the reader's "suspension of disbelief" to have an effect; in this respect, the discourse of authority (or power) is itself a narrative subject to these same considerations. See Louis Marin (117–43).

WORKS CITED

Anderson, Laurie. *Big Science*. Warner Bros, BSK 3674, 1982.

Castor, Graham. *Plêïade Poetics: A Study on Sixteenth-Century Thought and Terminology*. Cambridge: Cambridge University Press, 1964.

—— "The Theme of Illusion in Ronsard's *Sonets pour Hélène* and in the Variants of the 1552 *Amours*." *Forum for Modern Language Studies* (1971), 7:361–73.

Cave, Terence. "Ronsard's Mythological Universe." In *Ronsard the Poet*. Ed. Terence Cave. London: Methuen, 1973.

Desonay, Fernand. *Ronsard: Poète de l'amour*. 3 vols. Brussels: Ducelot, 1959.

Guilleragues, Gabriel de Lavergne, vicomte de. *Lettres portugaises*. Ed. Frédéric Deloffre and Jacques Rougeot. Geneva: Droz, 1972. All translations are mine.

Irigaray, Luce. "Quand nos lèvres se parlent." In *Ce Sexe qui n'en est pas un*. Paris: Editions de Minuit, 1977.

Kamuf, Peggy. *Fictions of Feminine Desire*. Lincoln and London: University of Nebraska Press, 1982.

Marin, Louis. *Le Récit est un piège*. Paris: Editions de Minuit, 1978.

Ronsard, Pierre de. *Les Amours*. Ed. H. and C. Weber. Paris: Garnier, 1963. "Sonets pour Hélène." All translations are mine.

Scudéry, Madeleine de. *Choix de conversations*. Ed. Phillip J. Wolfe. Ravenna: Longo, 1977.

Piecing and Writing

ELAINE SHOWALTER

Can you read it? Do you understand?
By squares, by inches, you are drawn in.
Your fingers read it like Braille.
History, their days, the quick deft fingers,
Their lives recorded in cloth.
A universe here, stitched to perfection.
You must be the child-witness,
You are the only survivor.
        —Joyce Carol Oates, "Celestial Timepiece" (1980)

As one of the critics from an English department to have invaded the hitherto French space of the poetics conference, I am faced with some special anxieties. I am going to look at the development of women's writing within a framework that is both historical and American—a critical position that may make me about as authentic in the Maison Française as a Pepperidge Farm croissant. But my purpose is in fact to ask about the difference of American women's writing, and less directly, about the difference of American feminist criticism, through the use of a downhome, downright Yankee historical approach which I hope will fit Alice Jardine's view of "American contextual feminism" and Susan Suleiman's definition of "thematic reading." If we move away from some of the universal, even global, constructs of psychoanalytical feminist criticism to consider American women's writing, will we find a literature of *our* own, and an American poetics of gender? Do we need to develop new forms of inquiry in order to account for a female tradition which is also multiracial? Does the special configuration of women's culture in the United States, the intimate world of female kinships, friendships, and rituals which has been so brilliantly studied by historians such as Gerda Lerner, Nancy Cott, and Carroll Smith-Rosenberg, suggest a special context for American feminist literary history?

Specifically, I want to ask whether the strongly marked American women's tradition of piecing, patchwork, and quilting has consequences for the structures, genres, themes, and meanings of American women's writing in the nineteenth and twentieth centuries. Here some quick definitions may be in order. "Piecing" means the sewing together of small fragments of fabric cut into geometric shapes, so that they form a pattern. The design unit is called the block or patch; "patchwork" is the joining of these design units into an overall design. The assembled patches are then attached to a heavy backing with either simple or elaborate stitches in the process called quilting. Thus the process of making a patchwork quilt involves three separate stages of artistic composition, with analogies to language use first on the level of the sentence, then in terms of the structure of a story or novel, and finally the images, motifs, or symbols—the "figure in the carpet"—that unify a fictional work.

While piecing, patchwork, and quilting have a long tradition in Europe, they became identified as specifically American feminine art forms in the nineteenth century. Quilting was an economic necessity in a society where readymade bedding could not be easily obtained before the 1890s, and where in the cold New England or prairie winter each family member might need five quilts. Nineteenth-century American women's autobiographies "frequently begin with a childhood memory of learning patchwork from a mother or grandmother" (Hedges, 295). Moreover, early art, writing, and mathematical exercises taught to little girls emphasized geometric principles of organization, and such lessons were applied practically to the design of quilts: "Obsessive repetition of the same small block pattern comprised the entire quilt, which was in essence a grid system, an emphasis on structure and organization" (Dewhurst et al., 139). Often, a little girl was encouraged to finish a small quilt in time for a fifth birthday, and the event was celebrated by a quilting bee; indeed, the making of textiles occasioned many of "the sanctioned social events of a young girl's life" (Dewhurst et al., 9; Hedges, 295–96). An American girl aspired to have a dozen quilts in her dower chest by the time she was engaged; the thirteenth quilt of the trousseau was the Bridal Quilt, made of the most expensive materials the family could afford, and assembled at a special quilting bee.[1]

Quilting was an art that crossed racial, regional, and class boundaries, produced by slave women in the south as well as by pioneer housewives on the trek west and by New England matrons in their homes. Alice Walker has suggested that the quilt was indeed a major form of creative expression for black women in this country. "In the Smithsonian Institution in Washington, D.C.," she writes,

there hangs a quilt unlike another in the world. In fanciful, inspired, and yet simple and identifiable figures, it portrays the story of the Crucifixion. . . . Though it follows no known pattern of quiltmaking, and though it is made of bits and pieces of worthless rags, it is obviously the work of a person of powerful imagination and deep spiritual feeling. Below this quilt I saw a note that says it was made by "an anonymous Black woman in Alabama a hundred years ago. (239)

The discourse of American quilting drew upon designs from African and from Native American culture, and from the nonrepresentational Amish and Mennonite traditions. Furthermore, the social institutions of quilting, such as quilting bees, figure in American women's history, as places where women came together to exchange information, learn new skills, and discuss political issues; it was at a church quilting bee in Cleveland, for example, that Susan B. Anthony gave her first speech on women's suffrage.

For at least the past decade, too, metaphors of pen and needle have been pervasive in feminist poetics and in a revived women's culture in the United States. The repertoire of the Victorian lady who could knit, net, knot, and tat, has become that of the feminist critic, in whose theoretical writing metaphors of text and textile, thread and theme, weaver and web, abound. The Spinster who spins stories, Ariadne and her labyrinthine thread, Penelope who weaves and un-weaves her theoretical tapestry in the halls of Ithaca or New Haven, are the feminist culture heroines of the critical age. Furthermore, metaphors of the female web of relationship have taken on positive associations with feminist psychology; as Carol Gilligan observes, "Women's place in man's life cycle has been that of nurturer, caretaker, and helpmate, the weaver of those networks of relationships on which she in turn relies" (17).

These theoretical images have material counterparts in the revival of feminine crafts which were despised in the early days of the women's movement but have been brought back into fashion under the auspices of a new women's culture, celebrated by such feminist art events as Judy Chicago's "The Dinner Party." The historical moment of transition, for me, was made vivid in 1980, when, at a scholarly conference in honor of the George Eliot centennial, Germaine Greer made a majestic entrance into the auditorium and withdrew a large roll of knitting from her briefcase. If, with her needles clicking loudly as the men read their papers, she hinted less of Mrs. Ramsay than of Madame Defarge, nonetheless her presence signaled a return of the repressed, a hint perhaps that, when in the early 1960s my Bryn Mawr classmates and I knitted as well as noted in lecture after lecture on the male literary classics, we were protesting against patriarchal culture in a secret women's language we used even if we did not fully understand it.

The patchwork quilt has become one of the most central images in this new feminist lexicon. As the art critic Lucy Lippard explains, "Since the new wave of feminist art began around 1970, the quilt has become the prime visual metaphor for women's lives, for women's culture. In properly prim grids or rebelliously 'crazy' fields, it incorporates Spider Woman's web, political networking, and the collage aesthetic" (32). The history of quilting is closely associated with the recording of American female experience; as one historian notes, women "were stitching together the history of the country, making the great American tapestry" (Cooper and Buferd, 18). Feminist poetry of the 1970s also celebrates the quilt as a female art of nurturance and sisterhood. In Marge Piercy's "Looking at Quilts," it is "art without frames," covering "the bed where the body knit/ to self and other and the/ dark wool of dreams" (35–36). In advertising, fashion, and the media, too, the quilt motif has been borrowed as an icon of feminist chic, from the short-lived Broadway musical "The Quilters," which opened and closed in fall 1984, to the designs for Ralph Lauren sweaters and Perry Ellis skirts.

Piecing and patchwork have also been widely discussed as models for a female aesthetic. As Patricia Mainardi explains,

because quiltmaking is so indisputably women's art, many of the issues women artists are attempting to clarify now—questions of feminine sensibility, of originality and tradition, of individuality versus collectivity, of content and values in art—can be illuminated by a study of this art form, its relation to the lives of the artists, and how it has been dealt with in art history. (36)

Among the leading feminist theoreticians of quilting is the Bulgarian artist and quiltmaker Radka Donnell-Vogt, who has written about piecing as a way of rethinking the maternal.[2] Donnell-Vogt views quilting as a primal women's art form, related to touch and texture, to the intimacy of the bed and the home, and to issues of sexuality. She believes that the basic quilt patterns are archetypal representations of the female body. In her own art, Donnell-Vogt explains, quiltmaking

was essential in giving me a base for exploring my situation as a woman and as an artist. . . quilts became for me a reconfirmation and restatement of women's toils in child-raising, of the physical labor in the cultural shaping and maintenance of persons. . . . Finally, I saw quilts as the bliss and the threat of the womb made visible, spread out as a separate object shaped by the imaginative wealth of women's work and body experience. (49–50)[3]

Insofar as she deals with piecing as jouissance, with quilting as an art expressive of the preverbal semiotic phase of mother-child bonding, with the aesthetic possibilities of the pre-Oedipal phase, and with the cultural significance of *écriture couverture*, Donnell-Vogt can be called the Kristeva of quilting, the Other Bulgarian.

In literary theories of a Female Aesthetic, the metaphor of piecing has been used as a model for the organization of language in the wild zone of the woman's text. According to Rachel Blau DuPlessis, a pure women's writing would be "nonhierarchic. . . breaking hierarchical structures, making an even display of elements over the surface with no climactic place or moment, having the materials organized into many centers." In the "verbal quilt" of the feminist text, there is "no subordination, no ranking" (274).

My approach to the poetics of gender in piecing and writing, however, will be through history, genre, and theme, rather than through a model of a female aesthetic, on the one hand, or a structuralist analysis of textual units, codes, sequences, and narrative functions, on the other. I would like to suggest that a knowledge of piecing, the technique of assembling fragments into an intricate and ingenious design, can provide the contexts in which we can interpret and understand the forms, meanings, and narrative traditions of American women's writing. But in order to understand the relationship between piecing and American women's writing, we must also deromanticize the art of the quilt, situate it in its historical contexts, and discard many of the sentimental stereotypes of an idealized, sisterly, and nonhierarchic women's culture that cling to it. We must then consider nineteenth-century women's writing with a similar detachment, avoiding a binary system in which we contrast women's art to male "high art" in an alternative vocabulary of anonymity, artlessness, privacy, and collaboration.

Piecing and quilting were not anonymous arts, although the names and identities of quiltmakers have frequently been suppressed by contemporary art history and museum curatorship. As Mainardi has pointed out, "the women who made quilts knew and valued what they were doing: frequently quilts were signed and dated by the maker, listed in her will with specific instructions as to who should inherit them, and treated with all the care that a fine piece of art deserves" (37). In addition, the myth of the quilting bee as the model of "an essentially nonhierarchical organization" (de Bretteville, 117–18) and as the place where women all collaborated on the making of a quilt comes from the cultural belief that women lack individuality, creativity, and initiative. In reality, expert needlewomen were invited to quilting bees to help the designer stitch her original pieced material to a heavy backing. Finally, the substitution of the term "pattern" for "design" in discussions of patchwork obscures the degree of intentionality and innovation possible within the form, and minimizes the autonomy and individuality of the artist. Piecing was not simply a repetitious and unoriginal recombining of design elements, but a creative manipulation of conventions. Even when working with such well-known patterns as the Star, Sun, or Rose, "the quilt artist exploited the design possibilities through her color relationships, value contrasts, and inventive variations on the original pattern" (Dewhurst, 48; Parker and Pollock, 71).

The relationship between piecing and writing has not been static, but has changed from one generation to another, along with changes in American women's culture. In antebellum American women's writing, piecing appears as a marker of female difference from the patriarchal literary tradition. The quilt is a moral artifact, an emblem of the deliberate ordering of women's separate cultural lives as well as fictions, and of the writer's control over her materials. After the Civil War, as women writers had to redefine themselves as artists working within two sexual and cultural traditions, the meaning of the quilt motif changed as well. Allusions to the structure and design of the pieces become more explicitly related to narrative problems and to the decline of a female aesthetic. And in contemporary writing, when quilts have been raised to the level of high art within a commodity market, and when a generation of feminists have returned to the past to reclaim a female heritage and its practices, the quilt stands for a vanished past experience to which we have a troubled and ambivalent cultural relationship.

Yet there are also significant historical continuities between these phases. As a twentieth-century quilter explains, piecing is an art of scarcity, ingenuity, conservation, and order: "You're given just so much to work with in a life and you have to do the best you can with what you got. That's what piecing is. The materials is passed on to you or is all you can afford to buy . . . that's just what's given to you. Your fate. But the way you put them together is your business. You can put them in any order you like. Piecing is orderly" (Cooper and Buferd, 20).

Furthermore, piecing is the art form which best reflects the fragmentation of women's time, the dailiness and repetitiveness of women's work. As Lucy Lippard observes, "the mixing and matching of fragments is the product of the interrupted life.... What is popularly seen as 'repetitive', 'obsessive', and 'compulsive' in women's art is in fact a necessity for those whose time comes in small squares" (32). I will be arguing that because of the structures and traditions of women's time, the dominant genre of American women's writing has been the short story, the short narrative piece. As the novel became the dominant genre of nineteenth-century American writing, women adapted the techniques of literary piecing to the structural and temporal demands of the new literary mode.

The women's novels which flourished before the Civil War have always been an anomalous form for literary history. Sometimes called sentimental, sometimes called domestic, and most recently named "woman's fiction," they do not seem to fit either the patterns of English women's novels, or the patterns of the American "romance." American women writers in fact did not self-consciously situate themselves in either artistic tradition. As Nina Baym has explained, "they saw themselves not as 'artists' but as professional writers with work to do": "The literary women conceptualized authorship as a profession rather than a calling, as work and not art. Women authors tended not to think of themselves as artists or justify themselves in the language of art until the 1870s   Often the women deliberately and even proudly disavowed membership in an artistic fraternity." Thus in their work, "the dimensions of formal self-consciousness, attachment to or quarrel with a grand tradition, aesthetic seriousness, all are missing" (32). Instead they wrote highly conventionalized novels, which, as Baym points out, all are variations on a single overplot: "the story of a young girl who is deprived of the supports she had . . . depended on to sustain her throughout life and is faced with the necessity of winning her own way in the world." In this system, like quiltmakers, "individual authors are distinguished from one another largely by the plot elements they select from the common repertory and by the varieties of setting and incident with which they embellish the basic tale" (11–12). As in piecing, in the hands of an imaginative writer, women's novels based upon conventional designs could achieve true artistic stature and power.

Before 1850, the standard genre of women's writing was the sketch or piece written for ladies' magazines or albums. While the sustained effort of a novel might be impossible for a woman whose day was shattered by constant interruption, the short narrative piece, quickly imagined and written, and usually based on a single idea,

could be more easily completed. When, in the 1850s, the "book became
the predominant mode of literary packaging, established authors such
as Harriet Beecher Stowe and Fanny Fern first gathered their sketches
into volumes with such titles as 'Fern Leaves from Fanny's Portfolio' "
(32). During the same period album quilts, the most prized and expensive examples of American quilt art, were a standard genre of
female craft. (See figure 1.) Album quilts are composed of pieced or
appliquéd squares "that are entirely different, even if their construction
has been carefully planned and orchestrated by a single quilter. The
effect is as if each square were a page in a remembrance book" (Pilling,
72).[4] They were made to be presented to young men on their 21st
birthdays (known as Liberty quilts), or exchanged among women
friends (Medley, Friendship, or Engagement quilts), and were signed
square by square. These squares, like the sketches in a literary album,
reflected the fragmentation of women's time.

       A number of nineteenth-century women's texts discuss
the problem of reading a quilt, of deciphering the language of piecing.
Most of these women's texts suggest that the language or meaning of
the quilt, its special symbolism, resides in the individual piece, the
fragment that recalls a costume and a memory. In "The Patchwork
Quilt," an anonymous essay by a factory girl printed in the Lowell Offering
in 1845, the author's quilt is described as "a bound volume of hieroglyphics." But only a certain kind of reader can decipher these female
signifiers. To the "uninterested observer," the narrator declares, it looks
like a "miscellaneous collection of odd bits and ends," but to me "it is
a precious reliquary of past treasure." The quilt's pieces, taken from
the writer's chilhood calico gowns, her dancing school dress, her fash-
ionable young ladies' gowns, her mother's mourning dress, her brother's
vest, are an album of the female life cycle from birth to death. Its
unmarried creator, a self-styled old maid aunt, recalls learning to piece
as part of that initiation into pain and blood that is recorded as part
of female destiny in texts from Sleeping Beauty to Helene Deutsch:
"O what a heroine was I in driving the stitches! What a martyr under
the pricks and inflictions of the needle. . . those were my first lessons
in heroism and fortitude." There is the record of "patchwork hopes," the
piecing done in the expectation of marriage. And there is the era in
the "history of my quilt" when it was given instead to the younger but

Figure 1. Baltimore album quilt, 1852; maker unknown.
(Courtesy America Hurrah Antiques, New York City)

married sister: "Yes, she was to be married and I not spoken for! She was to be taken, and I left. I gave her the patchwork. It seemed like a transference of girlish hopes and aspirations, or rather a finale to them all. Girlhood had gone and I was a woman" (150–54). Finally the quilt serves the sister on her deathbed after childbirth, and is stained by her blood; the woman artist survives to record this history through the hieroglyphics of the quilt.

Nineteenth-century women writers also drew attention to the way in which pieces were put together, as a moral allegory of the inventive and resourceful composition of a life. It was a quilter's truism that no two women would make the same design out of a given set of pieces. As "Aunt Jane of Kentucky," a character in the stories of Eliza Calvert Hall, comments, "How much piecing a quilt is like living a life! You can give the same pieces to two persons, and one will make a 'nine-patch' and one will make a 'wild-goose chase'. . . . And that is jest the way with livin' " (in Dewhurst, 138).

Louisa May Alcott's children's story, "Patty's Patchwork," combines a discussion of the emotional significance of the piece with a moralized account of the aesthetics of piecing and writing.[5] Ten-year-old Patty, visiting her Aunt Pen while her mother has a new baby, grows impatient with her patchwork, and flings the pieces into the air, declaring that "something dreadful ought to be done to the woman who invented it." But Aunt Pen has a different point of view. The quilt, she explains, is a "calico diary," a record of a female life composed of "bright and dark bits . . . put together so that the whole is neat, pretty, and useful." As a project, Patty sets out to make a "moral bed-quilt" for her aunt to read and decipher, while she herself is learning to become a "nice little comforter," the epitome of female patience, perseverance, good nature, and industry. When the infant sister dies, Patty nonetheless goes on to finish the quilt, which Aunt Pen not only reads and interprets as a journal of her psychological maturity, but also inscribes—that is, writes upon—with verses and drawings that become a textual criticism of both the work and the life. Aunt Pen is obviously a figure for Alcott herself, the woman writer, who is not the mother with the dead child, but who instead offers an alternative model of female power and creativity. While the discipline of the pieced quilt itself represents women's confinement within the grid of nineteenth-century feminine domestic morality, it also offers the potential creative freedom of textuality and design.

Like Alcott's, many stories about piecing, patchwork, and quilting use as their central figure a woman who is not a mother or a sister, but a maiden aunt, the creative female figure who is of the mother's generation but is not bound by the laws of reproduction. In the American tradition, it seems to be aunts who have organized the cultural activity of quilting, such as Aunt Dinah and her quilting party in a Stephen Foster song about seeing Nelly home. Aunts are also the organizers and custodians of folklore and stories, and these too are associated with piecing, as we see in the titles of such short story collections as Caroline Hentz's "Aunt Patty's Scrap Bag" (1846), or Louisa May Alcott's "Aunt Jo's Scrap Bag" (1872). Relationships between women in these stories are often represented as those of aunt and niece, rather than the more familiar and intense kinship bonds of mother and daughter, or the intense friendships of the female world of love and ritual. These stories are also about apprenticeship in an ongoing artistic tradition.

One of the most interesting examples of the relationship between piecing and writing in narrative design can be found in the work of Harriet Beecher Stowe. Stowe's literary career began in the 1840s with a series of sketches or pieces on various topics written for Christmas gift annuals, ladies' albums, and religious periodicals. As Mary Kelley has shown in her important study of the nineteenth-century American domestic novelists, Stowe thought of her writing in terms of temporal blocks; as she wrote an editor, she could not afford to write except by "buying my time." When the "family accounts wouldn't add up," Stowe recalled, "then I used to say to my faithful friend and factotum Anna . . . Now if you will keep the babies and attend to the things in the house for one day I'll write a piece and then we shall be out of the scrape" (169). A "piece" could be written in a day, and bring in $2.00 a page. Stowe regarded these short texts as pictorial, visual, grouped together less by plot than by principles of contrasting design. When she began to write Uncle Tom's Cabin, serialized in short weekly installments, Stowe continued to think of her writing as the stitching together of scenes. As Bruce Kirkland notes in his study of the manuscripts of Uncle Tom's Cabin, the novel was not a break with Stowe's narrative technique but rather developed out of her earlier writing and "was of a piece with it" (77).

Despite the unparalleled success of *Uncle Tom's Cabin*, and its current acclamation by feminist critics, however, Stowe's reputation has generally suffered from assumptions about her failure to live up to dominant standards of literary form. As one nineteenth-century critic complained, *Uncle Tom's Cabin* seemed to lack unity and formal design; "it is a rule of art," he declared, "that a work of fiction should be so joined together that every passage and incident should contribute to bring about an inevitable though unexpected catastrophe" (Holmes, in Ammons, 7–24). Even her feminist defenders have noted such flaws, and have had to explain them. While the book is "defective according to the rules of the modern French romance," George Sand wrote, the "conventional rules of art. . . never have been and never will be absolute. . . . In matters of art there is only one rule: to paint and to move" (in Ammons, 3–6). In our own day, feminist critics have interpreted Stowe's design in terms of male genres; Jane Tompkins, for example, calls it an American jeremiad; Ellen Moers sees it as a female epic structured geographically and metaphorically by the river (in Ammons, 135–38). Yet these redemptive readings, to some degree, cannot be produced without making the novel wrong in some other respect. In Moers's reading of the book as epic, for example, the title seems bizarre, or as she says, "misbegotten," for as Moers observes, "little of importance in the novel happens inside Uncle Tom's Cabin" (in Ammons, 136).

Uncle Tom's cabin, which Stowe first describes in the fourth chapter, is a log cabin whose facade is "covered by a large scarlet begonia and a native multiflora rose, which entwisting and interlacing, left scarcely a vestige of the rough logs to be seen." The title, I would suggest, is what Nancy K. Miller calls the "internal female signature: an icon or emblem within the fiction itself that obliquely figures the symbolic and material difficulties involved in becoming a woman writer."[6] "Uncle Tom's Cabin" is an allusion in the referential system of women's culture to the Log Cabin quilt, which by 1850 was the most popular American pieced quilt pattern. The basic Log Cabin pattern begins with a central square, often in red, which is sewn on to a larger block of fabric. "A narrow strip, or log, is then pieced to the edge of the center square. Subsequent strips are added, each perpendicular to the previous strip, until the center square is entirely bordered by logs" (Bishop et al., 74). The compositional principle of the Log Cabin quilt is the contrast between light and dark fabric. Each block is divided into two triangular sections, one section executed in light colored fabrics, the other in dark. When the blocks are pieced together to make the quilt, dramatic visual effects and variations can be created depending on the placement of the dark sections. We can see this first in the diagram of log cabin blocks, and then in quilts with such named variants as Light and Dark, Barn Raising, Courthouse Steps, and Streak of Lightning. (See figure 2.)

Radka Donnell-Vogt, moreover, sees the Log Cabin pattern as the most archetypal, profound, and symbolically significant of all quilt designs. It can also be found in the swaddling of infants, the wrapping of corpses, and in the inscriptions on sacred entrances. It can be read as either phallic or vaginal, depending on whether we see it as a projecting pyramid or a depression. "It is a universal convertible bisexual pattern protecting the union of opposites in human beings, and securing safe passage from one world into the other, from day to night, from life to death. Swaddling, doors, quilts, thus mediate in the dichotomy of inside and outside, that is, in the problems of physical, psychological, and social boundaries" (51). In its symbolic relationship to boundaries, the Log Cabin design is particularly apt for Stowe's novel of the borders between the states, the races, and the sexes.

We can understand the composition of the novel in relation to the elements of contrast and repetition in the Log Cabin pattern. As Stowe explained, she organized her text in terms of contrasting pieces of narrative. To the editor of the *National Era*, in which the novel was serialized, she wrote, "I am at present occupied upon a story which will be a much longer one than any I have ever written, embracing a series of sketches which give the lights and shadows of the 'patriarchal institution'. . . . My vocation is simply that of a painter. . . . There is no arguing with *pictures*, and everybody is impressed by them, whether they mean to be or not" (in Kirkland, 66–67). Uncle Tom's cabin becomes the iconographic center upon which narrative blocks are built up. Each block of the novel is similarly centered on a house, and around it Stowe constructs large contrasts of white and

Figure 2. Log cabin quilt, Barn Raising pattern, c. 1860.
(Courtesy America Hurrah Antiques, New York City)

slave society. The novel does not obey the rules which dictate a unity of action leading to a denouement, but rather operates through the cumulative effect of blocks of events structured on a parallel design.

Stowe's later New England local color novel, The Minister's Wooing (1859), is even more explicit about the structural and narrative correspondence between piecing and writing. The novel begins with a passage of authorial commentary: "When one has a story to tell, one is always puzzled which end of it to begin at. You have a whole corps of people to introduce that *you* know and your reader doesn't; and one thing so presupposes another that whichever way you turn your patchwork, the figures still seem ill-arranged" (527). In this story, Stowe chooses to begin with a particular female character, a widow who possesses the female art of order Stowe terms "faculty," and to build the design around her.

Stowe's purpose in The Minister's Wooing was to contrast the arid theology of New England Calvinism with the fertile spirituality of women's culture, and to balance the allegorical art of the Transcendentalists such as Hawthorne with the social art of the feminists. The motif of the pieced quilt recurs throughout the text to remind us of her design, and to emphasize the consequences for narrative of the difference between female realism and male romanticism. "Where theorists and philosophers tread with sublime assurance," Stowe comments in a chapter significantly titled "The Kitchen," "woman often follows with bleeding footsteps; women are always turning from the abstract to the individual, and feeling where the philosopher only thinks." The pieces of her plot are the chapters of the novel, with such titles as "the interview," "the letter," "the doctor," "the party," "the sermon," "the garret-boudoir," "the betrothed," and "the quilting." The artist in the novel, clearly a figure for Stowe herself, is the local dressmaker, Miss Prissy Diamond, another woman with "faculty," a genius at piecing, and a daring creative spirit who "never saw any trimming that she could not make" (p. 791). It is Miss Prissy who lies awake the night before the betrothal quilting party, thinking about a new way to get the quilt on to the frame, as Stowe is thinking about a new way to frame her text. The quilting bee is at the center of the book, epitomizing the aspirations of female artistic creation. As Stowe explains: "Many a maiden, as she sorted and arranged fluttering bits of green, yellow,

red, and blue, felt rising in her breast a passion for somewhat vague
and unknown, which came out at length in a new pattern of patchwork"
(788). Piecing these fragments together into a beautiful design is an
emblem of "that household life which is to be brought to stability and
beauty by reverent economy in husbanding and tact in arranging the
little. . . morsels of daily existence" (p. 789). Writing out of the security
of a historically strong women's culture, Stowe can assert that this
faculty is limited to women and alien to those whom she satirically
calls, in this self-consciously oppositional novel, "that ignorant and
incapable sex which could not quilt" (p. 789).

By the 1880s, the parallels between piecing and women's
writing were being more self-consciously, but much less happily, explored by a new generation of American women writers wishing to
assert themselves as artists rather than crafters, and looking towards
both native and foreign models of narrative design. That the transitional generation of the 1880s and 1890s who have been called the
first artistically respectable women writers in America are generally
referred to as the Local Colorists perhaps suggests their continuity
with the visual design traditions of their precursors. Their stories are
much more explicitly about the frustrations of the woman writer struggling to create an appropriate form for her experience within a literary
culture increasingly indifferent or even hostile to women's cultural
practices. As women's culture began to dissolve under pressures both
from the external male society, and from a younger female generation
demanding education, mobility, and sexual independence, older
women artists felt themselves isolated and uprooted. These are stories
that represent women's culture as sour and embittering, and that
frequently end in tragedy or defeat. Their quilts are crazy quilts, moving
away from the comforting design traditions of the past and unsure of
their coherence, structure, and form.

We can see the generational contrast in two related stories
about the quilting bee, Ann S. Stephens's "The Quilting-Party," written
in the 1850s, and Mary Wilkins Freeman's "A Quilting-Party in Our
Village," written in 1898.[7] In Stephens's story, the "quilting frolic" is an
all-day festival of female bonding; a bevy of girls in silk dresses stitch
merrily away on a rising-sun pattern while they sing romantic ballads.
At night there is a lavish feast, and the gentlemen arrive to dance in

a room filled "with a rich fruity smell left by dried apples and frost grapes" (209). In this story, women's culture is at its peak of plenitude, ripeness, and harmony. In Freeman's story, however, the quilting bee takes place on the hottest day of a July heat wave. Wearing their oldest dresses, the quilters set grimly to their task, gossiping among themselves about the bride's age, ugliness, and stinginess. The supper is sickening in its coarse abundance, and when the gentlemen arrive for a sweaty dance, the women nearly come to blows competing for their attention. The rising-sun pattern which they also quilt now seems like a mocking allusion to the setting sun of women's culture, and to the disappearance of its sustaining aesthetic rituals.

Freeman's story, "An Honest Soul," also mocks the conventions of quilting and female solidarity and nurturance. The quiltmaker Martha Patch—the name requires no comment—nearly starves to death in her dogged efforts to complete two pieced quilts for women clients named Mrs. Bennett and Mrs. Bliss, who seem to represent two traditions of quilting and women's writing. The pieces belonging to Bennett (the Austen heritage of the women's novel) and to Bliss (women's culture or literary jouissance) become confused in the mind of the old woman, whose claustrophobic separation from other sources of vision is signified by her windowless house. Rescued by neighbors after days of obsessive sewing and piecing which have brought her close to death, Martha Patch decides that she is "kinder sick of bed-quilts," and will make other things henceforth. A male neighbor cuts a front window in the blank wall of her house, and the story thus suggests that the traditional art of women is obsolete, blinded, claustrophobically and perhaps dangerously isolated from mainstream traditions.

"Elizabeth Stock's One Story," by Kate Chopin, also takes up this issue. It is the tale of an unmarried woman, a maiden aunt, whose desk after her death of consumption at the age of thirty-eight is found to contain "scraps and bits of writing." Out of this "conglomerate mass," the male editor, who may be either her nephew or her longtime suitor, assembles the only pages which seem to resemble a "connected or consecutive narration." They begin, however, with Elizabeth Stock's lament that she cannot write because of her inability to imagine a narrative both in conformity with a patriarchal literary tradition and in creative relation to it: "Since I was a girl I always felt as if I would like to write stories," but "whenever I tried to think of one, it always turned out to be something that some one else had thought about before me." Despairing of her efforts to imitate male traditions of plot that are "original, entertaining, full of action, and goodness knows what all," Elizabeth Stock turns to the female tradition, which seems to offer a more authentic but less orderly plot: "I . . . walked about days in a kind of a dream, twisting and twisting things in my mind just like I often saw old ladies twisting quilt patches to compose a design." But the one story she finally tells turns out to be the ironic account of her own betrayal, loss of employment, and death, as if women's one story were being fatally undermined by the pressure of new aesthetic expectations and competition. The designs of quilt patches are dreams of a past inhabited by old ladies, and finally her scraps and bits of writing, her stock of experience, will be edited, condensed, and preserved according to the consecutive and linear models of the male tradition.

Yet the feminist writers who come at the end of this transitional generation at the point where it begins to join with modernism, turn back to the model of piecing as a vehicle for discussing literary aspiration, and for altering the validity of a female tradition. Dorothy Canfield Fisher's story, "The Bedquilt," published in 1915, is a paradigmatic American women's text about piecing and writing. The story describes the design and creation of a magnificent quilt by an elderly woman, an unmarried dependent in her sister's household. At the age of sixty-eight, Aunt Mehetabel suddenly conceives a great artistic project: a spectacular quilt, pieced according to a dramatically difficult and original design. As Fisher writes,

She never knew how her great idea came to her. Sometimes she thought she must have dreamed it, sometimes she even wondered reverently, in the phraseology of her weekly prayer-meeting, if it had been "sent" to her. She never admitted to herself that she could have thought of it without other help. It was too great, too ambitious, too lofty a project for her humble mind to have conceived. . . . By some heaven-sent inspiration, she had invented a pattern beyond which no patchwork quilt could go. (36–37)

As Aunt Mehetabel becomes absorbed in the "orderly, complex, mosaic beauty" (39) of her pieces, so too her family begins to give her recognition, praise, and a sewing table of her own. She places the thimble on "her knotted, hard finger with the solemnity of a prophetess performing a rite." As the legend of the extraordinary quilt spreads through the region, "Mehetabel's quilt came little by little to become one of the local sights." No visitor to town went away without looking at it, and thus it becomes necessary for the aunt to be better dressed. One of her nieces even makes her a pretty little cap to wear on her thin white hair. At the end of five years the quilt is completed, and Mehetabel, who has never been more than six miles away from her home, is taken to the county fair to see it on display. The trip is the consummation of her life; at the Fair she can see nothing but her own quilt which has received the first prize; returning home, she can find no words to describe to her relatives what she has seen or felt, but "sat staring into the fire, on her tired old face the supreme content of the artist who has realized his ideal" (35–43).

The story is obviously a parable of the woman writer, and her creative fantasies. Fisher, who had received a Ph.D. in French from Columbia in 1905, and then abandoned academia to become a writer, confessed in an essay her anxieties about the "enormous difficulties of story telling, often too great for my powers to cope with" ("What My Mother Taught Me" 34). The writer's ambition to create an orderly and complex beauty of form, and the insecurities that make her attribute the power of design to a supernatural force rather than to skill, are figured in the image of the ultimate divinely inspired quilt.

Other feminist narratives used piecing as a metaphor for the difference between male and female discourse. This contrast is brilliantly represented in Susan Glaspell's story, "A Jury of Her Peers" (1917). Two women, the sheriff's wife, Mrs. Peters, and a neighbor, Mrs. Hale, accompany their husbands to a lonely farmhouse where the local miser has been strangled, and his wife, Minnie, jailed for the crime. Because there is no evidence of a motive for the murder, the men search the house and barn, while the women clean up the strangely disordered kitchen. Gradually they begin to notice domestic details which reveal Minnie Foster's troubled mind and hint of her oppression in a cruel marriage. The most telling clue is her unfinished quilt, which becomes a hieroglyphic or diary for these women who are skilled in its language. The "crazy sewing" of a block pieced all askew speaks powerfully of the anger and anguish of a woman who cannot control her feelings enough to create an orderly art. As Mrs. Hale and Mrs. Peters discover the other missing evidence—the body of a pet canary whose neck had been twisted by the husband—they recognize their own bonds within a cultural system meaningless to men, and their own complicity in the isolation of a woman who has been driven mad. In a moment of silent conspiracy, they resew the pieces and destroy the other evidence, under the very eyes of their husbands who are going over the evidence they can perceive "piece by piece." While the men laugh and tease their wives about whether Minnie Foster was going to knot or quilt her patchwork, the clue is in both the language and the act: it would have been knotted, as she has knotted the rope around her husband's neck, because knotting can be done alone; the solitary Minnie has no sisterhood of friends to join her in quilting (Alkaley-Gut, 8).[8] As Annette Kolodny observes, "Glaspell's narrative not only invites a semiotic analysis, but, indeed, performs that analysis for us. If the absent Minnie Foster is the 'transmitter' or 'sender' in this schema, then only the women are competent 'receivers' or 'readers' of her message, since they alone share not only her context (the supposed insignificance of kitchen things), but, as a result, the conceptual patterns which make up her world" (53).

To continue this analysis through modernist women's writing would take us perhaps to the fiction of Willa Cather, who learned to tell stories by sitting under the quilting frame listening to her mother's friends, and whose first serious novel, O Pioneers! (1913), was constructed by piecing together two short stories. We might also look at the modernist pieces of Gertrude Stein, or at the pieced narratives of Eudora Welty.

But a very recent quilt story, Bobbie Ann Mason's "Love Life," which appeared in the October 29, 1984, New Yorker, raises some of the most important issues of piecing, writing, and women's culture for literary historians. Mason is from Western Kentucky, a region in which most of her powerful and disturbing fiction is set, and her story alludes to the Kentucky tradition of the burial quilt. The best-known example is Elizabeth Roseberry Mitchell's Kentucky Graveyard Quilt, done in Lewis County in 1839, and now in the collection of the Kentucky

Historical Society. (See figure 3.) When a member of Mitchell's family died, she would remove a labelled coffin from the border and place it within the graveyard depicted in the center of the quilt.[9]

In Mason's story, two women represent two generations of women's culture—Aunt Opal, the retired schoolteacher, the old woman who is the caretaker of tradition; and her niece, Jenny, the New Woman of the 1980s, whose unfinished love affairs and backpack existence suggest the loss of traditions: "She's not in a hurry to get married, she says. She says she is going to buy a house trailer and live in the woods like a hermit. She's full of ideas and she exaggerates." Returning to Kentucky from her wanderings, Jenny pleads with Opal to see the family's celebrated but hidden burial quilt. "Did Jenny come back home just to hunt up that old rag? The thought makes Opal shudder." The burial quilt is made of dark pieced blocks, each with an appliquéd tombstone. Each tombstone has a name and date on it: "The shape is irregular, a rectangle with a clumsy foot sticking out from one corner. The quilt is knotted with yarn, and the edging is open, for more blocks to be added. "According to family legend, a block is added whenever someone dies; the quilt stops when the family name stops, so "the last old maids finish the quilt."

Who will be the last old maid? Ironically, Opal has rejected the cultural roles of the past. To her, the quilts mean only "a lot of desperate old women ruining their eyes." The burial quilt is a burden, "ugly as homemade sin," a depressing reminder of failure and loneliness. Opal plans to take up aerobic dancing, to be modern; meanwhile she spends all her time watching the video quilt of MTV. Jenny will finish the quilt. She will use it to mourn for relationships that never began, to stitch herself back into the past.

Like the Kentucky burial quilt, Mason's story is also composed of blocks of elegy, memory, and flashback, and remains open-ended, an irregular shape, with a clumsy foot of narrative (in this case the description of the video Opal is watching, Michael Jackson's "Thriller") sticking out from one corner. Using the familar nineteenth-century women's plot of an emotional interaction between aunt and niece, Mason brings us back, through Aunt Opal's Scrap Bag, to a sense of continuity in an American female literary and cultural tradition.

Figure 3. Elizabeth Roseberry Mitchell: Graveyard Quilt,
Lewis County, Kentucky, 1839.
(From the collection of the Kentucky Historical Society)

Yet does she really? The story also suggests that these traditions may be burdens rather than treasures of the past, and that there may be something mournful and even self-destructive in our feminist efforts to reclaim them. Is Jenny a feminist critic full of ideas who exaggerates the importance of women's culture? Are we ruining our eyes finishing a female heritage that may have become a museum piece? Is it time to bury the burial quilt rather than to praise it? Mason's story is a useful reminder of the complex relationship of women's culture and women's writing in any era, a warning that in tidily closing off our critical pieces we may miss some of the ragged edges that are a more accurate image of our literary history.

NOTES

This paper is dedicated to the members of the 1984 NEH Summer Seminar on "Women's Writing and Women's Culture": Joanne Braxton, Dorothy Berkson, Mary DeJong, Elizabeth Keyser, Peggy Lant, Joanne Karpinski, Andree Nicola-McLaughlin, Shirley Marchalonis, Ozzie Meyers, Adele McCullom, Sandee Potter, Cheryl Torsney, and Gail Kraidman.

1. See Mainardi (56–57), and Parker and Pollock (76).

2. See Burke, "Rethinking the Maternal," in *The Future of Difference* (107–13).

3. Thanks to Radka Donnell-Vogt for many helpful discussions of the quilt aesthetic, and to Lynn Miller for introducing me to her work. Donnell-Vogt is one of the women featured in the documentary film, "Quilts in Women's Lives."

4. Thanks to Gail Kraidman for this reference.

5. Thanks to Elizabeth Keyser for bringing this story to my attention; my analysis is indebted to her presentation in our NEH seminar. See also Marsella, *The Promise of Destiny*.

6. Thanks to Nancy K. Miller for this definition from her current work on French women's writing.

7. Thanks to Jeslyn Medoff for research assistance.

8. Log Cabin quilts were usually knotted rather than quilted. See Bishop et al. (74).

9. According to an unpublished letter by Mitchell's grand-daughter, the Graveyard Quilt was originally made as a memorial to two sons who had died in childhood. See Nina Mitchell Biggs, "Old Days, Old Ways," in the collection of the Kentucky Historical Museum.

WORKS CITED

Alcott, Louisa May. "Patty's Patchwork." In *Aunt Jo's Scrap Bag*. Boston: Roberts, 1872. Vol. 1, pp. 193–215.

Alkaley-Gut, Karen. "A Jury of Her Peers: The Importance of Trifles." *Studies in Short Fiction* (Winter 1984), 21:1–10.

Ammons, Elizabeth, ed. *Critical Essays on Harriet Beecher Stowe*. Boston: G. K. Hall, 1980.

"Annette" [Harriet Farley or Rebecca C. Thompson]. "The Patchwork Quilt." In *The Lowell Offering*. Ed. Benita Eisler. New York: Harper, 1977; pp. 150–54.

Baym, Nina. *Woman's Fiction: A Guide to Novels by and about Women in America 1820–1870*. Ithaca: Cornell University Press, 1978.

Bishop, Robert; Secord, William; and Weissman, Judith Reiter. *Quilts, Coverlets, Rugs and Samples*. New York: Knopf, 1982.

Bretteville, Sheila de. "A Re-examination of Some Aspects of the Design Arts from the Perspective of a Woman Designer. "*Women and the Arts: Arts in Society* (Spring–Summer 1974), 11:117–18.

Burke, Carolyn. "Rethinking the Maternal." In *The Future of Difference*. Ed. Alice Jardine and Hester Eisenstein. Boston: G. K. Hall, 1982.

Cahill, Susan, ed. *Women and Fiction* 2. New York: New American Library, 1978.

Chopin, Kate. "Elizabeth Stock's One Story." In *"The Awakening" and Selected Stories*. Ed. Sandra M. Gilbert. New York: Penguin, 1984; pp. 274–80.

Cooper, Patricia, and Buferd, Norma Bradley. *The Quilters: Women and Domestic Art*. New York: Doubleday, 1978.

Dewhurst, C. Kurt; MacDowell, Betty; and MacDowell, Marsha. *Artists in Aprons: Folk Art by American Women*. New York: E. P. Dutton, 1979.

Donnell-Vogt, Radka. Memoir in *Lives and Works: Talks with Women Artists*. Ed. Lynn F. Miller and Sally S. Swenson. Metuchen, N.J.: Scarecrow Press, 1981.

DuPlessis, Rachel Blau. "For the Etruscans." In *The New Feminist Criticism*. Ed. Elaine Showalter. New York: Pantheon, 1985.

Fisher, Dorothy Canfield. "What My Mother Taught Me" and "The Bedquilt." In *Women and Fiction* 2. Ed. Susan Cahill. New York: New American Library, 1978.

Freeman, Mary Wilkins. "A Quilting Bee in Our Village." In *The People of Our Neighborhood*. Philadelphia: Curtis, 1898; pp. 113–28.

Gilligan, Carol. *In a Different Voice*. Cambridge: Harvard University Press, 1982.

Hedges, Elaine. "The Nineteenth-Century Diarist and Her Quilts." *Feminist Studies* (Summer 1982), 8:293–99.

Holmes, George F. *The Southern Literary Messenger* (October 1852), vol. 18; repr. in *Critical Essays on Harriet Beecher Stowe*. Ed. Elizabeth Ammons. Boston: G. K. Hall, 1980.

Kelley, Mary. *Private Woman, Public Stage: Literary Domesticity in Nineteeth-Century America*. New York: Oxford University Press, 1984.

Kirkham, Bruce. *The Building of Uncle Tom's Cabin*. Knoxville: University of Tennessee Press, 1977.

Kolodny, Annette. "A Map for Rereading: Gender and the Interpretation of Literary Texts." In *The New Feminist Criticism*. Ed. Elaine Showalter. New York: Pantheon, 1985.

Lippard, Lucy. "Up, Down and Across: A New Frame for New Quilts." *The Artist and the Quilt*. Ed. Charlotte Robinson. New York: Knopf, 1983.

Mainardi, Patricia. "Quilts: The Great American Art." *Radical America* (1973), 7:36–68.

Marsella, Joy A. *The Promise of Destiny: Children and Women in the Short Stories of Louisa May Alcott*. Westport, Conn.: Greenwood, 1983.

Mason, Bobbie Ann. "Love Life," *New Yorker*, October 29, 1984, pp. 42–50.

Moers, Ellen. "Harriet Beecher Stowe." In *Critical Essays on Harriet Beecher Stowe*. Ed. Elizabeth Ammons. Boston: G. K. Hall, 1980.

Parker, Roszika, and Pollock, Griselda. *Old Mistresses: Women, Art and Ideology*. New York: Pantheon, 1981.

Piercy, Marge. "Looking at Quilts." In *In Her Own Image*. Ed. Elaine Hedges and Ingrid Wendt. New York: Feminist Press, 1980. pp. 35–36.

Pilling, Ron. "Album Quilts of the Mid-1800s." *Art & Antiques* (November–December 1982), pp. 72–79.

Stephens, P. "The Quilting Party." In *Female Prose Writers of America*. Ed. John S. Hart. Philadelphia: E. H. Butler, 1857); pp. 204–10.

Stowe, Harriet Beecher. *The Minister's Wooing*. New York: The Library of America, 1980.

Walker, Alice. *In Search of Our Mother's Gardens*. New York: Harcourt Brace Jovanovich, 1983.

Reading Double: Sand's Difference

NAOMI SCHOR

TRICKSTERISM

The trickster is, according to Lévi-Strauss, "a mediator." And he goes on to say: "Since his mediating function occupies a position halfway between two polar terms, he must retain something of that duality, namely an ambiguous and equivocal character" (223). The "transatlantic feminist" (Jardine), who ceaselessly shuttles between French texts and American contexts, is such a trickster figure, a mediatrix oscillating between the two often polar extremes she seeks to confront. What then are these polar extremes? They are the two poles of the axis of difference. Now, over the years these polar extremes have undergone a remarkable chiasmatic reversal, as France and America have shifted positions in relation to the central pivot of sexual difference. Whereas initially France was viewed as the chief purveyor of strong theories of a biologically rooted radical difference, an essential femininity (Irigaray), and America, as the home of androgyny (Heilbrun), recently France has disseminated a deconstruction of the paradigm of sexual difference that voids the feminine of any specific content or character, or of any necessary connection with femaleness (Derrida), while America has embraced the notion of socially fostered female specificity (Chodorow, Gilligan).

The chiasmus I have just traced is aesthetically pleasing but deceptive in that it masks the cracks and contradictions within each term of the chiasmus: there are, of course, advocates of both positions on both sides of the Atlantic. To consider only the French pole: at the very same moment when Hélène Cixous sounds the call, in "The Laugh of the Medusa," for the inscription of the female body in language, she calls into question the necessary connection between *écriture féminine* and female anatomy, asserting in a justly celebrated footnote that to date, "in France. . . the only inscriptions of femininity that I have seen were by Colette, Marguerite Duras. . . and Jean Genet" ("je n'ai vu inscrire de la féminité que par Colette, Marguerite Duras . . . et Jean Genet" (248–49/42). A different but homologous split is registered by Julia Kristeva in "Woman can never be defined." While interrogating the very referentiality of "woman" (Kristeva's piece appeared in 1974, one year after Lacan's Seminar XX on female sexuality and her "Woman can never be defined" echoes Lacan's "the woman does not exist") Kristeva concedes that, "we must use 'we are women' as an advertisement or slogan for our demands" (" 'nous sommes des femmes' est encore à maintenir comme publicité ou slogan de revendication") (137/379).

There seems to be a general recognition even among those most eager to dissolve traditional sexual opposition into the play of pure differences that political action requires a willing suspension of disbelief, an active assertion of female identity. My concern here is, however, with textual and not political strategies, if the two can ever be separated. More specifically my concern is with the status of difference as it is thematized in French women's writing, and even more specifically in the writing of a French woman conspicuously absent from Cixous's honor roll, George Sand, whose very pseudonym continues to body forth her difference. For, as is often forgotten, the dropping of the final s of Georges (the conventional French spelling of George), a gradual process according to Sand's biographers, signals a difference from the masculine at the same time as a rejection of the feminine. In French, George is an onomastic anomaly; being neither masculine nor feminine, or both, it subverts the taxonomic vocation of names. To read Sand's writing in a psychoanalytic perspective one must practice what I have called elsewhere "female fetishism," a simultaneous assertion and denial of sexual difference, rooted in woman's bisexuality. The increasingly urgent call to decide between two reading strategies, reading for specificity with the assumption of at least a fictive difference (the writer's, the protagonist's, the reader's) or beyond difference is blunted when confronted with a text such as Sand's *La Petite Fadette*, which is a doubly double text: first because it is the story of male doubles, second because it is also the story of the female protagonist whose name is featured in the title. I want to take *La Petite Fadette* as an allegory of the double reading—which is also a *doubling* reading, as the commentary *mimes* the text—that I think is now called for if we are to avoid the risks inherent in opting exclusively for either one of the positions now occupying the forefront of feminist literary criticism. To read beyond difference is inescapably to run the risk of reinforcing the canon and its founding sexual hierarchies and exclusions, while to read for difference is to risk relapsing into essentialism and its inevitable consequence, marginalization. Reading double presents, of course, its own dangers, those inherent in tricksterism: ambiguity and equivocation. But, as I hope to show, it offers a possible way out of the current impasse, by suggesting a way of reconceptualizing the problematics of sexual difference.

WEAVING IN THE REVOLUTION

Tryptichs, with the notable exception of Flaubert's *Trois Contes*, have not fared well in the hands of critics who prefer to analyze the intricacies of a single text rather than the complex interplay of three texts, which both stand alone and yet share a dense network of linking characters and themes. The case of *La Petite Fadette*, the third panel of Sand's pastoral trilogy, which also includes *La Mare au Diable* and *François le Champi*, is no exception to this rule. Invariably read, when it is read at all, as an autonomous work, *Fadette* is not seen for what it in fact is: the final elaboration of material already worked through in the previous texts: the difficulties of male object choice (*La Mare au Diable*) and the temptations of mother-son incest (*François le Champi*). My interest in reestablishing the connection between *Fadette* and the two previous pastoral tales is not, however, to emphasize continuity, rather the discontinuity that irrevocably separates them. For as Sand notes in the dialogue which serves as one of the two prefaces to *Fadette*, the writing of the trilogy was interrupted by an event so catastrophic that what was in fact a one-year hiatus in the composition of the series seems more like ten:

> "Do you remember," he said to me, "that we came this way *a year ago*, and that we stopped here for a whole evening? For it was here that you told me the story of *François le Champi* and that I advised you to write it in the same intimate style in which you told it to me."
>
> "And that I found by imitating the style of our hemp hackler. I remember, and it *seems like ten years ago*." (7; italics mine)

> —Te souviens-tu, me dit-il, que nous passions ici, *il y a un an*, et que nous nous y sommes arrêtés tout un soir? Car c'est ici que tu me racontas l'histoire du *Champi*, et que je te conseillai de l'écrire dans le style familier dont tu t'étais servi avec moi.
>
> —Et que j'imitais de la manière de notre *Chanvreur*. Je m'en souviens, et il me semble que, *depuis ce jour-là, nous avons vécu dix ans*. (33; italics mine)

The radical historical break which is the Revolution of 1848 introduces a cleft within the tryptich, which *Fadette* will attempt to suture by turning its back on history, a textual repression which I will argue was less than successful, but which draws our attention to a striking commonality in the two reading strategies outlined above: their isolation of the text from its historical context, their divorce of the problematics of sexual difference from the events of history.

In the second of her two prefaces, this one written in December 1851, after yet another major watershed in French history, Louis-Napoléon's coup d'état, Sand theorizes that there are two responses to civil war: that of men of action who are active participants in the events, and that of poets and "idle women" (*femmes oisives*), who watch events from the sidelines. It is of course true that a poet such as Dante managed to write his *Divine Comedy* without averting his gaze from contemporary horrors. But, according to Sand, today's artist— who is implicitly an "idle woman," reduced to the passive status of onlooker in the new historical era that 1848 ushers in (Lukács)—has the duty to represent an ideal world, avoiding any *direct* allusion to the terrible events at hand. The pressure of historical events only serves then to heighten Sand's persistent utopian tropism, her stated preference for representing ideal worlds.

Nous croyons que la mission de l'art est une mission de sentiment et d'amour, que le roman d'aujourd'hui devrait remplacer la parabole et l'apologue des temps naïfs, et que l'artiste a une tâche plus large et plus poétique que celle de proposer quelques mesures de prudence et de conciliation pour atténuer l'effroi qu'inspirent ses peintures. Son but devrait être de faire aimer les objets de sa sollicitude, et au besoin, je ne lui ferais pas un reproche de les embellir un peu. *L'art n'est pas une étude de la réalité positive; c'est une recherche de la vérité idéale. . . .* ("L'Auteur au lecteur," *La Mare au diable*, 30; italics mine)

We believe that the mission of art is a mission of feeling and love, that today's novel should take the place of the parables and apologia of more simple times, and that the artist has a greater and more poetic duty than to propose some measure of prudence and conciliation to mitigate the horror inspired by his depictions. His goal should be to make lovable the objects of his care and, if need be, I would not fault him for embellishing them just a little. *Art is not the study of positive reality; it is the search for an ideal truth.*

In the case of her pastoral trilogy, whose general title was to be *Les Veillées du Chanvreur*, the ideal world is a nostalgic evocation of pastoral simplicity. As if to underscore the distance that separates the reader from this lost world, the narrator adopts the persona of a mere translator, who transcribes and translates the tales told by the hemp-hackler in his native dialect into the more familiar Parisian French of the narratee. The pastoral tales are thus coded as translations from a minority language into the language of the dominant culture and troped as textiles. Sand's enlisting here of two recurrent tropes in French women's writing—translation and/or weaving[1]—for the act of writing as a woman suggests that Sand's predilection for the pastoral genre draws its impetus not only from her desire to idealize, to offer a corrective to the horrors of a then triumphant Balzacian realism, but from her sense that the tales she had to tell are so foreign and strange that they can only be told in the reassuring guise of what she referred to with mock modesty as her "bergeries," or shepherd's tales.

A MODEL PROTAGONIST: READING FOR DIFFERENCE (I)

La Petite Fadette is the story of Fadette, the ugly duckling tomboy who, loved by the handsome and well-to-do peasant Landry, metamorphoses into a beautiful and good woman who has lots of children and lives happily ever after. This brief plot summary is, of course, a caricature, but only barely, of one possible reading of La Petite Fadette: what we might call a "first-stage" reading focused on the female protagonist, her strengths and weaknesses.[2] Such a reading would follow the Bildung of the female character as she is integrated into patriarchal society. This is precisely the approach that prevails in psychoanalytically based interpretations of the tale. Let me give two examples. The first occurs in Helene Deutsch's The Psychology of Women, where in the course of an extended analysis of Sand's "masculinity complex," Deutsch offers a reading of Fadette which emphasizes its autobiographical nature. Deutsch recalls one of the most traumatic episodes recounted in Histoire de ma vie, the occasion on which Sand's grandmother, confronted with little Aurore's desperate desire to join her mother in Paris, tells her the truth about her mother's sordid past. "My thesis," writes Deutsch, "is that Sand's sadistic-masculine reactions to disappointment followed the pattern of her first reactions to her grandmother's destruction of her mother ideal" (304).[3] Little Fadette's rebellious attitude toward society—her refusal to conform to the sugar and spice model of femininity, her malicious habit of taunting her persecutors and flaunting her superior command of the logos—is closely patterned on little Aurore's response to her grandmother's revelation. Just as Aurore's mother went off to Paris, leaving her daughter in the custody of her paternal grandmother, Fadette's mother abandons her and her younger brother to become a campfollower, and Fadette, raised by a cold grandmother, faces a hostile community which condemns her mother as a whore and treats her abandoned children as pariahs. In Deutsch's words: "In her novel, La Petite Fadette ('The Cricket'), she describes a little girl who is exactly like the little Aurore of her diaries after the disclosures made by her grandmother. Little Fadette acts like a naughty, sadistic boy" (304–5). But, Deutsch goes on to say: "Fadette grows up to be a sweet and kindly woman; sadistic aggression in her is transformed into a woman's loving passive attitude. The transformation takes place when a man's love awakens her to femininity" (305).

Another psychoanalytic reading focused on the development of the female protagonist is the sympathetic feminist reading provided by Michael Danahy in his article, "Growing Up Female: George Sand's View in La Petite Fadette." The main theme of the tale, according to Danahy, is "the effect on a young woman growing up without the benefit of an adequate female role model" (50). Eventually, however, according to Danahy, Fadette does make it through to maturity by assuming her identification with her fallen mother. Growing up, then, in both these readings is growing up female, and the difficulties Fadette encounters in her development are bound up with a problematic identification with a mother who is closer to the whore than the angel. Emphasis is thus placed on Fadette's positive resolution of her sexual identity. In the syntagmatic logic of this reading the central scene in the tale is the one where Landry tells Fadette that she must give up her tomboy ways and take the conventional path toward normal femininity:

"Very well, Fanchon Fadet, since you speak so sensibly, and since, for the first time in your life, I see you gentle and docile, I'll tell you why people don't respect you in the way a girl of sixteen ought to be able to command respect. It's because you are not in the least like a girl and so like a boy in your looks and manners. . . . Well, do you think that's right and proper, at sixteen years of age, not to be in the least like a girl? You climb trees like a squirrel, and when you jump on the back of a mare, with no bridle and no saddle, you make her gallop as though the devil were on her back. It's a good thing to be strong and agile; it's also a good thing not to be afraid of anything, and for a man it is a natural advantage. But for a woman enough is enough, and you look as though you were trying to draw attention to yourself." (91)

—Eh bien, Fanchon Fadet, puisque tu parles si raisonnablement, et que, pour la première fois de ta vie, je te vois douce et traitable, je vas te dire pourquoi on ne te respecte pas comme une fille de seize ans devrait pouvoir l'exiger. C'est que tu n'as rien d'une fille et tout d'un garçon, dans ton air et dans tes manières; c'est que tu ne prends pas soin de ta personne. . . . Eh bien, crois-tu que ce soit à propos, à seize ans, de ne point ressembler encore à une fille? Tu montes sur les arbres comme un vrai chat-écurieux, et quand tu sautes sur une jument, sans bride ni selle, tu la fais galoper comme si le diable était dessus. C'est bon d'être forte et leste; c'est bon aussi de n'avoir peur de rien, et c'est un avantage de nature pour un homme. Mais pour une femme trop est trop, et tu as l'air de vouloir te faire remarquer. (136)

The affinity of psychoanalytic critics for this particular

Sand text seems to derive from its preinscription of Freud's teleological myth of female development. Landry speaks with the assurance of a spokesman for the patriarchal order, serenely articulating the laws of the symbolic, which enjoin the little girl to abandon the active mode of the phallic phase and accept the passive stance that will ensure her smooth development into femininity. The question arises: how do women readers respond to this scene? How does Sand go about making Fadette's relinquishing of her masculine attributes palatable to her female readers, who have identified, as female readers do, with the female protagonist? That women are charmed, indeed seduced by *Fadette* is attested to by Ellen Moers, who writes of Sand's peasant tales: "Here the critic of women's literature must simply abandon principle and, faced with George Sand, call the style of *La Mare au Diable* and *La Petite Fadette* plain seductive" (*Literary Women*, 53). These are strong words. Though Moers does not specify exactly what principles the critic of women's writing must abandon when confronted with Sand's "delicious" peasant tales, her call for a letting down of one's critical defenses testifies to the powerful charm exerted by Sand's text over the resisting woman reader. What Moers does make explicit is how Sand disarms her feminist reader: by an aesthetic benefit, a stylistic felicity that overcomes all resistance, what Freud in his essay, "The Relation of the Poet to Day-Dreaming," calls an "incitement premium" or "fore-pleasure."

I would suggest that there are elements other than Sand's untranslatable delicious prose style that work, in Teresa de Lauretis's phrase, to "seduce" the female reader of Fadette "into femininity" (137) and it is that more, that *seductive supplement* that must now be examined. To make palatable to the resisting reader Fadette's dwindling into femininity, Sand compensates for her renunciation of the strength and mobility that are, according to the doxa, essential male prerogatives by endowing her with an undeniable individual intellectual superiority and great wealth. Thus at the close of Landry's speech in praise of sexual difference, he offers Fadette a clever inducement to give up her inappropriate behavior:

"Think about it a little, and you'll see that if you were to be a bit more like other people they would be less resentful of the fact that you have more understanding than they have." (92)

—Rumine un peu la chose, et tu verras que si tu voulais être un peu comme les autres, on te saurait plus de gré de ce que tu as de plus qu'eux dans ton entendement. (137)

What Landry urges on Fadette is what we might call a "trade-off": in exchange for conforming to the cultural construction of the female, Fadette will be rewarded with the recognition of her *real* difference: her superior qualities of mind. For Landry is the first to recognize Fadette's quick wit, her superior command of language. At the same time as Fadette's intellectual gifts are valorized, the class difference which initially separates Fadette, the town marginal, from Landry, the son of prosperous peasants, is overturned when, after her grandmother's death, Fadette finds herself an immensely rich heiress, a reversal in fortune which is instrumental in overcoming the prejudices of the Landry family and especially its patriarch, Père Barbeau, against Fadette. Seduced, then, into identifying with Fadette's exceptional masculine intelligence—in her therapeutic use of herbs, Fadette displays the methodological skills of the experimental scientist—and independent means, the female reader is lulled into forgetting that the wages of genius and wealth are the acceptance of a definition of femininity that essentializes difference and naturalizes social inequity.

DOUBLE TROUBLE

These readings, centered on the female protagonist and grounded in the unproblematic assertion of absolute sexual difference, have at least one major drawback: they completely fail to take into account about one half of the text, since Fadette does not make her appearance until chapter 8 of the tale, and even after she appears her presence is fitful, intermittent, like that of the firefly ("follet") with which she is associated both metonymically and homonymically. As I have already indicated, despite the title that arouses and orients the reader's expectations, the tale is not focused on its eponymous heroine. For *La Petite Fadette* is not centered on an individual protagonist at all, rather on a unique set of doubles: the male twins, Sylvinet and Landry. Indeed, originally Sand had proposed to entitle her tale, "Les Bessons," an archaic dialectal word used throughout the tale to signify twins. As the author of the introduction to the Garnier-Flammarion edition writes:

In this world protected by its isolation and which remains true to the beliefs and social mores of the past, Sand has placed the story of two *bessons* and a wild young woman. Perhaps initially she had thought only of the former. It is indeed strange to observe that she had originally chosen as her title *The Twins (Les Bessons)*; in fact little Fadette only appears quite late in the first outline. (Van Den Bogaert, 18–19)

According to the author of this introduction, Sand's original inspiration came from a ballad, by the Provençal poet Jasmin, called precisely: "les deux bessons." What this author fails to note is the appeal this popular theme might have had for an author whose predilection for doubles is already a critical commonplace. Many recent readers of Sand's oeuvre have been struck by the proliferation of doubles in her work, doubles that tend to fall into two groups. One group consists of the female doubles, generally viewed as symptomatic of Sand's inability to overcome the traditional split (mother/whore) that governs the representation of women in male-authored fiction. The reinscription of the cleavage between the spiritual and the carnal produces such female doublets as: Indiana and Noun (*Indiana*), Valentine and Louise (*Valentine*), and Lélia and Pulchérie (*Lélia*). The other group, another modulation of the same obsession, consists of the doubles cast as male/female alter egos (*Jacques*). *Fadette* is, however, a limit case of a third, more problematic group of novels featuring male doubles as brothers or half brothers (*Les Maitres Mosaïstes, Le Marquis de Villemer, Les Deux Frères*). We are here of something on a different order from the split female or the ambi-sexual couple, both of which are in some sense ordained by the dream of an impossible integration of warring sexual selves. What then is the significance of this unique pair of doubles? What is the significance of this twinning, the always uncanny repetition of the identical?

THE USES OF TWINNING

In writing a tale about male twins, knowingly or unknowingly, Sand repeats an ancient motif. Indeed, according to Bruno Bettelheim: "The motif of the two brothers is central to the oldest fairy

tale, which was found in an Egyptian Papyrus of 1250 B.C. In over three
thousand years since then it has taken many forms. One study enum-
erates 70 different versions, but probably there are many more" (91).
Much of the extraordinary appeal of *Fadette* is rooted in its manipulation of material that is doubly archaic: archaic because of its venerable ancestry, archaic too because it centers on one of the earliest
stages of human development, individuation, the separation of the
self from Other. By making the two brothers twins Sand hyperbolizes
their initial indistinguishability. The very first gesture performed by
the midwife who delivers the babies, the wise mère Sagette, is to mark
the first born to distinguish him from his identical twin. Thus is the
disaster of violence averted for, as René Girard reminds us, the birth
of twins is viewed in many primitive societies with a special horror,
which has long puzzled anthroplogists. In keeping with his own theory
that violence is bred, paradoxically, by an excess of similarity, Girard
suggests that the fear inspired by the birth of twins is due to the
potentially dangerous crisis of difference their uncanny resemblance
figures:

Twins invariably share a cultural identity, and they often have a striking
physical resemblance to each other. Wherever differences are lacking,
violence threatens. . . . It is only natural that twins should awaken fear, for
they are harbingers of indiscriminate violence, the greatest menace to
primitive societies. (*Violence and the Sacred*, 57)

DIFFERENTIATION

From the outset the story of the twins bodies forth the
need to institute difference within sameness. We have already alluded
to the distinguishing mark etched onto the elder twin's skin by the
wise midwife in *Fadette*. This diacritical gesture is immediately followed
by another, indeed a doubly diacritical gesture which demonstrates
the inherently differential nature of language and of subjecthood ruled
by language. In being inscribed in the onomastic kinship system, the
twins are twice differentiated: the one from the other and each from
his godfather:

The older one was called Sylvain, which soon became Sylvinet, to *distinguish*
him from his older brother, who had acted as his godfather; and the younger

one was called Landry, a name which he kept unchanged from the time of his baptism because his uncle who was his godfather, had been called Landriche since he was very young. (10; italics mine)

L'aîné fut nommé Sylvain, dont on fit bientôt Sylvinet pour le *distinguer* de son frère aîné, qui lui avait servi de parrain; et le cadet fut appelé Landry, nom qu'il garda comme il l'avait reçu au baptême, parce que son oncle, qui était son parrain, avait gardé de son jeune âge la coutume d'être appelé Landriche. (42; italics mine)

But diacritical differences on the plane of the signifier are not sufficient guarantors of peace and happiness. The midwife sternly advises the parents to separate the twins from the outset or dire consequences will ensue: "by every means you can think of, stop them getting too involved with each other. . . if you don't follow my advice you will rue the day" (12) ("par tous les moyens que vous pourrez imaginer, empêchez-les de se confondre l'un avec l'autre. . . si vous ne le faites pas, vous vous en repentirez grandement un jour" [44]). Predictably, given the laws of the fairy-tale genre, the parents do not heed the midwife's warnings and the twins are suckled at the same breast and brought up as inseparable playmates. Throughout their childhood the twins are fused into a remarkably self-contained dyad that renders the grammar of possession and personal property inoperative:

Sometimes attempts were made to give something to only one of them, when they both wanted it; but if it was something good to eat, they would immediately share it; or if it was a little toy or small knife for their use, they would use it together or take turns, without bothering about what belonged to whom. (18)

On tenta aussi de donner, à l'un seulement, quelque chose dont tous deux avaient envie; mais tout aussitôt, si c'était chose bonne à manger, ils partageaient; ou si c'était toute autre amusette ou épelette à leur usage, ils le mettaient en commun, sans distinction du tien et du mien. (50)

In time, however, as they enter adolescence, practical considerations dictate the necessity for a physical separation of the two members of the dyad. It is at this critical juncture that Sand is closest to the ancient motif, for it is an invariant feature of the two brothers' tale that one brother leaves while the other stays home, that one brother successfully breaks the ties that bind while the other remains fixated at the earlier stage of symbiotic bonding.

Now it is of particular relevance to the argument I want to make that the differentiation between the twins will at one point be coded as sexual. Sylvinet, the stay-at-home brother, is the mother's favorite because of his feminizing attachment to the domestic sphere, while Landry enjoys the father's favor because of his superior virile strength. The mother makes the sexualization of the difference between the twins quite explicit when she says to herself:

My Landry is a *real boy*, he only want to live, move, work and move about. But this one here has *the heart of a girl*—he is so gentle and sweet that one cannot help loving him for it. (25; translation modified, italics mine)

Mon Landry est bien un *véritable garçon*, Ça ne demande qu'à vivre, à remuer, à travailler et à changer de place. Mais celui-ci a *le coeur d'une fille*; c'est si tendre et si doux qu'on ne peut pas s'empêcher d'aimer ça comme ses yeux. (58; italics mine)

For all its charming naiveté this is a complex passage: on the one hand the mother relies on preexisting notions of boyness and girlness to ground her sexual differentiation of her twin boys; on the other, her boys are boys, and sexual differentiation appears here to be merely a secondary, belated difference mapped onto anatomical sameness. Sexual difference is then arbitrary, and not essential. It is applied onto sameness to institute difference where difference is lacking. It is not the founding difference of the symbolic order, but merely *the difference of differences*. Indeed, invariably in Sand distinctions between same sex doubles are isomorphous with sexual difference, as can be seen in *Lélia*, where the difference between the female doublets, Lélia, the frigid intellectual, and Pulchérie, her orgasmic courtesan sister, involves the disparity not merely in their capacity for sexual pleasure, but in their very sexual inscription, Lélia being coded as masculine, Pulchérie as feminine. In enlisting sexual difference as a privileged mode of distinguishing members of the same sex Sand is not, I hasten to point out, innovating; she is adopting a conventional mode of exposing the conventionality of gender definitions. Her contemporary and friend Flaubert resorts to exactly the same means to introduce difference within sameness while at the same time subverting the sexual stereotypes of bourgeois patriarchal culture, first in *Sentimental Education*, where Frédéric plays woman to Deslauriers's man and, more strikingly still, in the case of his male couple of retirees, Bouvard and Pécuchet. Nevertheless, there is a difference between Sand's and Flaubert's deconstructions of the male-female paradigm and that difference coresponds to the difference between masculine and feminine forms of fetishism: whereas Flaubert consistently refuses to decide the question of sexual difference, Sand, as we observed in our first reading of *Fadette*, does on one level stop the endless oscillation of fetishism, in recognition of the inexorable force of cultural constraints in transforming anatomy into destiny. However arbitrary and unnatural sexual difference is, Fadette must give up her phallic attributes if she is to pursue the narrative destiny of woman, that is, marriage and motherhood.

　　　　The double strands of the plot I have teased out appear at this stage to resist any attempt to weave them into a seamless text: for if we read *Fadette*, as Sand explicitly instructs us to do, as the story of a female *Bildung*, then sexual difference in the traditional sense of opposition is assumed as the inevitable outcome, the *telos* of human development. If, however, we focus on the parallel plot, the maturational progress of the male twins, the assertion of an essential sexual difference is subverted; for the twins growing up is not bound up with assuming one's designated place within the binary sexual economy, rather with achieving differentiation. Whereas Fadette's growth consists in identification (with her mother), the twins consists in disidentification (with each other).

REREADING FEMININITY

　　　　The difference that must be instituted between the two brothers in order for them to enter the symbolic is the difference between self and other, the sundering of a symbiotic dyad. According to Lacan such a dyad is always, in the end, as in the beginning, the founding dyad constituted by the mother and child in the imaginary. However, as many commentators have noted, for Lacan the imaginary is unisexual, before rather than beyond difference. And yet ever since Freud began, somewhere around 1925, to recognize that the development of the little girl could not simply be traced from the template of male development, because of the whited-out continent of the female pre-Oedipus, psychoanalysts have argued that separation from the mother represents a far more complex task for the little girl than it does for the little boy. Indeed, if there is one thread than runs through the texts bearing on feminine specificity on both sides of the Atlantic it is the recovery and valorization of the mother-daughter bond. For Luce Irigaray, western phallocentric conceptual systems are grounded not so much in the repression of the female as in the suppression of women's essential bond with their mothers. A feminist psychoanalyst of the object-relations school, Nancy Chodorow, approaching the question from the angle of sociology, has placed particular emphasis on the almost insuperable difficulties the girl child encounters in achieving separation from the mother under current childrearing practices, where the primary caretaker is female. She concludes that the daughter does not ever really achieve total separation from the mother and that this continuousness with the mother is extended to her other relationships, making women more caring, more intimately connected to others than men.

While operating with different assumptions and different agendas, both Irigaray and Chodorow locate the specifically feminine in the intimate intensities of the mother-daughter relationship. By rewriting the traditional tale of the two brothers as an exemplary tale of separation and individuation, Sand has then stamped it with a distinctive sexual mark, one I will call feminine. To put it another, more paradoxical way: it is precisely Sand's insistence on the difference *before* sexual difference, on differentiation rather than difference,that constitutes the feminine specificity of her writing in this tale (as well as in many other of her works of fiction).

THE CUTTING EDGE

How then does this differentiation take place? Or rather, where? For invariably in Sand, differentiation, whether sexual or diacritical, is linked to a thematics of the liquid. If the Fadette plot line culminates in the scene where Landry tells Fadette she must renounce her unfeminine ways and become a woman, the "bessons" narrative I

am now foregrounding culminates in the scene where Landry, arche-
typally, enters the woods to find his lost brother, who, angered by
Landry's fancied neglect, has gone off to sulk. Just as he is about to
give in to his despair, Fadette materializes seemingly out of nowhere—
this is her first appearance in the novel and it is as a figure of the
good witch who helps the hero in his trial in the dark woods—and
tells Landry where to find his brother. He is on the other bank of the
portion of the river the twins call in their own idiolect, *la coupure*, with
a small c: "So Landry went to the cutting, which is what he and his
brother used to call this part of the field of rushes" (42) ("Landry
approcha donc de la coupure, car son frère et lui avaient la coutume
d'appeler comme cela cet endroit de leur joncière" [79]). What is
striking about the scene of their reunion is that throughout it the two
brothers are separated by the cutting waters and remain on opposite
banks of the stream. The *coupure* figures the diacritical slash that
institutes difference within sameness; topology is ontology.

From that day forward, the break between Landry and
Sylvinet will widen, as Landry goes forward into the world, eagerly
growing up, while Sylvinet, filled with envy and resentment at his
brother's betrayal of their symbiotic pact, remains at home, clinging
to his mother's apron-strings, hopelessly fixated at an early stage of
affective development. Sylvinet's bad feelings reach fever pitch when
Landry becomes involved with Fadette, who played such a crucial part
in the separation of the twins, since it was she who showed Landry
the way to *la coupure*. She comes on the scene of fiction at the precise
moment when the two brothers are to be definitively precipitated into
difference; in a word, far from representing the feminine side of the
sexual paradigm, when viewed from the perspective of the twins' story,
Fadette figures differentiation—she is la coupure.[4] Now, in true witchlike
fashion, when she appears to Landry in the dark woods, in exchange
for coming to his aid, she extracts from him a promise: that he will
do her bidding, whatever and whenever it will be. Months go by, and
Landry begins to forget his Faustian contract. Then one day Fadette
appears and makes known her wish: that Landry dance with her and
her only at the upcoming ball. Landry is extremely troubled by this
request because he had earlier promised his first dance to his sweet-
heart, the coquette Madelon, the opposition of the coquette to the

"natural woman" being a topos of nineteenth-century women's writing. The male protagonist must in the course of his erotic apprenticeship transfer his affections from the conventionally attractive coquette, whose attentions gratify his narcissism, to the less conventionally pretty and often poorer love-object, with whom he can have the anaclitic relationship appropriate to masculine eroticism. This transference is explicitly thematized in the first of Sand's three pastoral *contes*, *La Mare au Diable*. Because Landry has told no one, not even or least of all Sylvinet, of his encounter with Fadette, his selection of·the homely "little cricket" as a dance partner is largely viewed as incomprehensible. Sylvinet, in particular, is distressed and humiliated by his brother's bizarre and ridiculous object-choice and turns his hostility against Fadette.

INVENTING THE TALKING CURE

When, as the tale draws to a close, the break between the brothers appears irreversible, the case of Sylvinet attains pathological proportions. Finally he succumbs to what we might call anachronistically a nervous breakdown, taking to his bed and refusing to get up. After all efforts to cure Sylvinet fail, Landry asks Fadette to intervene. The method Fadette adopts to cure Sylvinet is, however, neither magical nor botanical, it is psychological. In order to deliver him from his pathological hostility toward herself, his rival for his brother's affections, Fadette devises a cure which consists in talking out the feelings whose repression has caused Sylvinet to fall ill and produce somatic symptoms:

"You are so learned, Fanchonette, you should find a way of curing him."
    "The only cure I know is reasoning," she answered, "for it is his mind which makes his body ill, and whoever can cure the one will cure the other." (156)

Toi, qui es si savante, Fanchonnette, tu devrais bien trouver un moyen de le guérir.
    —Je n'en connais pas d'autre que le raisonnement, répondit-elle; car c'est son esprit qui rend son corps malade, et qui pourrait guérir l'un, guérirait l'autre. (206)

Sand never stopped inventing psychoanalysis: the notion that neurosis and even the threat of psychosis can be averted only by passing through the straight gate of the symbolic is a reccurrent theme in her fiction (v. *Mauprat*). But, precisely because Fadette is an experimental scientist, the uncanny anticipation of another scene which was to unfold in Vienna, light years away from the rustic Berry setting of the tale, is more amply developed here than elsewhere in her fiction. Rehearsing the emergence of psychoanalysis from hypnosis, Fadette's initial treatment of her patient involves laying her hands first on his hand, then on his forehead, while he is plunged in a feverish sleep. By entering as it were into direct contact with Sylvinet's unconscious, Fadette succeeds in transforming his hostility toward her into that peculiar form of dependence Freud was to call transference. When Sylvinet emerges from his fever, he asks his mother: "Where's this Fadette, then? I think she helped me. Isn't she coming back?" (173) ("Où est donc cette Fadette? M'est avis qu'elle m'avait soulagé. Est-ce qu'elle ne reviendra plus?" [227]). Fadette returns and now begins the talking cure, as she instructs her patient to respect the cardinal rule of what was to become psychoanalysis, the uncensored articulation of all thoughts: "Say it all, Sylvain, you musn't keep anything back" (174) ("Dites tout, Sylvain, il ne me faut rien céler" [229]). The effect produced on Sylvinet by Fadette's novel treatment is spectacular and his condition improves markedly. There is, however, one major hitch: just as in the princeps case of psychoanalysis, Anna O., in the course of the treatment an unmastered transference has turned to love.

COMPULSORY HETEROSEXUALITY: READING FOR DIFFERENCE
(II)

Subverted on one level, sexual difference returns at another. Just as Fadette's social integration necessitates her renunciation of masculine behavior, Sylvinet's cure entails his substitution of a heterosexual object-choice for the homosexual one constituted by his brother. Thus one of the other wise women consulted by his parents in the course of his illness says in no uncertain terms: "There is only one thing which will save your child—to love women" (152) ("Il n'y aurait qu'une chose pour sauver votre enfant, c'est qu'il aimât les femmes" [201]). And she adds:

"He has an overabundance of affection in him, and always having turned it on his brother he has almost forgotten his sex, and in doing so he has gone against the Lord's law, which says that a man shall cherish a woman more than father and mother, more than sisters and brothers." (152)

—Il a une surabondance d'amitié dans le coeur, et, pour l'avoir toujours portée sur son besson, il a oublié quasiment son sexe, et, en cela, il a manqué à la loi du bon Dieu, qui veut que l'homme chérisse une femme plus que père et mère, plus que frères et soeurs. (201)

Before we condemn the utter conventionality of Sand's model of human desire, which is also to say of narrative closure, for the two are inseparable, we must take into account the perverse twist of the text's conclusion: when Sylvinet does make the transition to heterosexuality he chooses what is in fact an incestuous object of desire, his brother's wife. Thus, for him, far from providing any sort of resolution, the Oedipus consummates his sexual irresolution. The happy ending of the tale is purchased at the price of Sylvinet's self-imposed exile, for fated to love forever the first woman he falls in love with, Sylvinet takes himself out of the picture of domestic bliss and goes off to serve in Napoleon's army, rising rapidly in the ranks. The escape from incest signals the fall back into the history from whose bloody conflicts Sand sought to escape in her pastoral narrative. The reinscription of an absolute sexual difference signaled on the one hand by Sylvinet's love for Fadette and on the other by the apparently comedic closure of the tale—Landry's and Fadette's marriage—is undermined by the persistence of Sylvinet's unresolved sexual destiny. Heterosexuality, and the sexual difference that grounds it, is insepar-able from the incest taboo, and incest is here only averted, indefinitely deferred rather than definitively prohibited. We know that elsewhere in the tryptich of which *Fadette* constitutes the third panel, in that privileged Proustian intertext, *François le Champi*, incest is not only consummated, as François weds his adoptive mother, but happily so, as the mother-son couple live as happily ever after as any other fairy-tale couple. That Sylvinet's desire cannot achieve the same happy resolution, and that that impossibility drives him out of pastoral into epic suggests that in *Fadette*, that most immediately postrevolutionary of tales, a certain happy ending becomes unstuck and the fundamental unsociability of human desire cannot be accommodated within the framework of the narrative; the bloody civil war has left its mark on this tale of the impossibility of two brothers achieving happiness.

History returns and it returns at precisely the moment when one has one's back turned: while we peer obsessively into the abyss of sexual difference and its vicissitudes, history is already at work in that difference. If we are to go beyond the current split (when it is not an impasse) in feminist literary criticism, we will have to recognize that, to a degree that has perhaps not been sufficiently measured, *history inhabits sexual difference.*[5] The *coupure* which divides the text from itself may also be read as the most discreet of allusions to the gap constituted by 1848, an internal break mirroring in *abyme* the historical break Sand foregrounds in her preface. The text is thus traversed by a fissure that signals the return of the repressed historical reality, for in Sand's words: "Everything feeds into history, *everything is history, even the novels which seem* unrelated to the political situations which gave rise to them" ("Tout concourt à l'histoire, *tout est l'histoire, même les romans qui semblent* ne se rattacher en rien aux situations politiques qui les voient éclore)" (in Moers 1979, 224). Feminist theory has from the outset recognized the need to historicize, which is to say denaturalize notions of sexual difference. But studies of difference as it operates in literary texts have generally posited the nonhistoricity of the problematics of difference and to that extent reessentialized it. Reading double perhaps offers a way out of the impasse of many bicontinental feminist literary critics, in that it opens up a new space. Sexual difference can no longer be studied within the conceptual universe of psychoanalysis alone. A new articulation must be elaborated to take into account the place of history in the play of difference.

NOTES

1. Cf. in this volume Nancy Miller, "Arachnologies: The Woman, The Text, and The Critic"; see also her "The Knot, the Letter, and the Book."

2. My reference to a "first stage" feminist reading alludes to recent histories of

feminist criticism that generally equate the infancy of feminist criticism with a focus on "images of women" (particularly in male-authored texts). See, for example, Elizabeth Abel's fine "Editor's Introduction," to the Special Issue of *Critical Inquiry*, "Writing and Sexual Difference."

    3. Cf. Curtis Cate, *George Sand: A Biography*, for yet another biographical reading of what he terms a "juvenile version of *The Taming of the Shrew*": "the village brat was quite obviously (though the author may not consciously have realized it) her own daughter Solange" (606) with whom Sand had a famously stormy relationship.

    4. On woman as *coupure*, see Lemoine-Luccioni (91 and 98).

    5. In an essay on Sand that appeared several months after "Reading Double" had been completed, Wendy Deutelbaum and Cynthia Huff assert that a "feminist psychoanalytic approach, by its simultaneous focus on subjectivity and culturally constructed gender" is in a unique position to remedy a double lack: ideological criticism's lack of attention to "personal and psychic relations" and psychoanalytic theory's bracketing of "the social contexts of psychological processes" (Wendy Deutelbaum and Cynthia Huff, "Class, Gender, and Family System: The Case of George Sand," p. 260). Deutelbaum and Huff begin where I end and our approaches and specific concerns throughout our respective essays differ substantially. Nevertheless, the convergence of our essays on the paradigmatic figure of Sand is highly significant: it corroborates my sense that because of her peculiar "patriarchal family drama" (p. 277) and her vivid dramatization of the difficulties of conforming to the cultural construction of woman, more than any other French woman writer Sand renders urgent to think through the articulation of the categories of class and gender. Stated baldly—I hope to elaborate on this hypothesis more fully in a longer study on Sand—my contention is that Sand's sexual oscillation was the psychic acting out of the impossibility for her of surmounting the irreconcilable class differences that presided over her birth.

WORKS CITED

Abel, Elizabeth. "Editor's Introduction." *Critical Inquiry*. Special Issue: "Writing and Sexual Difference" (Winter 1981), 8:173–78.

Bettelheim, Bruno. *The Uses of Enchantment: The Meaning and Importance of Fairy Tales*. New York: Vintage Books, 1977.

Bogaert, Geneviève Van Den. "Introduction." *La Petite Fadette*. Paris: Garnier-Flammarion, 1967.

Cate, Curtis. *George Sand: A Biography*. New York: Avon, 1975.

Cixous, Hélène. "The Laugh of the Medusa." Trans. Keith Cohen and Paula Cohen. In *New French Feminisms*. Ed. Isabelle de Courtivron and Elaine Marks. Amherst: University of Massachusetts Press, 1980.

—— "Le Rire de la Méduse." *L'Arc* (1975), 61:39–54.

Danahy, Michael. "Growing Up Female: George Sand's View in *La Petite Fadette*." In

The George Sand Papers: Conference Proceedings 1978. Ed. Natalie Datlof et al. New York: AMS Press, 1982.

Deutelbaum, Wendy, and Huff, Cynthia. "Class, Gender, and Family System: The Case of George Sand." In *The (M)other Tongue: Essays in Feminist Psychoanalytic Interpretation.* Ed. Shirley Nelson Garner, Claire Kahane, and Madelon Sprengnether. Ithaca: Cornell University Press, 1985.

Deutsch, Helene. *The Psychology of Women: A Psychoanalytic Interpretation,* vol. 1. New York: Grune and Stratton, 1944.

Girard, René. *Violence and the Sacred.* Trans. Patrick Gregory. Baltimore: The Johns Hopkins University Press, 1972.

Kristeva, Julia. "Woman can never be defined." Trans. Marilyn A. August. In *New French Feminisms.* Amherst: University of Massachusetts Press, 1980.

—— "La femme, ce n'est jamais ça." *Polylogue.* Paris: Seuil, 1977.

Lauretis, Teresa de. *Alice Doesn't: Feminism, Semiotics, Cinema.* Bloomington: Indiana University Press, 1984.

Lemoine-Luccioni, Eugénie. *Partage des femmes.* Paris: Seuil, Points, 1976.

Lévi-Strauss, Claude. *Structural Anthropology.* Trans. Claire Jacobson and Brooke Grundfest Schoepf. Garden City: Anchor Books, 1967.

Miller, Nancy K. "Arachnologies: The Woman, The Text, and The Critic," in this volume.

—— "The Knot, the Letter, and the Book." Unpublished ms.

Moers, Ellen. *Literary Women: The Great Writers.* Garden City: Anchor Press/Doubleday, 1977.

—— "Fraternal George Sand." *American Scholar* (Spring 1979), 47:221–26.

Sand, George. *Little Fadette.* Trans. Eva Figes. London: Blackie, 1967. All references to the English text are to this edition.

—— *La Petite Fadette.* Paris: Garnier-Flammarion, 1967. All references to the French text are to this edition.

—— "L'Auteur au lecteur." *La Mare au Diable.* Paris: Garnier-Flammarion, 1964. The translations are mine.

Schor, Naomi. "Female Fetishism: The Case of George Sand." *Poetics Today* (1985), 6(1/2).

Arachnologies:
The Woman, The Text,
and the Critic

NANCY K. MILLER

> Most of the reasoning of women and poets is done in parables.
> Now think of a spider . . .
> —Diderot, *D'Alembert's Dream*

In one of the final segments of *The Pleasure of the Text* (1973), Roland Barthes elaborates an ostensibly etymological definition of one of the key words in his title:

Text means *Tissue*; but whereas hitherto we have always taken this tissue as a product, a ready-made veil behind which lies, more or less hidden, meaning (truth), we are now emphasizing, in the tissue, the generative idea that the text is made, is worked out in a perpetual interweaving; lost in this tissue—this texture—the subject unmakes himself, like a spider dissolving in the constructive secretions of [her] web. Were we fond of neologisms, we might define the theory of the text as an *hyphology* (*hyphos* is the tissue and the spider's web). (64)

As you may have guessed from the title of this paper, we too are fond of neologisms, and in a moment will offer our theory of the text as an arachnology. But first let us review this fable of metamorphosis. In the move from product to production, from work to text, as Barthes puts it in the earlier essay by that name, the emphasis moves also from the image of a centrally strong or unitary subject to a more ambiguous and fragile identity dependent upon the indeterminacy of *process*. The subject in this model is not fixed in time or space, but suspended in a continual moment of fabrication. In the theorizing on the status of the text—the modern text more specifically—that has taken place in this country over the past ten or so years, two fundamental assumptions of Barthes's position in this passage have become formulaic and axiomatic: that the textual is the textile; and that the text maker, previously known as the author, to the extent that he is still figurable, paradoxically owes his representation to an undoing: a destabilization of the terms of identity itself brought about by a breakdown in the boundaries between inside and outside (and other well-known binary oppositions). At issue, however, is not so much the "Death of the Author" himself—in so many ways, long overdue—but the effect the argument has had of killing off by delegitimating other discussions of the writing (and reading) subject.[1] This suppression is not simply the result of an arbitrary shift of emphasis: when a theory of the text called "hyphology" chooses the spider's *web* over the spider, and the concept of textuality called the "writerly" chooses the threads of lace over the lacemaker (S/Z, 160), the productive agency of the subject is self-consciously erased by a model of text production which acts to foreclose the question of identity itself.[2]

The recasting of the text as texture—the better to bring about the dissolution of any subjective agency—has other important, if ironic, implications for feminist critics (who themselves often favor the tropology of the loom) that parallel the effacement of the spider and the lacemaker. For one thing, and we return to the question in some detail at the end of this paper, the language of textiles tends to engender in the dominant discursive strategies of much contemporary literary criticism a metaphorics of femininity deeply marked by Freud's account of women and weaving.[3] For another, the discourse of the male weavers rhetorically stages "woman" without in any way addressing women. This "masculine recuperation" of the feminine[4] is a variant of the phenomenon Alice Jardine has named *gynesis*—"the putting into discourse of 'woman' "—and Gayatri Spivak has described, somewhat differently, as the "double displacement."[5]

In other words, if Barthes had been less fond of neologisms, and a feminist, he might have named his theory of text production an "arachnology." In English, the word exists to describe the study of spiders, so we would have had not a neologism, but a catachresis[6]; and to borrow Elaine Showalter's term, a "gynocritics" (185). We will want to remember, and we will rehearse her story in a moment, that Arachne, the spider artist, began as a woman weaver of texts. By arachnology, then, I mean a critical positioning which reads *against* the weave of indifferentiation to discover the embodiment in writing of a gendered subjectivity; to recover within representation the emblems of its construction. It is from that perspective that I propose now to read Arachne's story: both as a figuration of woman's relation of production to the dominant culture, and as a possible parable (or critical modeling) of a feminist poetics.[7] Arachnologies, thus, involve more broadly the interpretation and reappropriation of a story, like many in the history of Western literature that deploys the interwoven structures of power, gender, and identity inherent in the production of mimetic art.

The motherless daughter of a wool dyer, Arachne, though "low-born" herself had "gained fame [nomen memorabile] for her skill [studio]." In fact her accomplishments in the "art of spinning and weaving wool" [artis] made those who came to see her "finished work," or "watch her as she worked" assume that Pallas Athena (Minerva) had taught her (289). But Arachne refuses this implicit hierarchy of talents and claims equality in artistic skill with the goddess. Disguised as an old woman, Athena comes to warn Arachne against defiance of the gods, but Arachne persists in her daring, and the two engage in a contest of representation: "They weave in pliant threads of gold, and trace in the weft some ancient tale" (293). Athena "pictures [pingit] the hills of Mars . . . and that old dispute over the naming of the land. There sit twelve heavenly gods on lofty thrones in awful majesty, Jove in their midst; each god she pictures [inscribit] with his own familiar features" (293). Athena also represents herself separately armed and victorious. The central display of Olympian power is restaged in the margins: "she weaves in the four corners of the web four scenes of contest, each clear in its own colours, and in miniature design." In each of these "pictured warnings," a mortal is punished by transformation out of human identity for having challenged the gods. These embedded mininarratives may, I think, also be seen as self-reflexive, internal commentaries on the authority of representation itself. Thus, when she finishes her work at the loom, and in a final gesture of authorization, the goddess signs her text by a self-referring metonymy, with a "border of peaceful olive wreath. . . [from] her own tree" (295).

Against the classically theocentric balance of Athena's tapestry, Arachne constructs a feminocentric protest: Europa, Leda, Antiope, are the more familiar names of women, carried off against their will by the "heavenly crimes" of divine desire, whose stories she weaves; Medusa, and more obscurely Erigone, who in one account, deceived by Bacchus, "later hangs herself on a nearby tree."[8] When Arachne completes her "realistic" figuration of the ancient heroines of the oldest western stories of seduction and betrayal, like Athena she too frames the finished product, but the legibility of her signature is more ambiguous: "The edge of the web with its narrow border is filled with flowers and clinging ivy intertwined" [intertextos].[9]

As the exempla in the corners of Athena's tapestry had anticipated, this is not a contest for a mortal to win. And thus though the product is judged flawless in the signifiers of its art—the *verisimilitude* of its representation—"real bull and real waves you would think them"—its producer must be punished for its signified. Thus, outwomaned, and in phallic identification with Olympian authority, the goddess destroys the woman's countercultural account: she "rent the embroidered web with its heavenly crimes" (297). Symptomatically—we recall that Athena identifies not only with the gods, but with godhead, the cerebral male identity that bypasses the female— she goes on not only to mutilate the text, but to destroy its author by beating her over the head with the shuttle—their shared emblem.[10] Arachne, in indignation, tries to hang herself, at which point Athena both pities and transforms her; she is to hang and yet to live: her head shrinks, her legs become "slender fingers" and, virtually all body—the antithesis of the goddess—she continues the act of spinning: "and now a spider, she exercises her old-time weaver art."

In the neologism of the text as hyphology, we have said, the mode of production is privileged over the subject whose supervising identity is dissolved in the work of the web. But Arachne's story, as we have just seen, is not only the tale of a text as tissue: it evokes a bodily substance and a violence to the teller that is not adequately accounted for by an attention to a torn web. Represented in Ovid's writing representing the stories of sexual difference as a matter of interpretation, Arachne is punished for her point of view. For this, she is restricted to spinning outside representation, to a reproduction that turns back on itself. Cut off from the work of art, she spins like a woman.

Barthes maintains in S/Z that "there is no *first* reading"; that if we act as though "there were a beginning of reading, as if everything were not already read," we are "obliged to read the same story everywhere" (16). I want to suggest here that the poetics of the "already read," depends upon the same logic as that of the "subject lost in the tissue": in both cases the animating assumption of the critical model depends upon the confident posture of mastery that (paradoxically) a post-Cartesian subject enjoys—we should allow this verb its sexual valence in English as well as French—in relation to the texts of his culture. As Annette Kolodny argues in "Dancing Through the Minefield," "we read well, and with pleasure, what we *already know* how to read; and what we know how to read is to a large extent dependent upon what we have already read (works from which we've developed our expectations and learned our interpretive strategies)" (12; emphasis added). Only the subject who is both self-possessed and possesses access to the library of the already read has the luxury of flirting with the escape from identity—like the loss of Arachne's "head"—promised by an aesthetics of the decentered (decapitated, really) body.

What I want to propose instead as a counterweight to this story of the deconstructed subject, restless with what he already knows, is a poetics of the *underread* and a practice of "overreading." The aim of this practice is double. It aims first to unsettle the interpretive model which thinks that it knows *when* it is rereading, and what is in the library, confronting its claims with Kolodny's counterclaim that "what we engage are not texts but paradigms" (8). In a second, parallel gesture this practice, like Kolodny's "revisionary rereading" ("A Map," 465), constructs a new object of reading, women's writing. Specifically, the latter project involves reading women's writing not "as if it had already been read," but as if it had never been read, *as if* for the first time. Overreading also involves a focus on the moments in the narrative which by their representation of writing itself might be said to figure the production of the female artist. This might mean a scene like Arachne's that thematizes explicitly the conditions of text production under the classical sex/gender arrangements of Western culture, or more coded representations of female signature of a sort we will consider in a moment.

To overread is also to wonder, as Woolf puts it famously in A *Room of One's Own*, about the conditions for the production of literature: "fiction," she writes, "is like a spider's web, attached ever so lightly perhaps, but still attached to life at all four corners. . . . [W]hen the web is pulled askew, hooked up at the edge, torn in the middle, one remembers that these webs are not spun in mid air by incorporeal creatures, but are the work of suffering human beings, and are attached to grossly material things, like health and the houses we live in" (43–44).[11] When we tear the web of women's texts we may discover in the representations of writing itself the marks of the grossly material, the sometimes brutal traces of the culture of gender; the inscriptions of its political structures.

REPRESENTING WRITING: OPHELIA DROWNS

In his 1893 essay on George Sand in *French Poets and Novelists*, Henry James considers "what makes things classical," and contrasts Sand's novels to Balzac's. He concludes that Balzac will last longer: "We cannot easily imagine posterity travelling with 'Valentine' or 'Mauprat', 'Consuelo', or the 'Marquis de Villemer' in its trunk." But he also imagines that "if these admirable tales fall out of fashion, such of our descendants as stray upon them in the dusty corners of old libraries will sit down on the bookcase ladder with the open volume and turn it over with surprise and enchantment. What a beautiful mind! they will say; what an extraordinary style! Why have we not known more about these things?" (180–81).[12] It is against that question that I propose a novel of George Sand for an exercise in overreading. Taking more specifically the closural moves of *Indiana* (1832), I want to suggest the ways in which by an internal figuration of its own ambivalent relationship to the dominant literature and its critics the narrative itself stages the difficulty of reading women's writing.

Because the novel has remained largely unread "in the

dusty corners of old libraries," it may be useful to provide a brief account of its major events here.[13] Indiana is a young, beautiful creole from the Ile Bourbon married to a much older and thoroughly unpleasant man, the retired Colonel Delmare. Living with her husband and cousin in seclusion on a country estate in France, she meets Raymon, a handsome, aristocratic rake from a neighboring estate, who has already seduced her maid and foster sister, Noun. When Noun, who is pregnant, realizes that Raymon is falling in love with her mistress, she drowns herself. Indiana blindly continues to believe in Raymon and fantasize about love, but when Colonel Delmare's business fails, and he decides to return to the Ile Bourbon, Indiana suddenly throws caution to the winds and comes alone to Raymon's rooms. Appalled by the implications of her gesture of self-sacrifice, Raymon sends Indiana away, and in despair, she heads for the Seine. She is saved from drowning by her faithful cousin Ralph (led to her by her dog Ophelia). Ralph returns to the island with the unhappy couple, and continues to watch over Indiana, who continues to dream of Raymon and of another life. Then, in a repetition of the earlier episode, Indiana, encouraged by Raymon's rhetoric of love—he writes a letter of regret— returns to France alone, overcoming enormous physical difficulties (in a particularly brutal scene Ophelia is killed trying to follow her) only to find that he has married a rich woman, Laure de Nangy, and taken over her former property. Rejected once again, she is found and saved by Ralph, and the two return to the Ile Bourbon, this time making a joint suicide pact. (The husband has died during Indiana's trip to France). In the penultimate scene of the novel Ralph confesses his love to Indiana, then taking her in his arms in a final embrace they poise to plunge to their death into the ravine below.

The novel was an overnight success and "made" George Sand. But the ending Sand chose for her "signature" novel, the first novel she published without the collaboration of Jules Sandeau, then and now posed problems for its readers. In his review of the novel, reprinted in *Portraits Contemporains* (1870), Sainte-Beuve refers to "les étranges invraisemblances vers la fin" (471), the "strange implausibilities [that occur] toward the end of the novel"; and Pierre Salomon, in his introduction to the Garnier edition, speculates: "The . . . epilogue might have been added for purely opportunistic reasons. It is not absurd to imagine that the end volume was also considered too slim and that to have the right number of pages, the publisher proposed the addition of a commercially satisfying conclusion, not exactly a happy marriage, but something equivalent" (vi; my translation). I don't have the time to argue here all the ways in which ideology leads and misleads that interpretation of the conclusion, and the closure of women's fiction in general. I would like instead to consider briefly the metacritical function of the final volume. What might it tell us about *how to read* the novel it integrally frames? And, more generally, as I have asked elsewhere, what does the "strange" and implausible ending tell us about reading for the plot of women's fiction?[14]

In the pages often referred to as the epilogue, and which bears a separate address (to A. J. Néraud), the narrator, whom the reader meets for the first time, finds himself on the island, and meets the couple who in fact did not fall into the abyss; they are living together in their "Indian cottage" on the island, freeing the slaves, and caring for the poor. And we learn that it is from Ralph himself that the narrator has heard the story we have just read. The narrator, we are told in the preface, is a young man who "abstains from weaving into the woof of his narrative preconceived opinions, judgments all formed" (n.p./78). What are we now to make of this male "weaver" who wanders into the wilderness and tries to decipher the mysteries of its landscape?

I halted at the foot of a crystallized basaltic monument, about sixty feet high and cut with facets as if by a lapidary. At the top of this strange object an inscription seemed to have been traced in bold characters by an immortal hand . . . curious hieroglyphics, mysterious characters which seem to have been stamped there like the seal of some supernatural being, written in cabalistic letters. I stood there a long time, detained by a foolish idea that I might find a meaning for those ciphers. This profitless search caused me to fall into a profound meditation, during which I forgot that time was flying. (316/341)

Hieroglyphs are of course a commonplace of Romantic writing, and constitute by their semiotic protocol an automatic appeal to interpretation. But, in the pause, during which the narrator contemplates nature's messages, and tries to decipher the meaning of its "mysterious characters," the reader, I think, ponders more locally the fate of the lovers left on the "threshold of another life" and the meaning of their suspended narrative. In other words, I want to suggest that, coming after a certain narratological flamboyance, a literal cliffhanger marked by the (. . .) punctuation of suspense (deleted in the English translation), this sudden staging of the hermeneutic act forces us to pay particular attention to its operations. At stake here is what I think amounts to a *mise en abyme*, as it were (the pun is not only terrible and irresistible but important), of a female signature, the internal delineation of a writer's territory. For the "female landscape" is not only, as Ellen Moers has shown, a scene within which to read metaphors of sexuality, it is also an iconography of a desire for a revision of story, and in particular a revision of closure (255). This desire for another logic of plot which by definition cannot be narrated, looks elsewhere for expression: in the authorization provided by *discours*, and in descriptive emblems tied to the representation of writing itself. A practice of overreading self-consciously responds to the appeal of the abyss.[15]

Gilbert and Gubar have argued that the story of female authorship, its mode of self-division, is often read as a "palimpsest" (73) through the script of the dominant narrative. In *Indiana* that story is figured by this canonical representation of the romantic artist who measures his creativity against divine (or diabolical) makers. Thus the narrator speculates about the creators of this awesome scene, and wonders who could have "toyed with mountains as with grains of sand, and strewn, amid creations which man has tried to copy, these grand conceptions of art, these sublime contrasts impossible of realization which seem to defy the audacity of the artist and to say to him derisively: 'Try again' " (316/341). Against what model can a *female* artist measure herself in nineteenth-century France? Like the young male narrator who meditates upon nature's blueprint, Indiana perceives the poetic structures of landscape. But when she wanders over the island and contemplates the sails on the horizon, her vision does not translate into acts of representation. Instead, the woman is immobilized by her own imagination; she dreams not of making art, but of being in love in Paris (XXIV, 229/249).

And she writes. Like the heroine of an eighteenth-century epistolary novel prevented from acting in the world, Indiana writes as a way of establishing control over her lack of control. Indiana "had adopted the depressing habit of writing down every evening a narrative of the sorrowful thoughts of the day. This journal of her sufferings was addressed to Raymon, and, although she had no intention of sending it to him, she talked to him, sometimes passionately, sometimes bitterly, of the misery of her life and of the sentiments which she could not overcome" (XXVI, 248/268). That the construction of such a text is a gesture of potentially transgressive self-empowerment can be seen in her husband's response to discovering its existence. Having broken open the box that contained her papers—which included Raymon's letters—the husband, in his rage, "unable to utter a word . . . seized her by the hair, threw her down, and stamped on her forehead with his heel" (XXVI, 249/269). This marking—what we might think of as the dominant signature—generates the final sequences of the novel, and Indiana's heroinism. Clearly, however, Indiana's writing by itself cannot produce effective forms of protest against the powers of the social text, but Sand grants her heroine a literary victory of sorts. Thus, when Raymon panics at the social implications of Indiana's decision to live for love and beyond convention, and mocks her for having studied society in novels "written for the entertainment of lady's-maids" (XX, 191/210), Sand in *her* novel challenges the grounds of that literary judgment by returning it to him. Indiana writes from the island: "You see I was mad; according to your cynical expression I had acquired my knowledge of life from novels written for lady's-maids, from those gay, childish works of fiction in which the heart is interested in the success of wild enterprises and in impossible felicities" (XXIII, 222/240). Indiana's writing is incorporated within a critique of the love narrative itself which in turn becomes the frame for a different social realism. It is after all the dog named Ophelia who drowns. And unlike the victim of female plot, the darker double, Noun, in the end the heroine of these "strange implausibilities," does not die of unrequited love; indeed, she may, with Ralph, live the "impossible felicities" she had read about.[16]

In her autobiography, *Histoire de ma vie* Sand explains that writing *Indiana* also marked the end of a collaboration characterized by its inefficiency: one of them would spend the day unwriting what the other one had written the day before. This doing and undoing ("ce remaniement successif"), she explains, "made of our work an embroidery like Penelope's" ("faisait de notre ouvrage la broderie de Pénélope"

[V, 1, 174]). In *Indiana* the traces of a certain doubling seem to remain. A contemporary critic, thinking Sandeau was still on the scene, imagined that he saw what we might call today a "bisexual" origin in the authorship of *Indiana*: "One would say that this brilliant but unharmonious material [cette étoffe brillante mais sans harmonie] is the work [oeuvre] of two very different workers [ouvriers]; the hands of a young man stretched the strong, sturdy fabric and the hands of a woman embroidered flowers of silk and gold" (Vol. 2, 1343, n. 4). In a way, it is true that the novel offers a dual model of authorship, but the division of labor is not marked simply along the fault line of sexual difference. If we read the work of the feminine hand in Indiana's embroidery, "the flowers that had bloomed beneath the breath of fever, watered by her daily tears," we might also read the "masculine" identity figured in a less docile female figure, in Sand's other portrait of the female artist cast in the body of a woman who paints: Laure, a rich aristocratic young woman who appears fleetingly at the beginning of the novel long enough to label Raymon a ladies' man, a Lovelace. At the novel's close she sits at the place formerly occupied by the work table where Indiana embroidered, and to amuse herself copies the wall hangings of the chateau in watercolor. She parodies the rococo pastoral "fictions" of eighteenth-century France—which are already historical commentaries—and marks the ambiguous status of her signature in the corner of her painting: in the place of her name she writes the word "pastiche" (XXVIII, 266–67/288).[17]

Like Arachne at her loom, Laure at her easel offers a representation of the female signature of protest. An ironic nineteenth-century female artist refuses the pathos and limits of the woman who embroiders her way through the plot of her life: eighteenth-century woman, whose *proper* activity according to Laure is "paint[ing] fans and produc[ing] masterpieces of threadwork." Like Myth under Arachne's threads, History under Laure's satirical brush, derides pastoral, a Boucher-like landscape in which the "costumes of the boudoir and the shepherd's hut [are] curiously identical" (XXVIII, 267/288). But like "the engravings representing the pastoral attachment of Paul and Virginia" (VII, 59/82) that decorate Indiana's virginal bedroom, recontained by women's writing, pastoral comes back to indict history. Thus it is not so surprising that in the end Sand relocates Indiana on the island of her beginnings. The novel moves backwards from France to its colonies and at that distance points to the limits of the dominant narrative. Sand's nostalgic preromanticism—like George Eliot's insistence on the daisy fields of childhood in another watery text—is itself a mode of critique.

Pastiche is a term particularly charged for Sand, since it is the word with which her mentor Latouche measures her progress. As she tells the tale in Histoire de ma vie, his first reaction (flipping through the pages) to Indiana is not flattering: "Come now, this is a pastiche! School of Balzac! Pastiche! What do you mean by it?" (V, 1, 173). Latouche comes to regret his hasty evaluation, and writes the following morning: "Your book is a masterpiece. I stayed up all night to read it. No woman alive can sustain the insolence of a comparison with you. Successes like those of Lamartine await you . . . Balzac and Merimée lie dead under Indiana" (vol. 2, 1342, n. 1). Literary history has not borne out Latouche's judgment, but that is another story. The pleasure of the text is also a critical politics.

Toward the end of his essay on Sand, James explains that he has been trying to "read . . . over" the "author's romances," but that he must "frankly confess that we have found it impossible" (180). George Sand, he writes, "invites reperusal less than any mind of equal eminence," and wonders whether this is "because after all she was a woman, and the laxity of the feminine intellect could not fail to claim its part in her?" (181). The question, being after all rhetorical, is left without an answer. Although earlier in the essay, James accepts the apparently telling objection to the novels that they "contain no living figures . . . who like so many of the creations of other novelists, have become part of the public fund of allusion and quotation" (156), the invocation of sexual logic here suggests that the grounds of citational difference in fact derive, at least in part, from an older poetics of gender. It is precisely the persistence of that drift in critical discourse that overreading seeks to challenge.

THE ARIADNE COMPLEX

In a recent essay called "The Voice of the Shuttle is Ours," Patricia Joplin reviews Geoffrey Hartman's essay, "The Voice of the Shuttle: Language from the Point of View of Literature," which turns on a gloss of Aristotle's recording of a phrase from a lost play of

Sophocles based on Philomela's story: "As you know," Hartman explains, "Tereus, having raped Philomela, cut out her tongue to prevent discovery. But she weaves a tell-tale account of her violation into a tapestry (or robe) which Sophocles calls 'the voice of the shuttle.' If metaphors as well as plots or myths could be archetypal, I would nominate Sophocles' voice of the shuttle for that distinction" (25). Joplin argues, as does Jane Marcus in "Liberty, Sorority, Misogyny" (88), that when Hartman interrogates the power of the metaphor he "celebrates Language and not the violated woman's emergence from silence. He celebrates Literature and the male poet's trope, not the woman's elevation of her safe, feminine, domestic craft—weaving—into a new means of resistance.... When Hartman exuberantly analyzes the structure of the trope for voice, he makes an all too familiar elision of gender" (26). "The specific nature of the woman's double violation," she comments further, "disappears behind the apparently genderless (but actually male) language of 'us,' the 'I,' and the 'you,'" who in Hartman's account "attest to that which violates, deprives, silences only as a mysterious unnamed 'something.' For the feminist unwilling to let Philomela become universal before she has been met as female, this is the primary evasion" (30). Joplin's attention to the universalizing moves in Hartman's discourse away from the details of Philomela's silencing, and her reappropriation of the Philomela story, forcefully raise the question of a more specifically "*feminist* poetics" (28) that would reclaim the voice of the shuttle from the myth of a postgendered poetics.

I would like to turn now to an essay of J. Hillis Miller's which, I will argue, like Geoffrey Hartman's, fails to "meet" the female; in this case, the female in Arachne. The essay, which many of you will know, is entitled "Ariachne's Broken Woof." It takes as its pretext a passage from Shakespeare's *Troilus and Cressida* (Miller quotes from the Variorum):

> ... This is and is not *Cressid*:
> Within my soule, there doth conduce a fight
> Of this strange nature, that a thing inseperate,
> Divides more wider than the skie and earth:
> And yet the spacious bredth of this division,
> Admits no Orifex for a point as subtle,
> As *Ariachnes* broken woofe to enter: (45)

Much is at stake here, since to make sense of, or merely to decipher the phrase "Ariachne's broken woof"—is it a "slip of the tongue or of the pen?" (45)—involves nothing less than a gloss on the relations between the sexes, and a theory of the text. At stake as well in my choice of this essay is a look at the relations between deconstruction and feminism as practiced in the United States, two critical movements which like Arachne and Ariadne are both "alike and different" (57). The question through which I will more specifically address the problem of that relationship in these final pages is this: what grounds allow one to link or separate the two names Arachne and Ariadne which conflated in "a single word, Ariachne, mime the mode of relationship between two myths which exist side by side in a culture, and are similar without being identical"? (55).[18]

Miller comments on the sexual transpositions imaged in these ambiguous lines: "Ariachne's broken woof, figure of a torn or deflowered virginity, becomes, in a mind-twisting reversal of the sexes, itself a 'point' which might tear, though it can find in this case no orifex to penetrate.... Tearer and torn here change places, as Ariachne's broken woof both is and is not male and is and is not female, as the stories of Ariadne and Arachne are both alike and different" (57). But does the inversion of penetration, the blurring of the lines of sexual difference that Miller enlists to "justify" the yoking of the two women's names in the lines of *Troilus and Cressida* also inhabit their stories *outside* the Shakespearean context? Are all differences created equal? Put another way, if viewed from a position which favors the indeterminacy of meaning and the insecurity of all identity, tearer and torn trade places in a linguistic play of indifference, does it follow that no significant difference inhabits the two stories? Putting the matter politically, if we can't tell the difference between the stories, what are our chances of identifying the material differences between and among women that for feminist theory remains crucial? If Arachne and Ariadne change places in the threads of the loom, is nothing lost in this translation?

In a way this is also to worry whether we can, at least in critical practice, preserve women from the fate of "woman"?

As a way into and, by the logic of the labyrinth, out of these questions, let us briefly review Ariadne's story. In the *Metamorphoses*, Ariadne is never *named* in an account which figures a trajectory and an engagement that take place essentially between men: Minos, the father/King, to hide the monster produced by his wife and a sacrificial bull, commissions Daedalus, the architect/Artist to build an enclosure; a space designed to provide no exit. Theseus, the adventurer (and ladies' man) arrives to press his claim to fame. This heroic gesture brings death to the Minotaur "when, by the virgin Ariadne's help" (the Latin reads, *ope virginea*; *ops* means also might and power) the difficult entrance, which no former adventurer had ever reached again, was found by winding up the thread (419). Having provided the thread that unravels the maze, Ariadne, madly in love, is carried off, seduced and abandoned on the island of Naxos by the faithless hero. In alternate endings of the story, she is then either rescued and consoled by Dionysos, who marries her and offers her a crown of stars which he sends up to the skies; or, disconsolate like Arachne, hangs herself with her own thread.

What then is figured by Ariadne's thread, the woman or the thread? The agency of her desire or the process of solution she authorizes? When the critic suffering from what Naomi Schor has called an "Ariadne complex" (3) follows the thread of a reading practice common to the poststructuralist models of Barthes, Derrida, Deleuze—and more locally, of Hillis Miller—that by its metaphors and metonymies associates itself with the feminine, whose story is it? When the critic follows the thread handed to him by the "woman in the text," the thread that enables him to weave his way back through the meanders of the path already taken, whose powers do we admire?[19] The man who entered to kill, or the woman who allowed him to exit alive? Or is this a case, like the minotaur and the mermaid troped by Dorothy Dinnerstein, of an uneasy but no less powerful heterosexual arrangement founded on the deadly inseparable ("inseparate") relation between the two?

"Ariadne's thread," Miller writes in the essay by that name, "is both the labyrinth and a means of safely retracing the labyrinth" (156). Thus, in his textural metaphorics, within its reversible fabric Ariadne's story, like Arachne's, figures sexual difference only to undo it:

The stories turn on enigmatic oppositions: making/solving, hiding/revealing, male/female, or is it female/male united in ambiguous or androgynous figures. . . like Ariadne, who is perhaps too aggressive to be purely "feminine," in the male chauvinist sense of the word, or like Arachne, devouring phallic mother, weaver of a web, *erion* in Greek, which also, as Jacques Derrida observes in *Glas*, means wool, fleece, the ring of pubic hair. (154)

Philology makes odd bedfellows: how shall we square our account of Ariadne as the epitome of the resolutely feminine with Miller's "aggressive" type?[20] Or Arachne as "devouring phallic mother" with Joplin's reading of the woman artist battered into silence by the phallic woman? (49)

As the fixed expression "Ariadne's thread" confirms, Ariadne remains tied to her gift as a kind of package deal. Confident in her knowledge of the figures of the text, her feel for its turns, she rewards the seeker who makes his way to her with a way out. She is that which allows the male adventurer, the legislator, the ladies' man, the critic who fancies himself all of the above, to penetrate the space of the great artist like Daedalus (or Ovid himself), without the risk of getting stuck there. In this sense Ariadne is but the pre-text for the homosocial bond Eve Sedgwick has described that links and separates men in western culture.[21] Ariadne is thus the "woman in the text" the critic takes into the abyss of discourse that constructs his identity. Domesticated, female desire becomes the enabling fiction of a male need for mastery. Or, more perversely, as Nietzche's Dionysos sings to Ariadne's lament: "I am your Labyrinth."

Ovid in the *Heroides* represents Ariadne as an abandoned woman. Alone on the island, where Theseus has forgotten her, "abandoned on a solitary shore," Ariadne, like Indiana writing in her journal of lamentations, writes to Theseus and pleads not to "be stolen from the record of [his] honours," when he tells "gloriously" of "the death of the man-and-bull, and of the halls of rock cut out in winding ways" (X, 131). Lost or found, dead or married to the figure who represents the eternal return of male narcissistic desire, Ariadne's letter is written for the record of the already read; the question of her desire circulates only as repetition of the trope: the abandoned woman. Ovid in fact repeats Catullus who in *his* poem (64) details Ariadne's sufferings on "an embroidered. . . coverlet."

In a note to the title of "Ariachne's Broken Woof," Miller explains that the "essay is a segment cut from a work in progress . . . to be called *Ariadne's Thread*" (44). The choice of title for the forthcoming book—"on linear imagery and narrative form"—I think confirms a preference for the Ariadne matrix already at work in the body of both texts. In the choice between proper names, Miller takes the name of the woman who leaves the classical metaphors of representation intact.[22]

OVID'S SISTER[23]

I said at the beginning that we might want to read Arachne's story as a parable of women's writing, a model for understanding how it has classically been read. As in the standard library references, the dictionaries and the encyclopedias, the cultural text James called the "public fund of allusion and quotation," in Miller's account of Arachne reference is not made to the representations of Arachne's tapestry, to *what* she has been weaving.[24] Miller thus elides what I take to be the critical difference that separates, finally, Arachne from Ariadne: the making of a text. The image of Arachne Miller offers, the "arachnid who devours her mate, weaver of a web which is herself and which both hides or reveals an absence, the abyss" (161), is the image of the spider that Arachne the spinner *becomes*. When Miller moves from the abyss to Arachne's "text as *mise en abyme*" he installs a vacancy her tapestry refuses. Arachne in fact recontains the iconography of Ariadne's tale: according to Graves's etymologies, it turns out, Ariadne is also known in antiquity as Erigone, one of the despairing female bodies we saw earlier portrayed in Arachne's tapestry.[25]

Athena's punishment returns Arachne to the limits of femininity, to the eternal reproduction of female labor, to, precisely, the secretion of the spider, subject of Barthes's neologism, to the threads in the hands of the lacemaker he invokes in S/Z as a figure of text production. Despite the recognition Arachne's art is granted within the narrative of its production—after all (and this is not the case of the mortals in Athena's exempla) she does not *lose* the contest—her posterity as an artist is cut off by the female guardian of the law.[26] In a move analogous to Barthes's invention, then, of the spider and her web, Ovid on the one hand tells a story in which a female desire to produce art is staged, but on the other, no sooner does he textualize that agency than he deauthorizes the story that motivated its production in the first place. The artist is returned to "woman"; to the domain of the natural in which, as Joplin observes, she weaves only "literal webs, sticky, incomprehensible designs" (50–51).

If one of the tasks of feminist criticism in the age of poststructuralism is to read over the familiar texts of the library for the ideological support a culture supplies to its own self-representation, this sketchy revision of moments in the *Metamorphoses* which represent, among other things, the making of art, may help us to see the ways in which the representation of art in art affects the social construction of artists and their reception in the canons of culture. Ovid writes of changing bodies, he tells us at the end of his book, so that his name will live on, unchanging, forever. We will want, then, to remember which models of the artist have been retained from the *Metamorphoses*: Daedalus (revised, for example, by Joyce in *Portrait of the Artist*) and of course Pygmalion.

In the aftermath of her tale the spider woman seems to block completely the woman weaver of golden threads: it is as though Athena's punishment had destroyed not only the figures of a woman's text, but Ovid's. Or rather, Ovid has succeeded only too well, since his "intention," he writes in his opening lines, was to tell of "bodies changed to different forms." That we remember the spider and not the woman is in part of course the measure of the poet's mastery: the metonymies of narrative are subsumed by the metaphors of the trope as turn; good readers, we retain the metamorphosis. But in the many revisions of the *Metamorphoses* the images of Arachne's tapestry are similarly reappropriated by interpretive gestures that dematerialize the gender of cultural productions; and in the process aestheticize the referential claims of the female body in representation to representation.[27]

It is thus also the task of feminist criticism to read for Arachne, which is to say not only for her, but for emblems of a female signature elsewhere and otherwise as I have tried to do here for George Sand. In a tradition of recognition that Gilbert and Gubar have described, in a gesture meant to restore woman to her text the eighteenth-century century poet Anne Finch remembers nostalgically (in "A Description of One of the Pieces of Tapestry at Long-Heat") Arachne's contest with Athena as an earlier assertion of female agency and ambition (*Madwoman*, 525). In the "*Tapestry* of old," Finch writes, Arachne, "Whilst sharing in the Toil . . . shar'd the Fame,/ And with the *Heroes* mixt her interwoven *Name*./ No longer, *Females* to such Praise aspire,/ And serfdom now we rightly do admire." It is not so much the lament that interests me here, however, as the rendering of the signature: "The edge of the web with its narrow border is filled with flowers and clinging ivy intertwined" was the way, we remember, Arachne signed off her representation. The line in Latin ends on the word "*intertextos*." Reinscribing the "interwoven *Name*," the woman poet recognizes the signature of the female precursor. Curiously, however, Finch doesn't seem to remember the content of the representations that brought Arachne fame as a weaver. Pamela White Hadas does, though, in a poem called "Arachne"; she remembers the grounds of her protest as well: "My craft unwinds/ confabula beyond/ self-portrait: dense/ sublimities of rape: it takes all kinds/ to teach defeat./ I won so lost my head/ by blow and henbane/ hanged me/ by my thread" (*Designing Women*, 20–21).

To remember Arachne as the spider, or through the dangers of her web alone, is to retain the archetype and dismember, once again, with Athena, the subject of its history: to underread. The goal of overreading, of reading for the signature, is to put one's finger— figuratively—on the place of production that marks the spinner's attachment to her web. This is also, as luck would have it, to come closer to the art of natural spiders: the logic of reference may allow us to refuse and refigure the very opposition of the spider and her web.

This move, then, to recover the figurations of Arachne's tapestry—like the gold and silk flowers of Indiana's embroidery and the pastoral landscape of Laure's watercolors—is meant not only to retrieve those texts from the indifference of the aesthetic universal, but to identify the act of this reading as the enabling subjectivity of *another* poetics, a poetics attached to gendered bodies that may have lived in history.

NOTES

1. "The Death of the Author" (1968) and "From Work to Text" (1971) appeared in English in 1977 in a volume of essays translated by Stephen Heath, Image/Text/Music. "La mort de l'auteur" and "De l'oeuvre au texte" have only just been collected in France in Essais Critiques IV: Le bruissement de la langue, 1984. I think it is important to keep these dates in mind as markers of a powerful disjunction between French rhythms and contexts of production, and American cadences and frameworks of reception and consumption. The time lag and difference between institutional structures are perhaps more important to understanding Franco-American critical relations than the linguistic problems of translation.

I specifically address the relations between the deconstructive resonances of the "Death of the Author" and the reconstructive project of the feminist critic in "Changing the Subject," part of a work in progress. I make the point there that in the wake of the dead Author we might usefully distinguish between the discussions around patriarchal texts that move to dismantle the originating powers of authorship, and the readings of women's writing that seek to establish the material and figurative grounds for elaborating a history of female authorship.

2. It might also be noted in passing that both models are gendered. The spinning spider is after all female, as is the lacemaker. In both cases a female subject is bound to the mindless work now performed by women, overwhelmingly of the third world, in what has come to be known as the "integrated circuit."

3. Freud, in the essay on "Femininity," described weaving as women's unique contribution to civilization, an invention symbolically bound up with their "genital deficiency" (132). In weaving, the argument goes, women reenact nature's art of concealment by which pubic hair comes to hide what is said to be missing. In his essay, "The Clarification of Clara Middleton," J. Hillis Miller reads the weaving as a "metaphor claiming the existence of what is not there [a 'mock phallus'] so covering the fact that the phallus is not there" (109). It is this second degree of metaphor, I think, that leads him to argue so readily for the inter-changeability of male and female: "The phallic thicket becomes a vaginal gap" (109), etc.

4. In the essay "For a Restricted Thematics: Writing, Speech, and Difference in Madame Bovary," written in 1975 and reprinted in Breaking the Chain: Women, Theory, and French Realist Fiction (1985), Naomi Schor, citing the passage from Barthes with which I began, and the quotation from Freud, describes the persistent relationship between the "textural" and the textile as an "Ariadne Complex" (3–5). I am indebted to her for the formulation of the paradigm.

5. Gynesis: Configurations of Woman and Modernity; Spivak focuses more specifically on Derrida in "Displacement and the Discourse of Woman."

6. Barthes writes interestingly of catachresis in his "Conclusions" to the Collo-quium at Cerisy, 1977, of which he was the "pretext": "You remember that catachresis occurs when one says, for example: the arms of a chair . . . ; it's a way of speaking which produces an obvious effect of metaphor (arms), and yet behind these images there is no word in the language which allows one to denote the figure's referent; to designate the arms of the chair there are no other words than 'the arms of the chair.' Modern discourse is 'catachretic' because it produces a continuous effect of metaphorization, but on the other hand, because there is no possibility of saying things otherwise except by metaphor" (438–39); my translation. This has everything to do with the current feminist attempt to describe women's writing.

7. Early in the elaboration of this material, which then included a discussion of

the figures of Philomela and Penelope, I discovered Patricia Joplin's important work on Philomela and feminist poetics (see also below). My work on Arachne is greatly indebted to hers, as the subsequent acknowledgments in this essay should make clear.

I will be referring to Ovid's account of Arachne in the *Metamorphoses*. Book VI opens on Arachne's story and ends on Philomela's; the young women's stories frame the central moment of Niobe's text of maternal agony.

8. In "Ariadne's Thread: Repetition and the Narrative Line," Hillis Miller, by an associative logic that I will refer to later, connects Erigone to the story of Theseus and Ariadne via Dionysos (150).

9. In his extremely detailed and helpful commentary on the *Metamorphoses*, William Anderson suggests that Ovid seems generally (if ambivalently) to be attracted to Arachne's "kind of composition: freer, more mannered, more dramatic and distorted, less specifically didactic" (160). He specifically reads the "rhetorically ordered repetition [*verum taurum . . . freta vera*] as both an "editorial note on the realism" of her representation of Europa's fate, and "an appeal to the audience for agreement" (165).

At the Bunting Institute (Spring 1984), I learned from Blair Tate, who is a weaver, that Ovid, who gets most of the other details of the mechanisms of weaving right, misrepresents the framing of the border which produces the effect of a "signing." Since a tapestry moves up on the loom from the bottom, the border would be integrated from the beginning. I've taken the risk of drawing the inference that Ovid here insists on the mark of the signature as the locus of referring, the emblem pointing to subjective agency and identity.

10. Athena herself raises problems of identity and identification—whose side is she on?—I have not tried to answer in this paper. Nor have I addressed the ways in which this is a story (clearly) that takes place between women; in a context generated by women tellers and spinners. But briefly, on the level of representation itself I should at least observe here that in addition to the emblems of a masculine warlike identity—the shield, helmet, etc.—Athena is also associated with the domestic signs of the distaff and the spindle. On the ambivalences attached to these instruments for the female spinner who also wants to write, see Ann Jones's discussion of Renaissance women poets in this volume. On the relations between woven and written texts embedded *through* the figure of Athena herself, see François Rigolot's discussion of the role played by the Arachne/Athena story in the work of Louise Labé, "Les 'sutils ouvrages' de Louise Labé, ou: quand Pallas devient Arachné."

11. This quote from Woolf provides the epigraph to Susan Sniader Lanser's important book, *The Narrative Act: Point of View in Prose Fiction*. I'm grateful to her for inviting me to read "Arachnologies" at the Georgetown Conference on Literary Theory (June 1984), and for her exceptionally helpful comments on the paper in its earliest form.

12. James wrote several essays on Sand. Patricia Thompson's study, *George Sand and the Victorians*, discusses the evolution of his complex attitude toward her work in some detail (216–44).

13. Although the long out of print 1962 text of *Indiana* in the Classiques Garnier was reissued in 1983, the novel like most of Sand's fiction, despite the enormous impact it had on her contemporaries, has only recently received any serious critical attention. This neglect has begun to be repaired by the general interest in women's writing produced by feminist scholarship, and by a more specific interest in Sand herself stimulated in part by the centenary of her death in 1976, and largely sustained by a small committed group of scholars in France. Nonetheless, because Sand's work, unlike Balzac's, does not belong to the French canon of the nineteenth-century novel—which is essentially the realist tradition and its legacy—virtually no critical tradition of Sandian readings exists. The "underread" therefore

has important implications for the history of literary history itself. To what extent do we continue to read, teach, and write about the already read because it has *already been written about*? Some recent contributions to a new point of departure for readings of *Indiana* include Françoise van Rossum-Guyom's "Les enjeux d'*Indiana* I, Métadiscours et réception critique," in the collection *Recherches Nouvelles*; and her "A propos d'*Indiana*: La Préface de 1832. Problèmes du métadiscours" in the collection of papers (1983) from the George Sand Colloquium at Cerisy held in 1981.

14. James writes perversely: "We believe Balzac, we believe Gustave Flaubert, we believe Dickens and Thackeray and Miss Austen. Dickens is far more incredible than George Sand,.and yet he produces more illusion. In spite of her plausibility, the author of 'Consuelo' always appears to be telling a fairy-tale. We say in spite of her plausibility, but we might rather say that her excessive plausibility is the reason of our want of faith" (156). See also Arlette Béteille's "Où finit *Indiana*? Problématique d'un dénouement," and my "Emphasis Added: Plots and Plausibilities in Women's Fiction."

15. The abyss here is not infinitely (i.e., deconstructively) regressive. Mieke Bal argues that the *mise en abyme* always *interrupts* the linearity and the chronology of the text, and that we should therefore see its "effect . . . as a general mode of reading" (unpublished ms.). See also her "Mise en Abyme et Iconicité." Nancy Goulder, a recent Columbia Ph.D. in English, has done interesting work on the ways in which iconography in the novel carries its own (often disruptive) narrative.

16. The literariness of the critique of the love plot is doubled in the novel by Noun's letter to Raymon, a pleading love letter the reader is not given to read, a letter Raymon never finishes reading: "It was a masterpiece of ingenuous and graceful passion; it is doubtful if Virginia wrote Paul a more charming one after she left her native land." But the power of the pastoral model (see also below) is without effect in Raymon's economy: "Poor girl! That was the last stroke. A letter from a lady's maid! Yet she had taken satin finished paper and perfumed wax from Madame Delmare's desk, and her style from her heart" (IV, 32–33). Style is not enough, without class. On the woman who allows woman to write, see also Jane Gallop, in this volume.

Leslie Rabine argues in "George Sand and the Myth of Femininity" that "the use of Noun in the novel demonstrates how the prostitution of lower-class women was necessary to preserve the chastity of bourgeoise women for the sake of bourgeois men, and their system of property inheritance" (14). But Sand's rewriting of Bernardin de Saint-Pierre's drowning of the pure Virginia is still more complex, I think, and participates in the irony of pastiche.

17. The English translation, "copy," misses the painterly origins of the word, which appears in France for the first time at the end of the eighteenth century.

I am particularly indebted to Gina Kovarsky, a graduate student in the Department of Slavic Languages at Columbia, for her analysis of the double figure, romantic and ironic, of the artist, and for her attention to the notion of pastiche (Seminar, French Women Writers and the Novel, Fall 1983). P. Salomon, editor of the Garnier, also connects the use of the term pastiche to Latouche's language (288, n. 1); see also below.

18. In a feminist poetics the two names begin the alphabet of female precursors. "Like Ariadne, Penelope, and Philomela, women have used their loom, thread and needles both to defend themselves and silently to speak of themselves" (*Madwoman*, 642). Curiously, Arachne is not named in this discussion of Dickinson's "spider artist." Miller also, though to different ends, connects these women weavers and wonders "how to stop the widening circle of contextual echoes" (58).

19. I'm adapting the phrase to my purposes from Mary Jacobus's analysis of the

relations between women and theory, women and writing, in "Is There a Woman in This Text?"

20. I'm thinking of George Eliot's use of Ariadne (*Madwoman*, 526–28; also in those pages Eliot's use of the web). See also on Ariadne and Eliot, U. C. Knoeplflmacher's "Fusing Fact and Myth: The New Reality of Middlemarch." On Miller's version of the web and the "adventure of critical feminism," see Teresa de Lauretis in *Alice Doesn't* (2 and 187, n. 5).

21. See especially Sedgwick's "Introduction," *Between Men* (1–20). Like the little boy in Freud's fable who practices mastery by casting a reel out of his crib and pulling it back, thus dominating his passive anxiety about maternal absence; like Theseus rising to the challenge of the monster, the masculist critic uses Ariadne to negotiate his encounter with the woman, perhaps in himself, the monstrous self the male critic might meet at the heart of the maze of heterosexuality.

22. That is, Miller embraces a Freudian poetics. On the appeal of the labyrinth as abyss in critical discourse, see Frank Lentricchia's account of recent critical history, in particular the chapter, "History or the Abyss: Poststructuralism," which begins with Georges Poulet's metaphorics, and the latter's influential invocation of the "threshold of the labyrinth" (158).

Taking an altogether different perspective on the implications of Ariadne's fate, Carolyn Heilbrun, in "James Joyce and Virginia Woolf: Ariadne and the Labyrinth," argues for a positive, or at least less relentlessly "feminine" reading of Ariadne's destiny as metaphor after the labyrinth: "Theseus betrayed Ariadne, leaving her open to the world of female myth and female possibility. It was that world into which Woolf would follow Ariadne."

23. By this title, I refer of course to Woolf's tale of Shakespeare's sister. But I also want to invoke Ariadne's sister Phaedra, who offers a whole other network of associations for the French tradition of this myth. Lawrence Lipking has offered his provocative but finally problematic notion of a feminist poetics in "Aristole's Sister." And most recently, Jane Marcus reclaims Procne as Philomela's sister, and "socialist feminist critic" in "Still Practice, A/ Wrested Alphabet" (79).

24. A typical example reads: "In Greek mythology, woman of Lydia who challenged Athena to a trial of skill in weaving. Angered at such presumption, the goddess destroyed Arachne's work, whereupon the woman hanged herself. Athena then turned her into a spider." *The New Columbia Encyclopedia*, 1975 (132). In *Le dictionnaire des antiquités grecques et romaines*, Arachne's story appears only as a subset of Athena's (1915).

25. I discovered this in a novel by June Rachuy Brindel, *Ariadne: A Novel of Ancient Greece*, brought to my attention by Freda Gardner.

26. To what extent could we read the destruction of Arachne's text by Athena as a Bloomian symptom: the poet's need to vanquish the precursor? Is it completely farfetched to argue that Ovid stages here *through women* his own "anxiety of influence"? (For a feminist reading of the male paradigm, see *Madwoman in the Attic*, 46ff.) On Athena as an alibi or pseudowoman, Spivak writes: "If the situation of the Law is written into the situation of father-daughter incest, Athena the Law (-giving) daughter can be produced, and the phallic mother circumvented" (187); see also 174, 179.

27. It is the tendency to read allegorically, reading woman out—aren't these just stories of *human* overreaching? etc.—that overreading works self-consciously against: reading woman back in. My example here is the only visual representation of Arachne *as artist* I have encountered, Velasquez' *Fable of Arachne* (1644–68), often interpreted as an "allegory of the arts." I am grateful to Marcia Welles for bringing this work and its context to my attention. In *Arachne's Tapestry*, a study of parody in seventeenth-century Spain, Welles explains that Velasquez' painting ("Las Hilanderas") "was long thought to be a realistic view of the Royal

Tapestry factory of Santa Isabel of Madrid." Although in her discussion of the Ovidian matrix Welles does not address Arachne's attack on the prerogatives of sexual privilege, she reads subversiveness in a parodic stance, which " 'discrowns' the mythological gods in an act of carnivalistic reversal." It is of no small interest to my case that in the Velazquez painting Arachne's tapestry is *refigured*, in fact *replaced* by Titian's *Rape of Europa*, which then functions as a pictorial intertext. Arachne appears as an artist only to disappear, transformed into a woman in representation. In "Muiopotomos: or the Fate of the Butterflie," in which Spenser rewrites Ovid's account of Arachne's text, emphasis also falls on the representation (in detail) of the rape of Europa. I owe the reference to Ian Sowton.

WORKS CITED

Anderson, William S. *Ovid's Metamorphoses. Books 6–10.* Norman: Oklahoma University Press, 1972.

Bal, Mieke. "Mise en abyme et Iconicité." *Littérature* (1978), 29:116–28.

—— "Lethal Love," unpublished ms.

Barthes, Roland *The Pleasure of the Text.* Trans. Richard Howard. New York: Hill and Wang, 1975.

—— S/Z. Trans. Richard Miller. New York: Hill and Wang, 1974.

—— "The Death of the Author." In *Image/Text/Music.* Trans. Stephen Heath. New York: Hill and Wang, 1977.

—— *Prétexte: Roland Barthes. Colloque de Cerisy.* Paris: U.G.E., 1978.

Béteille, Arlette. "Où finit Indiana? Problématique d'un dénouement." *Recherches Nouvelles. Groupe de Recherches sur George Sand.* C.R.I.N. 6–7, 1983; pp. 62–73.

Brindel, June Rachuy. *Ariadne: A Novel of Ancient Greece.* New York: Saint Martin's Press, 1980.

De Lauretis, Teresa. *Alice Doesn't: Feminism, Semiotics, Cinema.* Bloomington: Indiana University Press, 1984.

Dictionnaire des antiquités grecques et romaines d'après les textes et les monuments, Le. Ed. Charles Darenberg and Edmond Saglio. Paris: Hachette, 1877–1919.

Freud, Sigmund. "Femininity." In *New Introductory Lectures on Psychoanalysis.* Trans. James Strachey. 1933; repr. New York: Norton, 1965.

Gilbert, Sandra M. and Gubar, Susan. *Madwoman in the Attic: The Woman Writer and The Nineteenth-Century Literary Imagination.* New Haven: Yale University Press, 1979.

Hadas, Pamela White. *Designing Women.* New York: Knopf, 1979.

Heilbrun, Carolyn G. "James Joyce and Virginia Woolf: Ariadne and the Labyrinth," unpublished ms.

Jacobus, Mary. "Is There a Woman in this Text?" *New Literary History* (Autumn 1982); 14(1):117–42.

James, Henry. "George Sand." *French Poets and Novelists*. 1893; repr. London and New York: Macmillan, 1977.

Jardine, Alice. *Gynesis: Configurations of Woman and Modernity*. Ithaca: Cornell University Press, 1985.

Joplin, Patricia Klindienst. "The Voice of the Shuttle is Ours." *Stanford Literature Review* (Spring 1984), 1(1):25–53.

Knoeplfmacher, U. C. "Fusing Fact and Myth: The New Reality of Middlemarch." In *This Particular Web: Essays on Middlemarch*. Ed. Ian Adams. Toronto and Buffalo: Toronto University Press, 1975; pp. 43–72.

Kolodny, Annette. "Dancing Through the Minefield: Some Observations on the Theory, Practice, and Politics of a Feminist Literary Criticism." *Feminist Studies* (Spring 1980) 6(1):1–25.

—— "A Map for Rereading: Or, Gender and the Interpretation of Literary Texts." *New Literary History* (Spring 1980), 11(3):451–68.

Lanser, Susan Sniader. *The Narrative Act: Point of View in Prose Fiction*. Princeton: Princeton University Press, 1981.

Lentricchia, Frank. *After the New Criticism*. Chicago: University of Chicago Press, 1980.

Lipking, Lawrence. "Aristotle's Sister: A Poetics of Abandonment. *Critical Inquiry* (September 1983), 10(1):61–81.

Marcus, Jane. "Liberty, Sorority, Misogyny." In *The Representation of Women in Fiction*. Ed. Carolyn G. Heilbrun and Margaret R. Higonnet. *Selected Papers from the English Institute*, 1981. Baltimore and London: Johns Hopkins University Press, 1983; pp. 60–97.

—— "Still Practice, A/Wrested Alphabet: Toward a Feminist Aesthetic." *Tulsa Studies in Women's Literature*. (Spring/Fall 1984), 3(1–2):79–98.

Miller, J. Hillis. "Ariadne's Thread: Repetition and the Narrative Line." In *Interpretation of Narrative*. Ed. Mario J. Valdes and Owen J. Miller. Toronto, Buffalo, London: University of Toronto Press, 1976; pp. 148–66.

—— "Ariachne's Broken Woof." *Georgia Review* (Spring 1977), 31(1):36–48.

—— "The Clarification of Clara Middleton." In *The Representation of Women in Fiction*. Ed. Carolyn G. Heilbrun and Margaret R. Higonnet. *Selected Papers from the English Institute*, 1981. Baltimore and London: Johns Hopkins University Press, 1983; pp. 98–123.

Miller, Nancy K. "Emphasis Added: Plots and Plausibilities in Women's Fiction." *PMLA* (January 1981), 96(1):36–48.

New Columbia Encyclopedia, The. Ed. William H. Harris and Judith S. Levey. New York: Columbia University Press, 1975.

Ovid. *Metamorphoses*. Trans. Frank Justice Miller. Cambridge and London: Harvard University Press and William Heinemann, 1966.

—— *Heroides*. Trans. Grant Showerman. Cambridge and London: Harvard University Press and William Heinemann, 1971.

Rabine, Leslie. "George Sand and the Myth of Femininity." *Women and Literature* (1976), 4(2):2–17.

Rigolot, François. "Les 'sutils ouvrages' de Louise Labé, ou: quand Pallas devient Arachné." In *Actes du Congrès de Macerata sur la Renaissance lyonnaise* (forthcoming).

Rossum-Guyom, Françoise van. "Les enjeux d'Indiana I, Métadiscours et réception critique." *George Sand. Recherches Nouvelles.* C.R.I.N. 6–7, 1983; pp. 1–35.

—— "A propos d'*Indiana*: La Préface de 1832. Problèmes du métadiscours." *George Sand.* Colloque de Cerisy. Paris: SEDES, 1983.

Sainte-Beuve, Charles-Augustin. *Portraits Contemporains.* Paris: Michel Lévy Frères, 1870.

Sand, George. *Indiana.* Ed. Pierre Salomon. Paris: Garnier, 1962.

—— *Indiana.* Trans. George Burnham Ives. 1900; repr. Chicago: Academy Press Ltd. Cassandra Editions, 1978.

—— *Oeuvres autobiographiques.* Vol. 2. Paris: Gallimard, 1971.

Schor, Naomi. *Breaking the Chain: Women, Theory, and French Realist Fiction.* New York: Columbia University Press, 1985.

Sedgwick, Eve Kosofsky. *Between Men: English Literature and Male Homosocial Desire.* New York: Columbia University Press, 1985.

Showalter, Elaine. "Feminist Criticism in the Wilderness." *Critical Inquiry* (Winter 1981), 8(2):179–206.

Spivak, Gayatri Chakravorty. "Displacement and the Discourse of Woman." In *Displacement: Derrida and After.* Ed. Mark Krupnick. Bloomington: Indiana University Press, 1983.

Thompson, Patricia. *George Sand and the Victorians: Her Influence and Reputation in Nineteenth-Century England.* New York: Columbia University Press, 1977.

Welles, Marcia. *Arachne's Tapestry: The Transformation of Myth in Seventeenth-Century Spain.* San Antonio: Trinity University Press, 1985.

Concluding Remarks

GITA MAY

It is hard to express in words the sense of exhilaration I feel at the conclusion of this memorable Colloquium.

As a member of what might be called the older generation of women in academia, I feel especially and personally gratified by the recognition feminist literary criticism and Women's Studies have achieved in such leading institutions of higher learning as Columbia. That the prestigious Colloquium on Poetics should have devoted its eighth international meeting to the Poetics of Gender, with Michael Riffaterre, our colleague and University Professor, and Nancy K. Miller, our colleague and Director of Women's Studies at Barnard, as coorganizers and comoderators, is, I think, what the French would call a "consécration." But more about that later.

For too many years, we your elder sisters have been loners in academia, laboring against traditional prejudices as well as against our own insecurities and shaky sense of self-identity. We rejoice over this triumph, and listening to the brilliant, exciting, and sometimes deeply moving papers at this Colloquium, admiring their intellectual scope and strength, their boldness and originality, their imaginative theoretical insights, and their methodological rigor, we feel proud of what has been achieved in a remarkably short span of time.

If anyone in this audience still had some doubts about the contribution feminist criticism has made to our understanding and appreciation of literature, art, psychology, philosophy, history, and politics, I am certain that by now those doubts have been completely dispelled.

But let me again address you, if I may, as one of your elder sisters. We hope that our painful, hard-earned experience and your enthusiasm and freshness of ideas will continue to be mutually beneficial. I think we need each other. I, for one, feel that we need your youthful energy, your confidence and self-assurance for our spiritual renewal and rejuvenation. And it may be useful for you to be reminded, now and then, of not so distant barriers. (To give but a small, mundane illustration of this: the Faculty House, where we have had such pleasant meals during the Colloquium, was not always called the Faculty House. Not very long ago it was the Men's Faculty Club, a forbidden territory for women, except as accompanied guests.)

May I, however, introduce a small cautionary note? Now that Women's Studies and feminist criticism have begun to be recognized within the institution, let us hope that they will not become sanitized and bureaucratized and that they will always remain a disquieting, unsettling force on the intellectual scene. Creativity feeds upon social marginality and alienation (or perhaps I am betraying here my own aesthetic prejudices).

I hope you will forgive me if I introduce a personal note in these brief remarks. When as a graduate student at Columbia, I mentioned (with some naïve pride) that an essay of mine had been accepted for publication (one is always proudest of one's first publication), the fact that it was on Germaine de Staël's novel, *Corinne*, hardly elicited an enthusiastic response on the part of my teachers and compeers. And when, a few years later, I embarked upon the project of writing a book about Madame Roland, French revolutionary and disciple of Rousseau, my best friends strongly advised me against wasting my time and energies on a meddlesome political intriguer and incorrigible scribbler who laid down her pen only at the foot of the guillotine (and even there, managed, I was reminded, to make a final melodramatic, self-serving statement, "O Liberty! what crimes are committed in thy name!").

To turn from such great writers and thinkers as Diderot and Rousseau to a Madame Roland seemed indeed rather peculiar, proof perhaps that my femininity, as might be expected, was getting in the way of my better critical judgment. Upon retrospect, I am glad I remained obdurate and decided to follow my own impulses rather than the dictates of professional common sense and practicality as they were then understood by the academic establishment.

Now, at long last, we all know better, including our enlightened, liberated male colleagues and friends. That feminist criticism is probably the most exciting, creative, and forward-looking movement in the last two decades is a point that hardly needs belaboring here. We owe a debt of gratitude to Michael Riffaterre and Nancy Miller for having collaborated so effectively and with such stunning results in gathering here an extraordinary group of feminist critics. I am sure I can speak for all of us when I say that these three days constitute a privileged moment, a benchmark in feminist criticism.

Notes on Contributors

ELIZABETH BERG is Visiting Assistant Professor of French Literature at the University of California, Santa Cruz. She has published articles on Racine, Sarah Kofman, Luce Irigaray, and other French writers.

MARY ANN CAWS is Distinguished Professor of French and Comparative Literature at the Graduate School, CUNY, and at Hunter College in New York. Among her most recent books are *Reading Frames in Modern Fiction*, *The Eye in the Text: Essays on Perception, Mannerist to Modern*, and A *Metapoetics of the Passage: Architectures in Surrealism and After*. She is the editor of *Le Siècle Eclaté* and *Reading Plus*, and the coeditor of *Dada-Surrealism* and *A French Modernist Library*.

JANE GALLOP is Professor of Humanities at Rice University and the author of *The Daughter's Seduction: Feminism and Psychoanalysis* and *Reading Lacan*.

SANDRA M. GILBERT teaches in the English Department of Princeton University; SUSAN GUBAR is a member of the English Department of Indiana University. Gilbert and Gubar are the coauthors of *The Madwoman in the Attic: The Woman Writer and the Nineteenth-Century Literary Imagination*; *Shakespeare's Sisters: Feminist Essays on Women Poets*; and *The Norton Anthology of Literature by Women: The Tradition in English*. They are currently working on a sequel to *The Madwoman in the Attic*, to be entitled "No-Man's Land: The Place of the Woman Writer in the Twentieth Century."

CAROLYN G. HEILBRUN is Professor of English and Comparative Literature at Columbia University. She is the author of *The Garnett Family*;

Christopher Isherwood; Toward a Recognition of Androgyny; and *Reinventing Womanhood.*

ALICE JARDINE is Associate Professor of Romance Languages and Literature at Harvard. She teaches feminist theory and contemporary literary criticism. She is the author of *Gynesis: Configurations of Women and Modernity,* and coeditor with Hester Eisenstein of *The Future of Difference.* She is also the cotranslator of Julia Kristeva's *Desire in Language.*

ANN ROSALIND JONES is Associate Professor and Director of the Comparative Literature Program at Smith College. Her research interests include Renaissance and twentieth-century ideologies of femininity, and women writers' responses to their social and cultural contexts. She has published articles on French feminisms and Renaissance lyric and narrative, and is currently completing a book on women's love poetry in early modern Europe.

GITA MAY is Professor of French and the Department Chair at Columbia University. She is the author of *Diderot et Baudelaire, critiques d'art; De Jean-Jacques Rousseau à Madame Roland: Essai sur la sensibilité préromantique et révolutionnaire; Madame Roland and the Age of Revolution* (Winner of Columbia University's Van Amringe Distinguished Book Award); *Stendhal and the Age of Napoleon;* and numerous articles and reviews. She edited Diderot's *Essais sur la peinture* and *Pensées détachées sur la peinture* for the complete critical edition of Diderot's works, and coedited *Diderot Studies III.*

NANCY K. MILLER is Professor of Women's Studies and Director of the Women's Studies Program at Barnard College. She is the author of *The Heroine's Text: Readings in the French and English Novel, 1722–1782,* and of essays on feminist literary theory and women's writing.

NAOMI SCHOR is Professor of French Studies at Brown University. Her books include *Zola's Crowds* and *Breaking the Chain: Women, Theory, and French Realist Fiction.* She has published numerous articles on nineteenth-century French fiction, feminism, and contemporary theory. The working title of her research in progress is "Sublime Details: From Reynolds to Barthes."

ELAINE SHOWALTER is Professor of English at Princeton University. She is the author of *A Literature of Their Own: British Women Novelists From Brontë to Lessing* and *The Female Malady* and has recently edited *The New*

Feminist Criticism: Essays on Women, Literature, and Theory. She is currently working on a literary history of American women writers.

DOMNA C. STANTON, Professor of French and Women's Studies at the University of Michigan, is the author of *The Aristocrat as Art: A Comparative Analysis of the 'Honnête Homme' and the Dandy,* and of articles on seventeenth-century French literature, women writers, and critical theory. She has also edited *The Female Autograph,* a collection of essays on women's memoirs, letters, and autobiographies; and a bilingual anthology of French feminist poetry for *The Defiant Muse,* a four-volume set published by The Feminist Press.

CATHARINE R. STIMPSON is Professor of English and Director of the Institute for Research on Women at Rutgers University. She is the author of fiction and nonfiction, the founding editor of SIGNS, and the editor of a book series on women in culture and society for the University of Chicago Press.

SUSAN RUBIN SULEIMAN is Professor of Romance and Comparative Literatures at Harvard University. She is the author of *Authoritarian Fictions: The Ideological Novel as a Literary Genre,* coeditor of *The Reader in the Text: Essays on Audience and Interpretation,* and editor of *The Female Body in Western Culture: Contemporary Perspectives.* She has published numerous articles on modern French literature and on literary theory, and is currently working on problems of avant-garde writing.

NANCY J. VICKERS is Associate Professor of French and Italian at Dartmouth College, and Chair of the Department of French and Italian. She is the author of articles on Dante, Petrarch, and Shakespeare, and is currently completing a book on French Mannerism and the female body. She is the coeditor of *Rewriting the Renaissance: The Discourses of Sexual Difference in Early Modern Europe.*

MONIQUE WITTIG is the author of *The Opoponax, Les Guérillères, The Lesbian Body,* and *Lesbian Peoples Material for a Dictionary* with Sande Zeig. In 1985 in Paris she published *Virgile, non,* her most recent novel; *The Constant Journey,* a play produced at the Théâtre du Rond-point; and "Paris-la-Politique," a fable published in a special issue of *Vlasta* devoted to her work. Wittig's critical essays are generally published in *Feminist Issues,* for which she is Advisory Editor. She has taught at the University of Southern California for the last two years.